P. Berresford Ellis

The Cornish Language and its Literature

Routledge & Kegan Paul
London and Boston

First published in 1974
by Routledge & Kegan Paul Ltd
Broadway House, 68–74 Carter Lane,
London EC4V 5EL and
9 Park Street,
Boston, Mass. 02108, USA
Set in Monotype Perpetua
and printed in Great Britain by
T. & A. Constable Ltd
Edinburgh, EH7 4NF

ISBN 0 7100 7928 1
Library of Congress Catalog Card No. 74-80103

Pan o marow,
dasserghys ve dhe Vewnans.
(Bewnans Meryasek, A.D. 1504)

When it was dead,
it was raised to life.
(Life of Meryasek, A.D. 1504)

Contents

Plates

A*

Introduction

Cornwall has often been referred to as 'the land beyond England'. Crossing the River Tamar into Cornwall one's first impression is of the un-English place names. Names such as Mawgan-in-Pydar, Treryn, Porthgwarra, Lostwithiel, Landewednack, Kennack, Gwithian, Caerhays and Boconnoc. They are names which remind one of Wales or Brittany. It is not really surprising. Cornwall is not really England nor can the Cornish be classified as English. They are a Celtic people, first cousins to the Welsh and Bretons and second cousins to the Irish, Scots and Manx. Cornwall was the first Celtic country to be conquered and annexed by England and, therefore, the Cornish became the first Celtic people to 'lose' their language. It died as a generally spoken vernacular in the eighteenth century. Even Manx, the language of the smallest of the Celtic nationalities, retained its native speakers until the twentieth century. The wonder is not that the language died but, indeed, how it survived eight centuries after the English conquest. Yet survive it did and until its death Cornwall still retained a quality of separateness from England so that in 1610 John Norden could write that 'they are among themselves litigious, so seem they yet to retayne a kind of concealed envy against the English who they yet affect with a desire of revenge for their fathers' sakes by whom their fathers received their repulse'.[1]

Although the spoken language died, Cornish still persisted in place names and in grammatical forms and words of the tongue of the ordinary people who spoke in the Cornish dialect of English. A Cornish poet, Richard Davies, expressed the survival of the older language through English in these words:[2]

We speak your language now . . .
But we sing it to our own tune
An ancient song
Lilting before you came
And the words in our way we say

I

In the old accents
Singing to a question
And because we say it is so
So chanting in our memories
It is not your language
It is ours.

The survival of the language through place names was expressed by
another Cornish poet, Katherine Lee Jenner, half a century earlier:[3]

The names of our dead speech are music still
In our dear living land
Which never can be void or desolate
While here on every hand
Is still the record of our fathers' lives
Though their old hopes and fears
Have passed away like sunlight on the hills
Down through the path of years.

And yet today the Cornish language is not merely confined to
snatches of dialect and place names. Today there are more people
with a knowledge of the language, who can read, write and speak it,
than at any time during the past 250 years. At the beginning of this
century some Cornish scholars started a language revival, inspired by
the bigger Celtic Renaissance taking place at the time in all the
Celtic countries. This language revival is continuing today with a
fair degree of success.

But it is not generally known outside Cornwall that there is a
Cornish language or that it is still a living thing to a great many.
There remains, instead, vague folk memories of the 'differentness'
of the Cornish people which have led many writers, who should know
better, to profess to see in the Cornish descendants of Spanish seamen
supposedly wrecked on the Cornish coasts, or descendants of a lost
tribe of Israel. This became a very popular belief in the nineteenth
century and one which was backed by learned discourses on Cornish
place names such as Marazion and Market Jew. The belief that the
Cornish were one of the lost tribes was half heartedly abandoned
when Professor Max Müller, professor of comparative philology at
Oxford, debunked the idea in a paper entitled 'Are there Jews in
Cornwall?'[4] Nevertheless, the mythologies that the Cornish have

a Spanish strain in them or that they are descended from the Phoenicians are still very popular. What is tragic is that there are still many Cornish people who have no knowledge of their ancient heritage or Celtic background: people who have become separated from their forefathers by a deep abyss and whose history has been set adrift because they have no knowledge of the language spoken by their ancestors until a few hundred years ago. In this respect the enthusiasts of the Cornish language revival have been and are doing exceptional work in the educational field by seeking to inform the Cornish man and woman about their history.

In editing a recent edition of a pamphlet history of the language, E. G. Retallack Hooper laments the fact that so far there has been no definitive history of the Cornish language and its literature.[5] Apart from a couple of pamphlet histories, one of them published in Esperanto, all the information on Cornish has been published in various academic journals and periodicals. 'A source book of reference, or perhaps summaries, is a desirable work, if it could be published.' Professor Charles Thomas, director of the Institute of Cornish Studies at Redruth, is currently working on such a source book with the aid of his assistant Miss Myrna Combellack. The work consists of a long and very detailed catalogue of all references to Cornish, in any language, in periodical literature, together with a discussion of all the existing manuscripts in Cornish, indicating what parts have been published, where and in what form. The projected title of this work is 'A Source Book for the Cornish Language (Old, Middle and Late)' and Professor Thomas hopes to have this published through the Institute in a few years' time.

The present volume is an attempt to present a general historical, not a linguistic, survey of the Cornish language and its literature, aimed essentially for the layman, although references are given to sources for those who wish to enlarge upon their studies. It is, in fact, an attempt to rectify what has been an important omission from literature on the British Isles: the presentation of a record of the language and literature of one of the smaller nationalities which comprises the multinational state of the United Kingdom.

I would like to record my thanks to the following people for their patience and help in my researches: Professor Charles Thomas, Director of the Institute of Cornish Studies; Miss F. J. Porter, Assistant Keeper, Department of Manuscripts, British Museum; Miss Mary Clapinson, Assistant Keeper, Department of Western Manuscripts,

Bodleian Library, Oxford; R. D. Hale, County Librarian, Cornwall; H. L. Douch, Curator, County Museum, Cornwall; J. G. Harries, Secretary for Education, Cornwall County Council; also the staffs of the Reading Room, British Museum, Public Record Office, etc.

Above all I would like to express my profound gratitude to G. Pawley White (Gunwyn), General Secretary of Kesva an Tavas Kernewek (The Cornish Language Board), and to E. G. Retallack Hooper (Talek), editor of *An Lef Kernewek*, both former Grand Bards of the Cornish Gorsedd, for answering my numerous queries, reading my manuscript and making so many helpful suggestions. Their encouragement, information and criticism has been invaluable. However, I hasten to add that any errors that may occur, and the opinions given in this work, are the responsibility of nobody but myself.

Chapter One

Old Cornish

The Cornish are a Celtic people, closely related to the Welsh and Bretons and less closely to the Irish, Manx and Scots. When we speak of the Celtic people we speak of a linguistic group and not of a race. By race we are considering the physical descent of people, regarding them purely as animals and judging such aspects as stature, complexion, shape of skull and the formation of features which have distinguished them notably from the rest of mankind. According to Johann Friedrich Blumenbach (1752-1840) there were five distinct types (or races) of the species *homo sapiens* (Man): white Caucasian, yellow Mongolian, black Ethiopian, red American and tawny Malay. But, as there are few biological differences between an African and a Scandinavian, race is largely a delusion and to talk of race, even if one is an eminent anthropometrist, is to talk about a field which is uncertain and confusing. In Europe no distinction of race may be found among the various nationalities. Writing about the old myth of the Aryan race, Professor Max Müller stated:[1]

> I have declared again and again that if I say Aryas, I mean neither blood nor bones, nor hair, nor skull; I mean simply those who speak an Aryan language. . . When I speak of them I commit myself to no anatomical characteristics. The blue-eyed and fair-haired Scandinavian may have been conquerors or conquered. They may have adopted the language to their darker lords or vice versa . . . To me an ethnologist who speaks of Aryan race, Aryan blood, Aryan eyes and hair, is as great a sinner as a linguist who speaks of a dolichocephalic dictionary or a brachycephalic grammar.

Professor Eoin Mac Neill has pointed out that there is no such thing as a Latin race, a Teutonic race, a Slavic race or a Celtic race.[2] The people of Europe are a mixture of several races and, for the most part, the same races though not in every case in the same proportions.

5

In the case of the populations recognised to be Celtic it is particularly true that no distinction of race is found among them and this was true even in ancient times as can be observed by a reading of their physical attributes recorded by ancient Greek and Latin writers. The term Celtic is thus used to describe groups who speak, or were known to have spoken, a Celtic language in which have been enshrined certain cultural ideas and philosophies. This must be made clear so that we may not be misled by ignorant people who insist on such nonsensical notions as 'racial differences' and 'racial purity'.

The Cornish language is one of six Celtic languages which have survived until modern times. These languages have been classified into two groups: Irish, Manx and Scottish Gaelic, known as Goidelic Celtic, and Welsh, Breton and Cornish, known as Brythonic Celtic or 'British'. The Celtic languages belong to the Indo-European family of languages whose linguistic territory stretches from Ireland as far as Tocharian Asia and includes such major languages as Latin, Greek, Sanskrit, English, French, Spanish and Russian. The main differences between the two branches of Celtic are that the Brythonic languages have simplified themselves in their case endings and in the loss of the neuter gender and dual number. The two groups also differ in the matter of initial mutation and aspiration. There is the famous substitution of P for Q in the Brythonic languages which has led some scholars to label the two branches P and Q Celtic. This was the sound in Indo-European which gave qu (kw). This sound qu in Goidelic later became represented by c. The qu sound in Brythonic was replaced by p. For example, the numeral 'four' in Irish is *ceathair* while in Cornish *peswar*. More examples can be found in the following:

English	son	head	worm	feather	everyone
Irish (Q)	mac	cenn	cruiv	cluv	cách
Cornish (P)	map	pen	pryf	plüf	pup
comparative ⎱ Welsh (P) ⎰	map	pen	pryv	pluv	paup

The close relationship between the Celtic languages can best be seen from the following examples. This is a selection of words which are of obvious relationship:

English	river	on	clean	island	full	land	wave
Cornish	avon	war	glán	enys	lün	tyr	ton
Welsh	avon	ar	glan	ynys	llawn	tir	ton
Breton	avon	war	glan	enez	leun	tir	tonn

Irish	abhann	ar	glan	inis	lán	tir	tonn
Scottish Gaelic	abhainn	air	glan	innis	làn	tir	tonn
Manx	awin	er	glan	innys	lane	cheer	tonn

The following words are examples of relationships that are fairly easy to recognise:

English	time/weather	year	bell/clock	good	sweet	auger
Cornish	amser	bledhen	clogh	da	melys	tardar
Welsh	amser	blwyddyn	cloch	da	melys	taradr
Breton	amzer	blizenn	kloc'h	da	milis	tarar
Irish	aimsir	bliain	clog	dea	milis	tarathar
Scottish Gaelic	aimsir	bliadna	clag	deagh	milis	tarachair
Manx	emshyr	blein	clag	jeih	millish	tharrar

The following words are also related but are not so easily recognisable:

English	money	cold	mouse	'to run'	apple
Cornish	arghans	or	lergh	resek	aval
Welsh	arian	oer	llwrw	rhed(eg)	afal
Breton	arc'hant		lerc'h	reizh	aval
Irish	airgead	fuar	luch	rith	üll
Scottish Gaelic	airgiod	fuar	luch	ruith	ubhal
Manx	argid	feayr	lugh	roie	ooyl

An excellent study on the relationship between the six Celtic languages, which compared about 120 words in varying stages of relationship, together with thirteen examples of parallel syntax, was recently completed by Liam Mac Mathúna.[3]

The Celtic languages are spoken by over two million people as their native tongue, the biggest group being speakers of Breton, said to number one million. But with each succeeding year the number of native speakers declines and the languages gradually fall into disuse, due to lack of interest and downright discouragement by state authorities. Trevor Fishlock, in a series of articles in the London *Times*, has observed:[4]

On the edges of north-west Europe the Celts are making their last stand. As distinct peoples they have been for 2,000 years a bright thread in the evolution of European civilisation and now

they have reached the ultimate crisis in their long march and decline. They are a tough remnant, not a relic, and by the end of the century it will be possible to judge whether they have gouged out for themselves a worthwhile and valid future existence, or have been effectively erased by the progress to which they have contributed much.

Professor David Greene has commented:[5]

The Celtic languages are not dead, since at least two million people speak one or other of them as their native tongue, but since none of them has succeeded in dominating a state, the vast majority of their speakers are perforce bilingual, and bilingualism under those conditions must ultimately lead to the loss of the less important language.

At the moment this statement still holds good but, as Trevor Fishlock pointed out, the Celtic world has of late been shaken by the rise of militant language movements which, in the space of a short decade, have achieved more concessions from the state authorities than a half century of pleading and coaxing by other language movements which sprung up with the Celtic Renaissance at the latter end of the nineteenth century. According to Mr Fishlock:

Wales is very much the cockpit of Celtic resistance. It is only here that people break the law and go to prison in pursuit of the greater security for their native language.
The steady and intensifying language campaign has a spearhead of militants who get the headlines. The rest of the iceberg is a body of support and sympathy and a lot of quieter and effective work for the language. The broad campaign has wrung concessions from the authorities, has improved the status of Welsh and has changed public attitudes. Welsh is no longer the quaint and patronised national pet which was dying nicely in the Celtic twilight.

The activities of Cymdeithas yr Iaith Gymraeg (Welsh Language Society) forced the granting of a quasi-official status to the Welsh language in Wales. In Ireland, where Irish is recognised in theory as 'the first official language', movements were formed to assert this

right in practice. In 1968 Coiste Troda na Gaeltachta (Gaeltacht Agitation Committee) was formed in the Donegal Gaeltacht (Irish-speaking area). In spring 1969 Gluaiseacht Chearta Sibhialta na Gaeltachta was formed in Galway to fight for civil rights for Irish speakers. This was followed in 1970 by Coiste Cearta Náisiúnta Chorca Dhuibhne, a National Rights Committee formed in the Munster Gaeltacht. Radical movements like these and Misneach (Courage), which staged a series of hunger strikes and demonstrations, are seeking to force Irish governments to do more than pay occasional lip service to the language. Their campaign has made Conradh na Gaeilge (The Gaelic League), the oldest of the language bodies, become more militant in outlook. In 1969 also, in Scotland, writer Seumas Mac a' Ghobhainn was the leading spirit in forming Comunn na Cànain Albannaich (Scottish Language Society) which is modelled on the Cymdeithas pattern but tailored to Scottish conditions. There is perhaps some hope for the survival of the Celtic languages in our growing world of deadly sameness and uniformity.

Trevor Fishlock says of the Celtic languages:

If they all succumb—that is, if they shrivel to a point where their use is minimal and artificial, and they cannot regenerate—the Celts, the last of those colourful and cultured warrior people who were the original Britons, may be said to have vanished.

They will leave a vast literature and mythology, monuments and the husks of languages, folk memories and a complete human experience with a beginning, a middle and an end.

The Celts are indeed possessed of 'a vast literature'. H.M. and N. K. Chadwick have stated:[6]

The Celtic literatures are practically unknown, except to persons who have spoken the languages from childhood. A few adaptations of early Irish sagas have recently had a certain vogue; but it may safely be said that very few people in this country have any conception of the extent and value of early Irish literature . . . The early Celtic literatures should not be ignored as they are at present.

Professor Calvert Watkins of Harvard has pointed out that the Irish language contains Europe's *oldest vernacular literature*. Both

Irish and Welsh literature, the oldest of the Celtic literatures, contain
a fabulous mythology with heroes, gods and tales of great loves which
are equal to the world's greatest mythologies. Proinsias Mac Cana's
Celtic Mythology[7] gives a magnificent introduction to the subject.
Although there have been a number of anthologies of translations
from Celtic literature since *Reliques of Irish Poetry* by Charlotte Brooke
in 1789, they have been limited to a selection from one particular
Celtic language. Professor Kenneth Jackson's *Celtic Miscellany* is a
superb introduction to general Celtic literature, translating works
from all six Celtic languages, although not dealing with modern works.

The ancient Celtic civilisation left its mark from Asia Minor to
Ireland. The Celts were the first Transalpine people to emerge into
recorded history. They were known as Keltoi to the Greeks, and
originated, according to the ancient chroniclers, from the region
around the Lower Danube. In the fourth century B.C. they began an
expansion through Europe and invaded Italy. They sacked Rome in
387-6 B.C. and Polybios tells us that the Romans remained under
Celtic domination until 349 B.C. when they began to fight back
successfully against the invaders. By 345 B.C. the Celtic conquest had
been turned back. A large proportion of Celts did remain in northern
Italy as settlers down to imperial times and evidence of their settlement
is shown in such place names as Trevi, Treviso, Treviglio, the River
Trebia, Reno and various other places which have obvious Celtic
names. A comparison with some of the Cornish place names is
interesting. This stay in Italy also resulted in some Celtic words being
borrowed by the Latins: words such as *gladius* (sword), *scutum*
(shield) and *vates* or *ovates* (philosopher or soothsayer). According to
Henri Hubert the Latin writers also benefited by the imagination of the
Celtic poets:[8]

> The story of the Gallic Wars, out of which Livy, a historian of
> genius gifted with the spirit of divination, has made a very
> remarkable historical work, is something quite by itself, rather
> fabulous and very epic. Monsieur Jullian [Camille Jullian,
> *Histoire de la Gaule,* Paris, 3rd ed., 1920] has suggested that the
> tradition was probably made up of Celtic epics. The well known
> story of Valerius Corvus who was rescued in single combat with
> a Gallic chief by a crow which pecked the Celt's face and hid
> the Roman from him with its wings, is an example. The episode
> is unlike anything else in Roman history and literature. But it is

like a famous episode in the great Irish epic of Ulster, the Táin Bó Chuailgne, in which the goddess Morrigu attacks Cuchulain, who has scorned her love, in the form of a crow. The crow is not a mere flight of fancy; it is the creature which stands for battle and the gods and goddesses of war.

An interesting, and perhaps ironic, sidelight to this period of Celtic empire emerges in the Roman Acta Triumphalia for the year 222 B.C. in the record of the battle of Clastidium (Casteggio, northern Italy). The Romans, led by the consul Marcellus, won a battle over the Celts, led by Virdumarus. This is the first time the Germanic peoples (ancestors of the English and the Franks) emerge into recorded history fighting for the Celts, according to Professor Mac Neill 'undoubtedly either as hired troops or as forces levied on a subject territory'. Professor Mac Neill is inclined to think, as does Professor Carl Marstrander, that the Germanic tribes were subjects of a Celtic empire. Mac Neill points out that a number of words of Celtic origin are found through the whole group of Germanic languages. 'Some of these words are especially connected with the political side of civilisation and are therefore especially indicative of Celtic political predominance at the time of their adoption into Germanic speech.'

The Celts also began to push into the Balkan Peninsula and during the next century entered Greece. The Macedonians tried to keep the Celts in check but they divided into three armies and began an advance in 260 B.C. The eastern army led by Cerethrios attacked Triballi on the Bulgarian side while the western army, commanded by Bolgios, entered Macedonia, defeated the Macedonian army and slew their king Ptolemy Cereaunos. The central army, commanded by Bran or Brennus and Achichorius, advanced successfully against Haemos and then against Thessaly. The Greek armies were scattered before the Celtic advance. Brennus came to Thermopylae where an Athenian army was gathered. He routed them and then turned on Aetolia and Callion, but his main force came by the gorges of Parnassos to Delphi, whose great temple was sacked. Although the Greeks finally turned back this Celtic invasion, Thrace remained a Celtic kingdom until 193 B.C. Some of the Celts also moved further eastwards and established a state called Galatia in Asia Minor. Hubert comments: 'What we know of the Galatian state gives us our first example of the organisation of a Celtic state.'[9]

What is astonishing is the intrinsic democratic character of Galatia, a state referred to by the chroniclers as the 'Commonwealth of the Galatians'. Government was by an assembly of 300 elected representatives and Galatia remained a Celtic speaking country until the fifth century A.D. In fact early Celtic society displayed a primitive communism, or community-ism, which, in the codification of the Brehon Laws of Ireland, became a very sophisticated social system. Evidence that such a social system was probably general to all Celtic societies may be seen by a comparison of the Brehon Laws with the Laws of Hywel Dda of Wales and some Breton laws embodied in the Treaty of 1532.[10] Even in the laws of the mythical king of Cornwall, Dunwallo Molmutius, one finds an intense regard for democracy and the rights of the individual. Dunwallo was said, by Geoffrey of Monmouth, to have been son of Cloten, king of Cornwall (circa 450 B.C.), and 'who established among the Britons the so called Molmutine Laws which are still famous today'.[11] It has been suggested that when King Alfred (871-99) compiled his famous Anglo-Saxon laws, Asser, abbot of Amesbury and bishop of Sherborne, a Welsh monk from St David's, translated the Molmutine Laws for the English king, who incorporated some of them into his code. Asser was certainly one of the authors of the 'Anglo-Saxon Chronicle'.[12] While the history is highly suspect the spirit of what are purported to be the Molmutine Laws agrees with the spirit of the Brehon Laws and those of Hywel Dda.

The contacts between the Celts and the Greeks resulted in some Celtic words being adopted into Greek, such as *leiousmata* or *leloumata* (a kind of body armour); *ernbrektou* (a kind of soup or porridge); *os* (the kermes oak); *taskos* (a stake) and *karuos* (a trumpet).

In the Celtic civilisation the Druids were the philosophers, teachers, exponents of the Celtic religion and natural scientists. They were well known and respected in the ancient world. The Celtic religion was one of the first to evolve a doctrine of immortality and the Druids taught that death is only a changing of place and that life goes on with all its forms and goods in another world, a world of the dead which gives up living souls. Therefore a constant exchange of souls takes place between the two worlds . . . death in this world brings a soul to the other and death in the other world brings a soul to this world. Julius Caesar observed that this religious outlook could have accounted for the reckless bravery of the Celts in battle, with their apparently complete lack of any fear of death. As to the philosophies of the

Druids, Aristotle, Sotion and Clement all state that early Greek philosophers borrowed much of their philosophy from the Celts. The similarity of Druidic philosophy, especially on immortality, and Pythagorean philosophy, has frequently been stated. Pythagoras had a slave named Zalmoxis of Thrace, who appears to have been a Celt. But while Clement of Alexandria says that Pythagoras and the Greeks acquired philosophy from the Celts, presumably through Zalmoxis, Hippolytus claims that Zalmoxis took Pythagoras's philosophy to the Druids, 'he, after the death of Pythagoras, having made his way there became the founder of this philosophy for them'.[13] Cicero pays tribute to the Druids as great natural scientists who had a knowledge of physics and astronomy applied in the construction of calendars. The earliest known Celtic calendar, and, incidentally, the earliest piece of Celtic writing, dates from the first century A.D. and is far more elaborate than the rudimentary Julian one. This is the 'Calendrier de Coligny' now in the Palais des Arts in Lyons, France.

There are numerous works on the social life of the Celts, such as Nora Chadwick's *The Celts*, Jan Filip's *Celtic Civilisation and Its Heritage* and the widely readable *Everyday Life of the Pagan Celts* by Anne Ross.[14] But Celtic studies is a changing field and old theories are constantly being discarded as new evidence—particularly archaeological evidence —comes to light. Patrick Crampton's *Stonehenge of the Kings*[15] presents just such startling new insights into Celtic life.

Here we can give no more than a brief glimpse of the ancient civilisation from which the Cornish people sprung. It is thought that the Celts reached the shores of Britain about 600 B.C. and began a series of immigrations which ended a few hundred years before the birth of Christ. Again modern research tends to put the date of the first Celtic migrations to Britain at a far earlier date. What is certain, however, is that by the time the Romans first arrived in Britain in 55 B.C. they found the island populated by Celtic tribes. It also appears from the evidence that when the Celts arrived in Britain they found another people occupying the island whom they absorbed in the same way as the English and French are absorbing the Celts today. A unique feature of the Celtic languages is that while they are classified as Indo-European, and have Indo-European vocabularies, much of their syntax is *not* Indo-European. Sir John Morris-Jones suggested that the survivals were similar to the idiom of the Hamitic languages.[16] The Hamito-Semitic group of languages includes Arabic, Hebrew, Ethiopic, Berber and ancient Egyptian, a linguistic area occupying the greater

part of northern Africa and the Near East. Professor Kenneth Jackson says of these non Indo-European remains:[17]

> It may be that some of these are due to the speech habits of a pre-Celtic population, who, when they learned the language of their Celtic conquerors, introduced the manners and construction, and 'accent', of their own tongue in their efforts to reproduce the new language they were learning.

In Chapter Six we will be seeing how the syntax of a language can survive after the language has ceased to be spoken.

Sometime around 325 B.C. a Greek mariner named Pytheas of Massilia (Marseilles) journeyed to Britain and wrote an account of the journey calling the islands of Britain and Ireland *Pretannikae* or the Pretanic Isles, a presumptively Celtic name. He wrote about 'a stormy strait [which] separates the shores of Britain, which the Dumnonii hold, from the Silurian island'. The Silures were a tribe living in the east of South Wales, thus the 'stormy strait' must be the Bristol Channel. 'This people,' says Pytheas speaking about the Dumnonii, 'still retain their ancient customs; they refuse to accept coin and insist on barter, preferring to exchange necessities rather than fix prices.' This is perhaps our first glimpse of the Celts of Cornwall. But it is from Diodorus Siculus (who died *circa* 21 B.C.), the author of a world history, that we get our first close look at Cornwall:

> The inhabitants of that part of Britain which is called Belerion [Land's End] are very fond of strangers, and from their intercourse with foreign merchants, are civilised in their manner of life. They prepare tin, working very carefully the earth in which it is produced. The ground is rocky, but it contains earthy veins, the produce of which is ground down, smelted and purified. They beat the metal into masses like astragli and carry it to a certain island lying off Britain called Ictis . . . here then the merchants buy the tin from the natives and carry it over to Gaul, and after travelling over land for about thirty days, they finally bring their loads on horses to the mouth of the Rhone.

Diodorus Siculus's account is extremely accurate. Land's End is certainly a place of rocky ground and the tin always occurs near granite. Charles Woolf says:[18]

The working of 'earthy veins' certainly refers to tin streaming, which means the winning of surface tin from soft ground or streams running from it. The 'certain island' is considered to be St. Michael's Mount. The 'astragalus' of tin dredged from the river at St. Mawes many years ago may well be one of those referred to . . . Archaeology has revealed the home of the 'natives' and has confirmed barter—the Grecian mirror from a grave at St. Keverne and Iberian brooches from Harlyn—treasured possessions from over the seas of a simple hard working people who received them in exchange for their tin.

After Julius Caesar's two abortive expeditions in 55 and 54 B.C. 40,000 Roman troops commanded by General Aulus Plautius, consisting of four legions, II Augusta, XIV Gemina, XX Valeria Victrix and IX Hispana, with their auxiliaries, secured a hold in Britain in A.D. 43. By A.D. 61, after the suppression of an uprising led by Boudicca (or Boadicea) the Romans were clearly in Britain to stay. It is generally supposed that the Romans did not enter Cornwall and halted their conquest at Exeter. Certainly Exeter was the nearest point of Roman civilisation to Cornwall. But the Romans did enter Cornwall and this is borne out by the finding of twenty-four earthworks of typical Roman type, many of which appear to be the small legionary 'marching camps', thrown up by the legions as a small fortress in which to spend the night. Five Roman milestones have also been discovered—these do not indicate distances from place to place but are monoliths usually erected on the completion of a road and dedicated to the honour of the emperor of the time. The inscriptions are in abbreviated Latin. The dates of the milestones range from A.D. 244 to 308. In 1931 at Magor Farm near Camborne, a Roman villa was discovered which appears to have been occupied in about A.D. 150 and eventually abandoned in A.D. 230 to 240. Woolf comments: 'Certain crudities of construction and lack of amenities suggests that it was not built by a Roman at all but possibly by a local person who had seen such villas outside Cornwall and had attempted to copy them on his return home.' It is interesting to note that Cornish word *magor* means an ancient ruin. Was the ruined villa still visible when the old Cornish farm was named? As Woolf says: 'Much work has yet to be done towards the elucidation of Cornwall in Roman times.' This does not only apply to the archaeological field but to the linguistic field. It might be possible to ascertain, as the Welsh have done, what

influence the lingua franca of the Roman Empire had on Cornish, if any, during this period. At the present time one is tempted to say that life in Cornwall was by-passed by the Roman occupation of the rest of the country.

The Romans pulled out of Britain in the fifth century A.D. and the fierce pagan Saxons began to invade the country. It was from the fifth century that vast waves of Celtic immigrants left Britain. Early writers, such as Gildas Albanius in the sixth century, claim that the Celts fled in the face of the Anglo-Saxon invasions. The Breton traditions of the eighth and ninth centuries, recorded by Eginhard (Einhardi Annales) and Ermold Le Noir (Ermoldi Nigelli Carmina) support this idea. But Nora Chadwick says that the Celts did not migrate under pressure from the Saxons.[19] Tradition and language alike lead to the conclusion that the earliest immigration to Armorica (now Brittany) came almost wholly from the Devon-Cornwall peninsula, which was, at this time, virtually untouched by Saxon aggression. According to Mrs Chadwick, the impetus for the migrations from Dumnonia came from Irish aggression. In her excellent study, Mrs Chadwick presents brief evidence showing the extent of Irish excursions to Wales and south-west Britain. Professor Jackson says: 'The Irish who settled on the west coast of Britain shortly before the end of Roman rule lived side by side with the British speaking population on terms of close companionship.'[20]

He presents evidence to show that the Irish language was spoken in south-western Wales and on the Dumnonian peninsula. But for all the 'close companionship' the British Celts still felt threatened by the Irish invaders and so began their exodus to Armorica. Mrs Chadwick points out four important facts. (1) That according to tradition the majority of the leaders of the emigration seem to have come from east central Wales, where no Saxon threat was felt. (2) While traditions of Irish saints are not lacking, even for the earliest period, the majority are from Wales. (3) Linguistic evidence suggests the majority of the settlers came from the Devon-Cornwall peninsula. (4) Most important of all, none of the early Breton settlers seems to have come from eastern or south-eastern, or even from mid-southern, England.

The British Celts, arriving among their fellow Gaulish Celts of Armorica, took with them many place names. The Breton kingdoms of Dumnonia and Cornouaille were of course taken from the British Dumnonia and Cornwall, which were certainly well secure from

Saxon incursions at this time. Likewise the British Celts also took with them the name of their country—Britain—and transposed it to Armorica as Brittany, or little Britain. There is also evidence that some Celtic rulers ruled in Cornwall and in Brittany. A *Life of Leonorus* claims that King Rhiwal 'took possession of Little Britain, and ruled jointly on both sides of the sea. . .'. Then there is the Breton tyrant Cunomorus of Carhaix, and King Mark Cunomorius, owner of Castle Dore, at Carhays, not far from Fowey, Cornwall. It is possible that they are one and the same.

The British Celts did not only migrate to Armorica: they also established settlements in Galicia in north-western Spain about the end of the fifth or the beginning of the sixth century. It has been suggested that the name derives from the Brythonic Celtic word *gallu*—strong men. Their religious leaders founded a diocese of Bretoña and the Celtic monastery of Santa Maria de Bretoña, Pastoriza near Mondonedo. The Council of Lugo, held by King Thiudemir in A.D. 567, records a division of the realm into two provinces and thirty dioceses nine of these belonging to Galicia. In A.D. 572 a council of bishops at Braga was attended by Mahiloc (Celtic—Mailoc), *Britonensis ecclesiae episcopus*. The Celtic influence in Galicia has lingered on even today with such survivals as the single drone *gaita* or bagpipe. Dances such as the Muneira show close kinship to Breton dances while traditional art forms rely a lot on circular designs with spiralesque movements common to the Celtic tradition. There are, of course, a lot of Celtic word roots in the Galician language (Galego) which is different from the other languages of Spain. Today Galicia has a population of two millions but due to the advance of Castilian Spanish and the suppression of the other languages of Spain (Basque, Catalan and Galician), especially in the recent years of the Fascist dictatorship, Galego is a dying language. It first appeared in written documents in A.D. 1192 and became the medium of a rich lyric poetry in the thirteenth and four- teenth centuries. In the sixteenth century the majority of speakers crystallised into Portuguese but the linguistic minority in the north west of the Iberian peninsula fell under the influence of the Castilian- speaking orbit. In the early 1960s the Galician national movement applied to join the League of Celtic Nations but their application was refused because, apart from the odd folkloric survivals, any Celtic foundation to Galicia has long since ceased to be.

With the coming of the Irish and Welsh, particularly during the period A.D. 450 to 550, the evangelising men and women of the

growing Christian Church started to arrive leaving as their memorial
hundreds of place names in Cornwall: St Breoc, St Buryan, St Columb,
St Endellion, St Ives, St Mawes, St Mawgan, St Tudy, St Mabyn, etc.
The Irish brought with them their Ogham script, the first written form
of the Irish language consisting of short lines drawn to or crossing a
base line. The Latin alphabet, a semi-unical script, which was adopted
with Christianity, was soon to replace this early form of Irish. There
are 315 inscriptions in Ogham in Ireland compared with forty-eight
in England and Wales. Cornwall has six such inscriptions. These
inscriptions consist almost entirely of proper names in the genitive
case, and although they are of no historical value, they tell us something about the Irish language in its early stages. Ogham bears the
same relation to the Irish of a later period as Latin does to French.
'Thus Ogham Dovatuci is the forerunner of Old Irish Dubhthaich
[still surviving in the surname Duffy] just as Latin avicellus is the
forerunner of the French oiseau.'[21] Professor Greene continues:

> When we find Irish written in Roman letters, from the seventh
> century onwards, a linguistic revolution had taken place, with
> words greatly reduced from their Ogam forms. This is parallel
> to the changes which took place in France and the other Roman
> languages as compared to Latin, and it is possible that the historic
> process was the same.

He adds:

> It may well be that the form of Irish found in the Ogam
> inscriptions was already archaic, and confined to the learned
> class, when the Christian missionaries came, and that it was
> discarded and replaced by the speech of the people when
> writing in Irish started in earnest in the seventh century.

According to Professor Greene Ogham was the archaic speech of the
Druids and incomprehensible to the ordinary man. 'And it is at least
possible that the Ogam inscriptions were carved in a language which
was no longer generally spoken, just as we to the present day use
Latin for monumental purposes.'
Of the six Ogham inscriptions in Cornwall, all carry an inscription
in Latin repeating the name of the commemorated person. There are
also numerous Latin inscriptions, some bearing the Chi Rho, one of the

earliest Christian symbols derived from the first two letters of the Greek word for Christ. Unfortunately this is a shadowy period in history, a Cornwall where legendary kings ruled of whom we can only get occasional glimpses. The Men Scryfa (or Men Scryfys), the written stone, standing high on the moors of West Penwith, is dated to the early sixth century and its inscription reads—RIALOBRANI CUNOVALI FILI (Rialobran son of Cunoval)—the names meaning 'Royal Raven' and 'Worthy Fame' respectively. Gereint is mentioned in the 'Anglo-Saxon Chronicle' in A.D. 710 as 'king of the Britons'— his name is popularly connected with the Roseland district of Cornwall. Another shadowy Cornish king referred to in the 'Anglo-Saxon Chronicle' is commemorated on a stone in the parish of St Cleer, north of Liskeard. The inscription reads—DONIERT ROGAVIT PRO ANIMA (Doniert ordered (this to be set up) for (the good of) his soul). Doniert has been identified with Dungarth, a Cornish king who was accidentally drowned in A.D. 878—the lettering and ornament of the stone agreeing with this date. Doniert is considered to be the last Cornish ruler to have controlled the whole of Cornwall as the Saxons had already inflicted a defeat on the Cornish in the east by A.D. 838.

As the Anglo-Saxons began to settle in Britain, the Celtic inhabitants were either slain or pushed slowly westwards. Nora Chadwick is of the opinion that the English and Celts intermarried as the English began to get a stronger grip on the island.[22] But this would have meant a number of Celtic loan words being drawn into the language. There were a few such words in pre-Conquest English but these were mainly of deep geographical significance (such as crag, dun, coomb, avon, etc.) and one or two religious words taken from the missionary Irish. The most prominent of these words was 'cross' (Gaelic *crois*) which fought a battle with the native English word 'rood' for several centuries before it was finally adopted into the language. Other Celtic words such as bucket, car, nook, crockery, noggin, gob, slogan, flannel, etc. were drawn into English at a much later date. Mario Pei comments:[23]

One might imagine that the Celtic of the original Britons would have supplied a fertile field for loan words to the Anglo-Saxon. Such is emphatically not the case . . . The reason for this seems to lie in the scantiness of social relations between the two races, the English considering the Celts as inferior and their own race and tongue superior.

Soon the Celts were pushed into the western part of the island, their territory extending from Dumnonia (Devon and Cornwall) across Wales to Cumberland and into Scotland where the British Celts mingled with the Goidelic Celts. After two centuries of struggle the Celtic Confederation was broken and the Celtic peoples were divided. The 'weahlas' or 'foreigners' as the English called the Celts, were pushed into 'the land of the foreigners'—or Wales. The Welsh called their country Cymru. Another land called Cymru was established in northern Britain but this small kingdom of Cymru (pronounced Cum-ree) was incorporated into the Gaelic Celtic kingdom of Scotland in the eleventh century. By the end of the following century the Scottish ruler, Calum a' chinn mhoir (Malcolm III, Malcolm Canmore or, in English, Malcolm the Bighead) was defeated by the English and had to surrender the territory as the price of defeat. The ancient name of Cymru is still retained in the form of Cumbria and Cumberland. The Brythonic language of Cumbria, of which no written records remain, died out in the twelfth century. Professor Jackson points out that Cumberland still has many Celtic place names.[24] The peculiar style of Cumberland wrestling is remarkably similar to that in Cornwall and Brittany.

Most of the earliest Welsh poetry that is extant was written in 'lowland' Scotland about the sixth century A.D., though to call it 'Welsh' is an anachronism. It was written in a Brythonic Celtic language which later developed into Welsh, Breton and Cornish and so the poems of Taliesin and Aneirin could equally be claimed in the Cornish literary tradition. Aneirin wrote the famous poem ' Y Gododdin'. The Gododdin were a British tribe which lived in south-east Scotland who, during the sixth century, led by their chief Mynyddawg Mwynfawr, lord of Dineiddyn (Edinburgh), sent 300 warriors in an attempt to recapture the stronghold of Catraeth (Catterick, Yorkshire) from the English. The expedition was a disastrous failure and in the poem Aneirin tells the unhappy story. Aneirin and Taliesin are not the only early 'Welsh' poets from 'lowland' Scotland. Llywarch Hen, another famous sixth-century poet, began his life in south-east Scotland.[25]

As the Anglo-Saxons began to push towards Cornwall, penetrating deep into the once unified Dumnonia kingdom, the name of Cornwall became known to written history. Kernow may have derived from the name of a tribe (such as the Cornavi—a Celtic tribal name that occurs frequently—the Celts of Caithness and Chester were also called

Cornavi as well as Carnabi). The name could also derive from 'the Rock land', 'land of Carns' or 'the Horn Shaped land'. Whatever its original meaning, to the Celtic word *Kern* or *Corn*, the Saxons fixed the name 'weahlas' (foreigners) and arrived at Corn-weahlas or Cornwall.[26]

According to Jenner the Cornish tried to fight off the Saxons by joining forces with their fellow Celts:

> The Cornish did join the Welsh and Bretons on occasion, under, perhaps, their own Arthur, in the 6th Century, and under Rhodri Molwynog of Gwynedd and Ifor map Alan of Brittany in the 8th Century but these were only temporary alliances and they continued to be governed by their own kings such as Cador, Conan, Gerrans, Teuder, Blederic, Doniert, Hoel etc.

Jenner refers to Cornwall's 'own Arthur'; was the legendary King Arthur really a Cornish ruler fighting against the invading English? If so, is the provenance of the Arthurian legends attributable to Cornwall and even to the Cornish language? Arthur was most definitely a Celtic ruler born in the late fifth century A.D. who led the last big Celtic resistance against the Anglo-Saxon invasion and conquest of Britain. This much is clear. But the legends of Arthur, now completely swamped with medieval tales of chivalry and knighthood, have obscured the reality of Arthur. Legends of Arthur persist in Brittany, Wales and Scotland as well as Cornwall. According to Geoffrey Ashe:[27]

> First: Where was Arthur's home territory? Here, all tradition converges. The problem is whether tradition can be trusted. It makes him a West Countryman. Even such nebulous clues as place names and local legend point that way. They cover, indeed, a vast stretch of Britain (nobody else is commemorated so widely, except the Devil); and, as Tennyson said, Arthur's name streams over the land like a cloud. But the cloud has shape as well as extent. In all its length, from the Isles of Scilly to Perth, only the West Country supplies Arthur with dwelling places. His Cornish home is Kelliwic, probably a hill fort in the parish of Egloshayle near Padstow. Cadbury Castle (formerly plain Camel) has been identified with Camelot from time immemorial. The oldest triads locate Arthur in Cornwall. The Life of St. Carannog

connects him with Dunster. The Life of St. Gildas portrays him
summoning his troops of [sic] Cornwall and Devon. If Kelliwic,
Dunster and Cadbury are all authentic, he must have moved as his
power increased. But the vital point is that no comparable places
exist outside of the West Country. The courts of Caerleon
and Winchester are found only in medieval literature. Geoffrey
of Monmouth himself gives the same testimony. His story of the
birth of Tintagel is not evidence as to history, but it shows that
Arthur was supposed, even in Wales, to have come from that
quarter. Likewise, even the Welsh bard who spoke to Henry II
indicated that Somerset, not Wales, was thought of as the right
place for his burial.

The famous 'Black Book of Carmarthen', referring to Arthur's son
Llacheu, calls a group of West Country soldiers 'Arthur's men'. Of
course, Arthur's alleged birth at Tintagel cannot be true. There was
no fortress or castle there until Norman times.

The main source we have for the Arthurian legends on which the
authors Malory (*Morte d'Arthur*) and Tennyson (*Idylls of the King*)
based their work is, of course, Geoffrey of Monmouth's famous
History of the Kings of Britain. Geoffrey lived in the early part of the
twelfth century and if the doubtful evidence of the Welsh chroniclers
is accepted he died in A.D. 1155. For his source material Geoffrey
refers to only one work:

Walter, Archdeacon of Oxford, a man skilled in the art of
public speaking and well informed about the history of foreign
countries, presented me with a certain very ancient book written
in the British language. The book, attractively composed to form
a consecutive and orderly narrative, set out all the deeds of these
men, from Brutus, the first king of the Britons, down to
Cadwallader the son of Cadwallo. At Walter's request I have taken
the trouble to translate the book into Latin. . .

The book to which Geoffrey refers is lost if, point out the more
cynical scholars, such a book ever existed. Sir John Lloyd wrote: 'No
Welsh composition exists which can be reasonably looked upon as
the original or even the groundwork of the *History of the Kings of
Britain*.' But could this book, written in 'the British language', have
had its birth in Cornwall? The theory is not so far fetched when one

considers the poem produced by John of Cornwall in the same century in Latin, which he said he had translated from an old manuscript in Cornish. John, who reproduced notes from the original manuscript, called his work 'The Prophecy of Merlin'. Geoffrey's *History* contains a section entitled 'The Prophecies of Merlin' which he originally conceived as a separate volume. Jenner's remark that 'it looks as if some of the so called Mabinogion of Arthur were known in Cornwall also' is a valid one. But unless there is a growth of a bigger corpus of scholars and the discovery of new manuscript evidence, we can only speculate. But while we can only speculate on the provenance of the Arthurian legends we can offer more informed opinion of that other world famous romance, the story of Tristan and Iseult.

It was Joseph Bédier[28] who made the significant discovery that all the stories of Tristan and Iseult could be traced back to a single poem. Thomas, a French poet of the twelfth century, is perhaps the oldest Tristan writer and from this version Gottfried von Strassburg, a German poet, composed his fine epic on which Wagner based his opera. An English version, in a north English dialect, was composed in the thirteenth century by Thomas the Rhymer of Ercildoun and a Scandinavian version was composed by Brother Robert. But there are only 3,000 lines of the Thomas poem extant. Another twelfth-century French poet Béroul made a version and from this Eilhart von Oberge derived his version. Chretien de Troyes (author of the Perceval Grail story) also wrote a Tristan poem which has been lost but which is said to have been the basis of a long romance by Luce de Gas and Helie de Barron entitled *Prose Tristan*. This tends to mix up the story with Arthurian legends. The earliest known full length version in a Celtic language is the sixteenth-century Welsh *Ystoria Trystan*, now in Cardiff Library. Béroul also gave the basis to Malory's *Morte d'Arthur* which, in its turn, inspired such poets as Matthew Arnold, Swinburne and Tennyson.

Professor Joseph Loth, professor of Celtic at Rennes and Paris put forward the theory that both Béroul and Thomas derived their poems from a single Cornish source. Addressing the Penzance Natural History and Antiquarian Society on 28 November 1913, in support of Loth's theory of the Cornish provenance of the Tristan romance, Jenner described Loth as 'the greatest living authority on Celtic Cornwall'.[29] In advancing his theories Jenner pointed out that the author of the original tale was remarkably informed about Cornish topography. Loth, in a work *Contributions a l'étude de la Table Ronde*,[30]

said he felt that the story was first written down at the time of the Saxon and Norman influence in Cornwall.

Loth makes two main points. (1) That the author of the original story from which Béroul and Thomas derived their versions, and upon which the entire literature of the Tristan romance is founded, was, if not actually a Cornishman, well acquainted with Cornwall. (2) The scenes of the story are clearly laid from Fowey along the south coast to St Michael's Mount, taking real and identifiable places for reference. Not only real places were taken as setting for the tale but *likely* places.

King Mark of Cornwall, the husband of Iseult (in Cornish Ysolt), was a real Cornish ruler in the sixth century A.D. It is possible that the name Mark derives from the ordinary Roman praenomen Marcus but it seems more likely that the name is genuinely Celtic meaning 'horse'. Béroul actually mentions that Mark has horse's ears. Animal names for people were fairly common in the Celtic languages. The Welsh make Mark's name March (horse), and there is a Welsh/Irish story of a king called March and also Eachaidh (Irish for horse). Loth mentions a similar Breton story of a ruler called Guimarc'h or Gwrac'h at Prat-an-Rous in Denhars. King Mark comes into the lives of several Celtic saints. In the 'Life of St Pol de Leon', written in A.D. 880 by Urmonek, a monk of Landévennec, we are told that St Pol (or St Paul, the saint of the next parish to Penzance) was King Mark's chaplain before he was sent to Brittany. A story is told of how Mark had a beautiful set of hand bells. Paul begged for one of the bells to take with him but Mark refused. While Paul was on the Isle de Baz, near Roscoff, a fisherman caught a large fish and when it was cut open one of the bells was found. A sixth-century Celtic hand bell is now preserved in the Cathedral of St Pol de Leon—did Iseult summon her maid Brangien with it? Several romantic conjectures have been made. In this 'Life of St Pol de Leon' we also read of 'King Marc whose other name is Quonomorius' (*quem alio nomine Quonomorium vocant*) and that he is a powerful monarch under whose rule lived peoples speaking four different languages. It seems highly likely that Mark ruled not only in Cornwall but in Brittany also for there was a Marcus Cunomorus of Carhaix, Count of Poher, who comes down in Breton tradition as a tyrant. He is reported to have usurped the rule of Dumnonia from King Judal till defeated by the diplomacy of St Samson. In Cornwall Mark's capital was at the fifth-century fort at Castle Dore, at Carhays, not far from Fowey. It is here we get our most striking

evidence of the real Mark and his connection with Tristan. Near Fowey stands a pillar stone over seven feet high bearing a worn Latin inscription dating from the middle of the sixth-century— DRUSTANUS HIC IACIT CUNOMORI FILIUS.[31] Drustanus on the inscription is philologically identical with Tristan.[32] The inscription therefore reads: 'Tristan lies here, the son of Cunomorus.' In the legend Tristan is made the nephew of Mark. How much more dramatic is his love affair with Iseult, Mark's young bride, if, as the inscription states, he was Mark's son and Iseult his stepmother.

Professor Loth also found that Iseult's name was used as a place name in a charter of A.D. 967 when some lands of Lesmanaoc in St Keverne, were described by the boundaries of Porth Alow, along the brook to Hryt Eselt—the Ford of Iseult. According to Jenner, Loth proves 'without dogmatising too much, that it is not Breton *lais* worked up by Frenchmen, as used to be the theory, but a lost literature of our own Cornwall'. He adds, 'we may claim even the nucleus of the great Grail allegory as of Cornish origin'. Perhaps, and it seems exceedingly likely, the Tristan romance was part of Cornish folklore: a tale based on the historical events of the sixth century, embellished, told and retold by many a Cornish bard. But was the tale ever written down in Cornish? Perhaps the original Cornish stories, like a vast number of Celtic tales, were never committed to paper and so perished with their reciters. Perhaps a Cornishman took the story to Brittany where it became part of Breton folklore which was translated and written by Béroul or Thomas.[33] Again we are left to speculate, but it is, at least, a speculation based upon some established facts, unlike the tales of Arthur.

By A.D. 700 the West Saxons had reached as far as Taunton and Exeter and the Celts of Dumnonia were severed from their fellow Celts of Wales and the north, and the defeat of the Dumnonii was merely a matter of time. As the Saxons pushed westwards towards the Tamar, along the north side of Devon, the Celts of the peninsula, whom the Saxons called the 'west Welsh' in contrast to the 'foreigners' of Wales, managed to inflict a defeat on the Saxons at Camel in A.D. 721/2. Despite considerable resistance, the Saxons pressed on and were soon raiding into Cornish territory. By the parish church of Lanteglos by Camelford, in north Cornwall, there is a stone written in the English of the period: 'Ælseth 7 Genereth whote thisne sybstel for Ælwines soul 7 heysel' (Aelseth and Genereth made this monument for the soul of Aelwine and for themselves). In A.D. 825 the Cornish

fought another battle in Devon and in A.D. 838 they enlisted the help
of the Danes. A combined army of Cornishmen and Danes met the
English at Hingston Down, near Callington, but were defeated by
Ecgberht of Wessex (802-39). For another century the Cornish
managed to put off the subjugation of their country but resistance was
finally overcome in A.D. 936 by Athelstan, king of Wessex (925-39),
who drove the Cornish out of Exeter and fixed the River Tamar as the
boundary between his Saxon kingdom and the 'west wealhas'.
Cornwall, although it had ceased to be an independent state, retained
some independence (more or less as the Indian princes did under
British Imperial rule in India) under the suzerainty of the kings of
Wessex and, in A.D. 954 when the Saxon kingdoms joined together,
England.

Under English rule the individuality of Cornwall was at least
recognised. Eadmund (939-46) of Wessex had a charter drawn up in
A.D. 944 in which he styles himself as the 'King of the English and
ruler of this British province'.[34] According to Jenner: 'Even the
English did not consider Cornwall to be part of England, but a
separate earldom or duchy attached to the English Crown. All through
the Middle Ages the official expression "in Anglia et Cornubia" was
as common as England and Wales is now.'[35] In fact 'west Wales' was
marked on some maps until Tudor times and as late as 1485 certain
laws were passed which were peculiar to Cornwall.

It was during this century of the conquest of Cornwall that a
Welsh poet wrote 'Armes Prydain' (the Prophecy of Britain). The
poem was written in A.D. 930, six years before the conquest of
Cornwall, consisting of 199 lines. It calls upon the Celts of Wales,
Cornwall, Scotland, Ireland and the Isle of Man, to unite and throw the
English out of Britain led by Cadwaladr and Cynan:

And concord of Welshmen and Dublin's men,
Gaelic men of Ireland, Man and Scotland,
Cornishmen and Clydesmen at one with us.

The poem is written with great vigour but its call to throw out
the conquerors, in Cornwall's case, was a forlorn one.

Athelstan divided his conquest into areas called 'hundreds'—a
division of English land said to have originally contained a hundred
families. Although Kenstec, a bishop of the Cornish, had written a
letter giving his allegiance to Ceolnoth of Canterbury in A.D. 865,

Athelstan decided to reform the church in Cornwall for it still retained much of its independence, particularly its Celtic monasticism. The parochial system was introduced and the diocese of Cornwall, which had been created in A.D. 931 under a Cornish bishop named Conan, had its See established at St Germans. In A.D. 981, along with many other seats of Celtic learning, St Petroc's monastery was sacked and its remaining possessions were transferred to Bodmin. The old Celtic church had been centred at Petroc's monastery which the English called Petrocys Stow (Padstow). After the death of Athelstan all the bishops of Cornwall were appointed from Englishmen, the last being Burhwold, who died in 1040. It was in that year that St German's lost its cathedral status and an independent diocese of Cornwall was dissolved. The diocese was combined with Crediton. Not until 1876 was a diocese of Cornwall re-established with its See at Truro. Under Bishop Burhwold the parishes of Cornwall were reorganised and the Celtic forms of the church services were slowly abandoned. Celtic monasticism, such as the community at St Michael's Mount, long a centre of Celtic scholarship, was dissolved. St Michael's was reconstituted, however, as a collegiate college in 1050 and we find English already competing with the Cornish language.[36]

It is more than a probability that, in the reform of the Celtic monastic centres, some Cornish manuscripts were destroyed and this could account for our sad lack of remains from this period. It may even lead us to suppose that perhaps the stories of Tristan and Iseult and Arthur were lost in this manner. In the twelfth century, for example, we have the poem written by John of Cornwall in Latin hexameters, 'The Prophecy of Merlin', dedicated to Bishop Warelwast. John claims that it is a translation of a very early Cornish manuscript and he gives notes in the original Cornish. The only known manuscript of his work that survives, a fifteenth-century copy, is in the Vatican Library and dated 8 October 1474.[37] It was the Celtic scholar Dr Whitley Stokes who pointed out this survival in the latter part of the nineteenth century. Yet while the Cornish scholar, Jenner, accepted the manuscript on face value in 1904, by 1913 he maintained that it was 'a medieval fake'.[38] Yet there is, so far, no concrete reason to doubt John of Cornwall's word that he translated the manuscript from an old Cornish original. Certainly, judging from the words he wrote on the manuscript, he had a knowledge of Cornish.

It is from this period that we begin to get our first glimpses of the language that we can recognise as Old Cornish. English pressure had

separated the Welsh from the Cornish in the sixth century, and
similarly, the Bretons were now leading their own existence. The
once common British Celtic language now began to follow different
paths of development.

Throughout the old territory of Dumnonia there are a number of
inscribed stones bearing, in the main, names of rulers which throw
very little light on the Cornish language.[39] Unfortunately most of the
readings of these stones date from the nineteenth century and are
dubious. An example of such an inscription, noted in the mid-
eighteenth century, found on the threshold stone of the south door of
the parish church of Lustleigh, near Moreton, Devon, reads:
DXXTUIDOC: CONHINOC. According to one interpretation:[40]

> The language is Cornish and I take the second and third letter to
> represent the ET ligature & and the stone to be the boundary
> stone or tombstone of Dettuidoc son of Conhinoc. This part of
> Devon was not conquered by Saxons until after 925 but the
> inscription looks to be not later than 9th Century and to be
> possibly of the 8th Century.

Fortunately new research into the corpus of the fifth to eighth
century south-western inscribed stones as a source of Celtic names is
being undertaken by the Institute of Cornish Studies under its director
Professor Charles Thomas.

Our first real knowledge of Cornish comes from glosses, notes on
manuscripts in the language of the writer to explain a Latin text,
written between the lines and in the margin, just as a schoolboy
of today marks his Latin, Greek, French or German grammar.
Sometimes the glosses are single words, sometimes long sentences
explaining the meaning of a phrase. The first Cornish glosses are found
in a treatise on Donatus by Smaragdus, abbot of Mihiel, now in the
Bibliothèque Nationale, Paris; together with three glosses now in the
Bodleian Library[41], these are all from the tenth century and the Celtic
scholar Zeuss first published them as Old Welsh glosses in his
Grammatica Celtica.[42] This mistake was corrected by Whitley Stokes
in his work *Old Breton Glosses*, which he had privately printed in
Calcutta in 1879.

Glosses come from St Petroc's Gospels, which contain 141 leaves,
and were written in the ninth or tenth century.[43] The gospels were
housed in Petroc's monastery (Padstow) until its sack in A.D. 981.

On the fly-leaves of this manuscript is the record of ceremonies of manumissions, or the freeing of slaves, covering the period A.D. 940-1040 when 122 slaves were freed. The overwhelming number of names, ninety-eight, are Cornish, with twelve Saxon names and twelve Latin or Biblical names. Halliday maintains: 'The Cornishmen were probably descendants of slaves of the period of Cornish kings and not wretches enslaved by the Saxon for the Saxons were not much given to slavery and of the thirty-three liberators twenty-four have Saxon names and only five Celtic.'[44] In fact the opposite is probably true. Celtic society, as may be judged by the Brehon Laws and those of Hywel Dda, was not given to the practice of slavery. Loss of civil rights punished criminals but even those suffering 'civil degradation' had certain rights and were not treated as chattels as under the Saxon system. The 'Colloquies' of Aelfric, monk of Winchester, is explicit about Saxon slavery.[45] Far from the small number of Celtic slave owners listed as freeing slaves indicating a reluctance on the part of the Cornish to free slaves, it could be more readily argued that they had no slaves to free.

It is from the twelfth century that we get a more extensive picture of the language with a manuscript which has become known as the 'Cottonian Vocabulary' or 'Vocabularium Cornicum', which appears to have been based on the earlier 'English–Latin Lexicon' of Aelfric. The manuscript was mistakenly classified as an early Welsh vocabulary until a Mr Antis discovered it in the Cottonian Library and brought it to the attention of the eminent Celtic scholar Edward Lhuyd. Lhuyd examined it between 1701 and 1707 and wrote: 'When I had seen the book I knew very well that it was not a Welsh vocabulary as it appeared by the Latin title "Vocabularium Wallicum" written at the end of it, but a Cornish vocabulary.' The manuscript covers seven pages of Cornish nouns, concerning parts of the human body, birds, animals, fish, trees, herbs, ecclesiastical and liturgical terms plus a number of adjectives. Preceding the vocabulary is a calendar containing many Cornish words and the lives of Cornish and Welsh saints. This manuscript is very basic to the history of the Cornish language as it is almost the whole body of Old Cornish.[46] The text was not edited until 1859 when Dr Edwin Norris appended it to his edition of *The Old Cornish Drama* which was studied and used by Nance in the *Cornish–English Dictionary* of 1938. In 1964 Dr E. van T. Graves of Columbia University published the vocabulary as *The Old Cornish Vocabulary*[47] which contained 961 entries, printed with corresponding

Breton forms and Middle and Modern forms in all three Brythonic Celtic languages.

These few remains of the period of the language classified as Old Cornish lead one to speculate on the loss of other linguistic remains from this period. Commenting on such manuscripts Jenner says: 'There may be others of very early date, which have been hitherto classified as Old Welsh or Breton, such as the lament for Geraint of Devon generally attributed to Llywarch Hen, and certain glosses in Latin manuscripts.'[48] There is still a field for exploration.

From this period we also get our first comment on the Cornish language from Gerald the Welshman (Giraldus Cambrensis):[49]

Cornubia vero et Amorica Britannia lingua utuntur fere persimili, cambris tamen propter originalem convenientiam in multis adhuc et fere cunctis intelligibli. Quae, quanto delicata minus et incomposita magis tanto antiquo linguae Britanniae idiomati, ut arbitror, est appropriata.

When the Normans invaded England, Cador, or Condor, was the name of the earl of Cornwall. According to Jenner he was a descendant of the Cornish kings, although his predecessors in office from the time of Athelstan were Ordgar, Eadulf, Ethelmar, and Algar, plainly Saxon names.[50] Cador, or Condor, it appears, made common cause with the Normans, and the army of William of Normandy contained many Bretons. Having gained control of Cornwall, however, William deposed Cador, or Condor, and made Robert, earl of Mortain, its ruler. A number of Bretons were rewarded by grants of land in Cornwall; Bretons such as Blokin, founder of the Bloyou family; Alvred, founder of the Montague family and Gunnar, who held Dimelihoc and Wilhuniow. Several Breton names appear as holders of Cornish manors in the Domesday Book. It was not until much later that more humble Bretons came to Cornwall where they could earn higher wages, learn trades or do missionary work as clergymen. The deposed Cador, or Condor, however, had a son named Cadoc, Caradoc or Condor II, who was restored to the earldom after the attainder of William, son of Robert of Mortain. In 1104 he had a daughter named Avice or Beatrix who married Reginald Fitz Henry, son of Henry I, who had the earldom by right of inheritance through his wife.[51]

The Normans interfered little with the Cornish. They went to

Cornwall mainly as landowners, speaking Norman-French among themselves; they used Cornish to communicate with the people. But the English, who had settled in Cornwall, were now placed in the position of a 'middle class' and resented being caught between two cultures.

B*

Chapter Two

Middle Cornish

Medieval Cornwall is very little known to us. Between us and it there is the barrier of a lost language and perhaps a lost literature as well, for in a change of language, as in moving house, a good many things get lost and broken.[1]

Jenner's statement has been echoed by Elliott-Binns who points out that since written records are lacking, the extent to which Cornish was used in the medieval period is largely a matter for surmise.[2] But we can base our surmise on fragments of knowledge. For example, Cornish, which had now entered a softer sounding period known as Middle Cornish, had sufficient prestige for the gentlemen of Cornwall to use it in their mottoes for their coats-of-arms. Some of these were gathered during the seventeenth century. Perhaps the most interesting of these is that belonging to Carminow of Carminow in the parish of Mawgan Meneg: 'Cala rag Whethlow'—A Straw for Tales. The motto may be seen carved on the sixteenth-century pulpit in the church of St Teath. In the reign of Edward III, Lord Scroope, a baron of the realm, commenced a law suit against Carminow for bearing the same coat-of-arms as himself. Reference was made to John of Gaunt as a judge in such matters and on 16 June 1386, John of Gaunt stated that the Carminows had borne the arms before the Norman Conquest but, as Lord Scroope was a baron of the realm, Carminow was ordered to add to his arms 'a pile in chief gules' for distinction. It was, according to tradition, at this time that Carminow took up the motto 'Cala rag Whethlow'.[3]

The Tonkin family (earls of Godolphin) had a motto 'Frank ha leal ettoga' or 'Franc ha leal atho ve'—Free and Loyal Forever, or, Free and Loyal Am I. The Boscawen family (Viscounts Falmouth) used the motto 'Bosco, Pasco, Karenza Venza'. The first two words are meaningless as recorded. The second two words belong to a Cornish saying: Kerensa a vynsa, covaytys ny vynsa—Love would, greed wouldn't. E. G. R. Hooper, in Cornish Nation, September 1972, says the motto

seems an attempt at a pun. The Polwhele family used the motto 'Karenza whelas karenza'—Love Worketh Love; the Tonkins of Trevaunance used 'Kenz ol tra, Tonkin, ouna Deu Mahtern yn'—Tonkin, above all things, Fear God and the King. Other mottoes known to have been used were 'Car Deu reyz pub tra'—Love God Above All (Harris of Keneggy); 'Teg yw hedhwch'—Fair is Peace (Noye of St Buryan); 'En Hav perkou Gwav'—In Summer Remember Winter (Gwavas); 'Rag a Mahtern a Pow'—For King and Country (Polkinhorne) and 'Bethoh Dur'—Be Bold (Sloggett of Tresloggett).[4]

If the gentry of Cornwall still respected the language enough to use it in their mottoes, the language should therefore have been in a fairly strong position when, on 17 March 1337, Cornwall became the first duchy created since the Conquest in recognition of its peculiar position in the kingdom. A few years before the creation of the duchy the bishop of Exeter, John de Grandisson (1327-69), writing to some cardinals in 1329, pointed out that 'furthermore, the language known in the extremities of Cornwall is still not English but British'. In 1336, according to the Register of John de Grandisson, there arose a quarrel in the parish of St Buryan, four miles from Land's End. The bishop had to travel to the parish to sort out matters in person. Formal submissions were made to him in French and English by thirteen prominent parishioners while the rest of the evidence was given in Cornish and had to be translated by Henry Marseley, the rector of St Just. After the hearing, the bishop preached a sermon which was then translated into Cornish by Marseley. De Grandisson also mentions a Cornish priest named Ralph de Tremur of Lanivet who had studied at Oxford and was instituted to the rectory of Warleggan. De Grandisson says he was a Master of Arts able to speak fluently in Latin, French, English and Cornish. But Tremur had lapsed into heresy and wandered through the diocese spreading his heterodox views. De Grandisson was forced to excommunicate him for his denials, in particular, that of the doctrine of transubstantiation. De Grandisson seems to have been very conscientious of his role as administrator of the church in Cornwall by the appointment of people who could preach to the Cornish in their own language. In 1339 he licensed J. Polmarke to help the vicar of St Merryn, near Padstow, 'expound the Word of God in the said church in the Cornish language'. A few years previously, in 1335, Brother Roger of Truro was listed as being able to hear confessions in Cornish and Brother John of Bodmin was to preach and hear confessions in Cornish and English.[5] Elliott-Binns

points out that Brother Roger was a Dominican named Roger Tyrela and he appears to have been the only confessor provided for those knowing Cornish only. He concludes that this indicates that most Cornish people were bilingual at the time and that English was fairly common.[6] However, as late as 1538, John Veysey, bishop of Exeter, specifically ordered that all or part of the Epistle or Gospel of the day, or else the Paternoster, Ave Maria, Creed and Ten Commandments, should be read in Cornish in those parishes where English was not spoken. Chantry priests were told to teach children the Seven Works of Mercy in Cornish or in English as required. There are even instances, at this time, of familiarity with Cornish being stipulated for the appointment of parish priests.[7] As late as 1560 it was directed by the bishop that Cornish should be used in teaching the Catechism where the English language was not understood. So perhaps Mr Elliott-Binns leaps to a too simplistic conclusion on the observation that only one confessor was appointed in 1335 to hear confessions from Cornish monoglots. Jenner went so far as to say, 'there is said to be some evidence that even as late as the reign of Elizabeth, Cornish was spoken in a few places to the east of the Tamar, notably in South Hams. Polwhele, however, limits the South Hams use of Cornish to the time of Edward I.[8] While geographically it is quite possible that the old Celtic speech of Dumnonia survived in South Hams, east of Plymouth, in the area around Kingsbridge to Bolt Tail, Bolt Head and Prawle Point to Start Point, until the time of the Norman Conquest, there seems no evidence, certainly not in place names, to suggest the Celtic language survived there for any longer period. Indeed, Nance has written: 'Some of the statements in Jenner's *Handbook* he would have altered himself if he had brought out a new edition: as I know, from having discussed these points with him.'[9] Nance agrees there is no evidence of Cornish having been spoken in Devon in Edward I's reign and still less in the time of Elizabeth I.

The church, as the centre of learning, played an extremely important part in the history of the language and the collegiate church of St Thomas of Canterbury at Glasney, Penryn, became the centre of literary activity in the Cornish language during this period. The suppression of Glasney during the Reformation doubtless contributed to the failure of Cornwall to produce a distinctive literature of its own.[10] Penryn, the site of Glasney, stands at the head of the Penryn river, three miles north west of Falmouth and, at the time of the Domesday survey, it was already an established seaport and trading town. It is

from the cartulary of the collegiate church of St Thomas of Canterbury at Glasney that we get what is possibly the earliest known complete sentence in the Cornish language which has survived. This fifteenth-century manuscript[11] contains the story of the foundation of the college in 1265 by Walter Brandscombe, bishop of Exeter, in consequence of the appearance to him, in a vision, of St Thomas. The bishop is directed to go to Penryn at a certain place near the River Autre called Polsethow, the mere or pit to which animals wounded by arrows (*sethow*) were wont to run. Here he would find a swarm of bees in a large willow tree and at that spot he was to put up a High Altar. The manuscript says: '*De quo loco in lingua cornubica quia prophatusm fuit ab antiquo . . . in Polsethow ywhylvr anethow*'—Of which place it has been prophesied in Cornish . . . in Polsethow shall dwellings or marvels be seen.[12]

Glasneth, old Cornish loosing the final *th* sound, means green vegetation and Glasney stood on a heavily wooded area of Penryn, bordering a river. Whether the foundation of the college happened as recorded, Walter Brandscombe laid the foundation stone, brought from Caen, on the day of the Annunciation of Our Lady, in 1265, and two years later the church was consecrated. It became the place of learning in the south west and had the Reformation not destroyed it Glasney might well have become the university of Cornwall. Several leading Oxford scholars became provosts at Glasney such as William Trengofe of Exeter College (fellow of the college between 1403 and 1417 and rector and chancellor of the university from 1418 to 1420). He was provost of Glasney in 1427-36. Michael Trewynnard, also a fellow of Exeter College, was provost in 1436-8 and yet another fellow of Exeter College, John Evelyng, who was rector of the college in 1438-51, was provost at Glasney in 1471. Glasney, after building up a wide reputation for its scholarship, was suppressed in 1535, the year Henry VIII was excommunicated by the church and Thomas Cromwell became vicar-general. The college lingered on, however, and it is listed in 1545 among the chantries granted to Henry by Act of Parliament. Master John Libbe became the last provost on 30 September 1546. John Leland, during his tour of Cornwall in the 1530s, describes the college 'as strongly walled and encastled, having three towers and guns at the butt of the creek'. The land passed into the possession of the Godolphin family and then to the duke of Leeds. Glasney eventually became the borough gaol and was finally pulled down in the nineteenth century.

Glasney was the centre where the Middle Cornish miracle plays

appear to have been written. It was the popularity of this medieval drama that provided the only bulwark against the increasing pressures on the language. In Cornwall the village amphitheatre, or *plen an gwary,* held an important position in Cornish life. In such amphitheatres, a remarkable survival of which can still be seen in Bank Square, St Just-in-Penwith, seven miles from Penzance, a series of religious plays were acted. Richard Carew (1555-1620) in his famous *Survey of Cornwall,* published in 1602, describes the *plen an gwary* by saying they were mostly fifty feet across. The one at St Just, however, when it was measured by Dr Borlase in 1750, was 126 feet across. It was still encased in granite but since then the stones have disappeared. According to Carew:

> The guary miracle (in English, a miracle play) is a kind of interlude compiled in Cornish out of some scripture history with that grossness which accompanied the old Roman comedy. For representing it, they raise an earthen amphitheatre in some open field, having the diameter of it enclosed plain some 40 or 50 foot. The country people flock from all sides, many miles off, to hear and see it; for they have therein devils and devices to delight as well the eye and the ear; the players con not their parts without book, but are prompted by one called the ordinary who followeth at their back with the book in one hand and telleth them softly what they must pronounced aloud, which manner once gave occasion to a pleasant conceited gentleman of practising a merry prank: for he undertaking (perhaps a set purpose) an actor's room, was accordingly lessoned before hand by the ordinary: 'Go forth, man, and shew thyself.' The gentleman steps out upon the stage and, like a bad clerk in scripture manners, cleaving more to the letter than to the sense, pronounced those words aloud. 'Oh' (says the fellow softly in his ear) 'you mar all the play'. And with this his passion, the actor makes the audience in like sort acquainted. Hereon the promptor falls to flat railings and cursing in the bitterest terms he could devise: which the gentlemen with a set gesture and countenance still soberly related, until the ordinary, driven at last into a mad rage, was fain to give over all. With trousse, though it brake off the interlude, yet defrauded the beholders, but dismissed them with a great deal more sport and laughter than twenty such guares could have afforded.

It must be remembered, of course, that Carew was totally un-sympathetic to Cornish and never lost a chance to present the ordinary Cornish folk in an unfavourable light.

It is the survival of the scripts of these miracle plays performed in the *plen an gwary* that constitute the bulk of early Cornish literature. While their literary merit is not of any startling significance, A. S. D. Smith has pointed out 'the mature Cornish in which these plays were written can only be the outcome of a long tradition of Cornish writing'.[13] The miracle play was, of course, known throughout medieval Europe. William Sandys, in comparing the Cornish plays to their English equivalents, comments:[14]

> The Cornish Drama appears to have less of the comic character
> than the other mysteries with which we are acquainted. There
> are in the latter, scenes and passages that are quaint and
> laughable, even in our present advanced state of dramatic literature;
> while in the former the few passages that occur, as with the
> executions & etc., are generally coarse.

Sandys comes into direct conflict with Nance who claims: 'Compared with the English plays contemporary, the Cornish plays are dignified.' There was, perhaps, a certain amount of 'coarseness' in the actual production which caused Bishop Beaupré of Exeter to issue a positive prohibition against the mysteries being performed in the Exeter diocese in 1360. He notes that 'in one of these plays Adam and Eve appear naked, the Devil displayed his horns and tail, and Noah's wife boxed the Patriarch's ears before entering the Ark'. All highly immoral for the time. But the miracle plays were too popular to suppress. In England, in fact, the English miracle plays were very much encouraged. As in Cornwall, all who saw the miracle plays paid nothing, and in 1328 all who saw the Chester miracles were promised 100 days pardon from the Pope and forty days pardon from the bishop of Chester.

Perhaps the Cornish drama should be compared more closely with the Breton mystery plays rather than the English, although Middle Breton literature obviously lacks originality and does not really reflect Breton life of the period. However, Jean Lagadeuc's *Catholicon*, the first Breton–French lexicon, dated 1464 and printed in 1499, gave a tremendous boost to Breton writing—a boost lacking in Cornish. Plays such as *Buez Santez Nonn* (fifteenth century), *Burzu bras Jean* (1530) and *Buhez santes Barba* (1557) were produced as well

as the writing of significant poetical works such as *Tremenvan an itron gwerches Maria* (The passing of the Virgin Mary), *Pemzec levenez Maria* (The fifteen joys of Mary) and *Buhez Mabden* (Life of Man). To this period also belongs *Mellezour an Mary* (The Mirror of Death), composed in 1519 and printed in 1575. Breton literature had, in this period, become a printed literature; this was not the case with Cornish, and whereas the development of Cornish literature stopped with its miracle play output, in Brittany, with the publication of Quiquer di Roscoff's French–Breton dictionary and conversational pieces in 1616, Breton literature began to grow in strength and output.

The biggest work of the Cornish miracle plays is the *Ordinalia*, a cycle of three dramas said to have originated from Glasney sometime during the period 1275, a date given by E. H. Pedler, and 1450, a date given by Nance. Dr David C. Fowler, however, after an exhaustive study based on the evidence of place names mentioned in the text, claims: 'It is possible to affirm, I believe, with some measure of confidence, that the evidence thus far considered points to the third quarter of the fourteenth century as the period in which to place the composition of the Cornish *Ordinalia*.'[15]

In his work *The Medieval Stage*, Sir E. K. Chambers, referring to the 'great cycle' of the *Ordinalia*, points out that the dramas are extremely important parts of the medieval history of these islands, deserving to be compared with the more widely known medieval English plays of Chester, Coventry and Beverley. The first drama of the *Ordinalia* is called *The Creation of the World* and illustrates a number of Biblical stories from the Creation to the building of Solomon's Temple but winding up in a curious fashion with the martyrdom of St Maximilla *as a Christian* by the priest in charge of the temple. The second play is called *The Passion of Christ* and the third play is called *The Resurrection of Our Lord*. The earliest manuscript of this cycle, written in the first half of the fifteenth century, is now in the Bodleian Library.[16]

While there is nothing spectacular about the *Ordinalia* cycle as literature there are certain passages which are extremely poetical and Nance, in fact, claims that a Cornish poem has been borrowed by the author of *The Passion of Christ* and inserted into the play. According to Nance:[17]

it is into this Passion Play also that has been inserted, I think, a far shorter religious poem in which the Mater Dolorosa in

beautiful Cornish verse makes what in the English of the time would be described as 'grete laymentacyoun'. In spite of being broken up so as to fit into three separate scenes of the play, none of it seems lost, and its singular metrical arrangement makes it easy to sort out and put it together again as forming two verses, each of twenty-five lines.

The poem is reproduced here as Nance restored it in Unified Cornish which gives a clear indication of the poetical value of some of the passages in the *Ordinalia* cycle.

1

Ellas! A gryst, ow map ker,
  Yn mur bayn pan y-th-whelaf,
Ellas! dre guth pan yn clamder
  Dhe'n dor prag na omwhelaf?
Dre ow map pyth yu ow cher?
  Pup ur-oll y-n-benygaf!
Ellas! ny-won py tyller,
  Byth moy py le, y-trygaf,
    Eghan!
      Rag y-fynnyr,
      Mara kyllur
      Gans paynys mur
        Ow dyswul glan!
Ogh, govy, ellas, ellas,
Gweles ow map mar dhyflas
  Gans tebel wesyon dyghtys!
A vap, dha guth re-m-ladhas,
Na allaf gweles yn-fas
  Kemmys dagrow re-olys!
Govy, ny-won pandr 'a wraf
Gallas ow holon pur glaf
    Dre brederow!
Ny-allaf sevel yn-fas
War ow threys, ellas, ellas,
    Rak Galarow!

2

Ellas, ellas! ogh, tru tru!
  Yn ow holon ass-yu bern
Pan whelaf ow map jhesu
  Adro dh'y ben curun spern,
Hag ef Map Dew a vertu
  Ha gans henna gwyr Vyghtern,
Treys ha dywluf a bup tu,
  Fast takkyes gans kentrow hern,
    Ellas!
      Y-fyth deth brus
      Mur a anfus
      Y gyk ha'y gnas
        Nep a-n-gwerthas!
Ogh, govy rag ow map ker,
Dh'y weles y'n keth vaner
  May whelaf lemmyn dyghtys!
Ellas, na-varwen ynweth,
Na-ve kensa ow deweth
  Es dweth ow map y'n bys!
My a-yl bos morethek,
Gweles ow map mar anwhek
    Dyghtys del yu,
Nep yu Arluth lun a ras!
Govy vyth, ellas, ellas,
    Ragos, Jhesu!

Verse 1 Alas, O Christ, my dear son, when in great suffering I see Thee. Alas, for grief, why do I not fall in a swoon? Through my Son, what is my state? All the time I bless Him!

Alas, I know not on what spot, nor yet in what place I shall abide.
O, woe, for it is wished, if possible, with great sufferings to
destroy me utterly! O woe is me! Alas! Alas, to see my Son so
shamefully used by wicked fellows! O Son, Thy sorrow hath
slain me, so that I can scarce see, so many tears have I shed!
Woe is me, I know not what I shall do! My heart has become
right sick through care: hardly can I stand upon my feet. Alas,
for my sorrow.

Verse 2   Alas! Alas! O, sad, sad! What care is in my heart
when I see my Son, Jesu, with a crown of thorns about His head,
and He the Son of God, of Power, and therewithal a rightful
King! Feet and hands nailed fast on either side with spikes of
iron. Alas! On the Day of Doom shalt thou have much misery
who didst sell Him, both flesh and fell! O woe is me, for my
dear Son, to see Him treated in the same way which now I see!
Alas, that I might not also die, that my end might not sooner
be on earth than the end of my Son! Well may I be sorrowful
to see my Son so ungently treated as He is; He who is the lord
in grace abounding! Woe is me forever! Alas! Alas! for Thee, Jhesu!

The most interesting play surviving from this period, however,
is *Beunans Meriasek* (in Unified Cornish *Bewnans Meryasek*), the life of
St Meriasek or Meriadoc, bishop of Vannes. The play appears to
have been written for a performance over a two-day period and it
deals with the life of Meriasek, a Breton, who became a priest in
Cornwall and was the patron saint of Camborne. His name survived
in the nickname used for Camborne people—'merry geeks' or 'mera-
jacks'. Speaking of its literary quality, the play is very long and ill
constructed, yet it contains many beautiful philosophical passages,
such as the long disputation between Meriasek and Teudar, a pagan
Cornish ruler, on the respective merits of Christianity and Moham-
medanism in which the position of Moslems on the subject of the
Virgin Birth is fairly put. Thurstan Peter believes that the play was not
an original Cornish one but merely a translation of a Breton play.
He also reasons the translator to be John Nans of Illogan who was
probably a canon of Glasney:[18]

One of the reasons that makes me think it was a translation, and
not an original composition, is that the saint's name appears

both in its Breton form Meriadoc and in its Cornish form
Meriasek. Moreover, it is clear that the translator had only an
imperfect vocabulary of Cornish, as he is often reduced to use
an English word.

This still does not seem enough evidence on which to base the
assumption that the play is of Breton provenance. Middle Cornish is
riddled with a number of English loan words so the basis for Peter's
assumption must rest merely on the two spellings of the saint's name.
The oldest manuscript that survives of this play is entitled '*Ordinale
de Meradoc, episcopi et confessori*' and it is signed by Dominus Rad Ton
and dated 1504.[19]

The name has frequently been mis-read as 'Hadton' but Nance,
in his unpublished report on the manuscript, observes that the name
is 'Rad. Ton' and probably is Radulphus or Ricardus. There was, in
fact, a priest of Crowan, near Camborne, in 1537 named Dominus
Ricardus Ton.

The cycle of the *Ordinalia* and *Beunans Meriasek* constitute the only
complete miracle plays which have survived. Dr Rowse comments:[20]

> These plays then give an extraordinary insight into the mental
> life of the people, moulded as it largely was by the Catholic
> faith. They enable one to form a coherent picture of the fabric
> of belief and teaching which held them up, the imagined world
> into which they lived and moved. It gave them standards,
> administered consolation in suffering, explained in terms of the
> universally accepted Faith how evil and good were rewarded,
> and so played an essential part in enabling society to discipline
> its members and hold itself together.

There also remains a fragment of another play which was discovered
by Jenner in 1877 and which he described as 'probably the oldest
existing piece of Cornish literature'. The fragment consists of forty-
one lines of Middle Cornish, hardly differing from the *Ordinalia* dramas
in spelling, which Jenner significantly points out 'was fairly uniform
and systematic, more so than contemporary English'. This seems to
endorse the view that Smith took of a long tradition of Cornish writing.
The verses, however, are irregular and Jenner puts this down to the
fact that they may have been drafted for a projected play or simply
were an actor's part roughly jotted down on the first piece of

parchment to hand, in this case a land charter dated 1340. The story of Jenner's discovery is told in Chapter Six. Jenner first published the verses in the *Athenaeum*, 1 December 1877, and another version appeared in the *Revue Celtique* (vol. iv, p. 258), edited and translated by Dr Whitley Stokes. Dr Stokes disagreed with Jenner's translation: 'Mr. Jenner's readings seem to be, in some cases, clearly wrong . . .' The version printed here is that of Dr Stokes.[21]

1	golsow ty cowez	1	Hearken, thou comrade
	byz na borz nez		Be not ashamed
	dyyskyn ha powes		alight and rest,
4	ha zymo dus nes	4	and draw nearer me
	mar cozes ze les		If thou kno'st thine advantage
	ha zys y rof mowes		And to thee I will give a maiden
	ha fest vnan dek		And one very fair
8	genes mar a plek	8	If she pleases thee
	ha tanha y		Go take her
	kymmerry zoz wrek		Take her for thy wife
	sconye zys ny vek		She will not say thee nay
12	ha ty a vyz by.	12	And thou shalt have her.
	hy a vyz gwreg ty da		She shall be a good housewife
	zys ze synsych		For thee to hold
	pur wyr a laura		Right truly I say it
16	ha govyn worty	16	Go, then, ask of her
	lemmen yz torn my as re		Now into thy hand I give her
	ha war an greyz my an te		And by the faith I swear it
	nag vsy far		It is not far
20	an bar ma ze pons tamar	20	On this side to the Tamar bridge
	my ad pes' worty byz fa		I pray thee be good to her
	ag ol ze voz hy a wra		And all thy pleasures she will do
	rag flog yw ha gensy doz		For she is a child and withal sweet
24	ha gaffy ze gafus y boz	24	. . . to find her desire
	kennes mes zymmo ymmyug		Though it is a shame to me, kiss ye,
	eug alemma ha tystynyug		Go ye hence and hasten.

	Dallaz a infez dar war		Begin early
28	oun na porz o	28	that he hath no fear
	ef emsettye worzesy		to set himself against thee
	kam na vezo		would not be a step
	mar az herg zys gul neb tra		He commands thee to do something
32	lauar ze sy byz ny venna	32	say to thyself, never will I (do it)
	lauar zozo gwra mar mennyz		say to him, I will do (it) if thou wishest
	awos a gallo na wra tra vyz		Though he could, he will do nothing
	in vrna yz sens ze vos meystres		Then hold thyself to be mistress
36	hedyr vywy hag arluzes	36	and lady, as long as thou livest.
	ras o ganso re nofferen		Grace was with him, by the mass
	curtes yw ha deboner		courteous is he and gentle
	zys dregyn ny wra		he will not do evil to thee
40	mar an kefyz in danger	40	if thou wilt get him into (thy) power
	sense fast in dell		hold him fast.

One more work dates from this period, entitled *Pascon agan Arluth* (Unified Cornish: *Passyon agan Arluth*) or the Passion Poem or, as Davies Gilbert titled it, the Poem of Mount Calvary. This is a versified narrative of the events of the Passion of Christ from Palm Sunday to Easter Morning taken from the four gospels with an addition from the legendary Gospel of Nicodemus. The metre is of eight-line stanzas with seven syllables per line which illustrate the degree of sophistication reached in Cornish poetry. The entire poem consists of 259 stanzas. E. G. R. Hooper, in his introduction to the Unified Cornish version of the poem, published by Kesva an Tavas Kernewek in 1972, comments: 'The "Passion Poem" is a Cornish treasure and equivalent to good poetry in any language; every Cornish student ought to know it and it is with this aim that it is presented in "unified" or "modern standard" spelling.' The following three verses from the 'unified' version give one example of the prosody of the work:

168 Benenes prest a holyas
Jhesu Cryst yn un arma
Jhesus worta a vyras
Has a leverys dhedha,
'Fleghes mur ha benenes
A Jerusalem y'n dre
A wor bos ow faynys bras,
Ragof na whyleugh ola.

Women ever followed
Jesus Christ making an outcry.
Jesus looked at them
and said to them,
'Many children and women
of Jerusalem in the town
who knows that my pains are great
for me seek not to weep.

169 'Oleugh rag agas fleghes
Ha ragough agas honen:
An dedhyow a vyth gwelys
Hag a dhe, sur, yntredhon,
May fyth torrow benygys
Bythqueth na allas omdhon,
Ha'n benenes kekefrys,
Na ve dhedha denys bron.

'Weep for your children,
and for your own selves:
the days shall be seen,
and will come, surely, among us
when wombs will be blessed
that could never conceive,
and the women likewise,
who have not had a breast suckled.

170 'Y'n ur-na dhe'n
menydhyow
Why a ergh warnough
codha
Yn ketella an nansow
Why a bys rag' gas cudha,
Del lavaraf war anow,
War an pren glas mara te,
Y'n pren segh ha casadow,
Sur, y'n ur'na fatel ve?'

'Then you will command the
mountains

to fall on you,
in the same way the valleys
you will beseech to hide you,
as I say openly,
on the green tree if it comes
in the dry hateful tree,
surely, then how might it be?'

There are five manuscript copies of the work but the earliest surviving version of the poem, which is claimed to be the original, dates from the fifteenth century and was found in the church of Sancreed. The small, quarto volume, written on rough vellum and embellished with pictures, is now in the British Museum.[22]

Since 1869 there have been three major 'accidental' discoveries of Middle Cornish literature. The discovery of the entire play of *Beunans Meriasek*, the discovery of the Charter Fragment by Jenner and, in 1949, a translation of Bishop Bonner's book of *Homilies* (dated *circa* 1560). Such discoveries, despite the meagreness of the current Middle Cornish literature, lead one to hope that more discoveries may be made—that other Cornish manuscripts may be tucked away

in various museums and libraries either wrongly classified, as happened with *Beunans Meriasek*, or simply overlooked as with Bonner's *Homilies* (which we shall deal with in Chapter Three). There are enough references to various pieces of lost Cornish literature, as will be seen in subsequent chapters, to back up this hope which is further increased by the foundation of the Institute of Cornish Studies to help encourage such research.

Before leaving the miracle play period it is sad to observe, as Nance pointed out,[23] that we know little about the people who acted in these dramas. In fact we know nothing except the name of one actor— John Ergudyn—who doubled parts in the Meriasek drama. After playing the part of a rustic with Constantine, Ergudyn had to be 'ready a horse back for to play the merchant'. Nance says the name Ergudyn is probably *erghudyn* meaning 'snowlock'. We know little else about the plays apart from accounts that the authorities in St Ives left. They made £17 from the plays during six days in May 1575. One item reads 'spent upon carpenter that made heaven 4d'. We also know of two dramatic incidents which happened during performances at Sancreed and at Penryn. The first happened in 1568 when, during a performance, a man named Quennall, a servant of Sir John Trevyre, quarrelled with Richard James Veane. They left the amphitheatre and fought a duel with swords. Veane was killed and Quennall was confined in Conerton gaol and eventually hanged on Conerton Downs.[24] The second incident took place at Penryn in 1587 when the entire town had gone to the local amphitheatre. A small body of Spanish raiders landed hoping to sack the town: they found it deserted and were about to set to looting when a mighty shout was heard from nearby. The Spanish fled to their boats thinking the townspeople were attacking them. The townspeople were merely watching the drama of St Samson—the gates of Gaza had just fallen and the crowd raised a deafening cheer.[25] One wonders whether Henry VI saw some of this Cornish drama because, in 1482, it is recorded that a Cornishman named Jakke Trevaill presented various plays and interludes before the king.[26]

Before leaving the medieval period mention must be made of the part that Cornishmen played in saving the English language from destruction, ironic though it must seem to Cornish language enthusiasts of today. Following the Norman Conquest of 1066 Norman–French was imposed as the language of the ruling class. The Normans had raged mercilessly through the country in such a fashion that for

centuries afterwards Yorkshire was a near desert. English resistance
to the Normans finally died away when Hereward the Wake, partisan
leader of the last band of English fenmen, was subdued in 1072.
Mario Pei comments: 'Saxon nobility, robbed of everything in favour
of William's followers, sank sullenly to the level of their own
peasantry, while the ancient freemen of England now undistinguished
from the churls, turned into villeins of the new seigneurs.'[27]

All patronage of the English language ceased and 'the speech of
the conquered was banned from all polite society and official usage, it
was despised as the jargon of peasants and practically ceased to be
a written language'. French bishops and abbots were appointed in
place of English ones and a flourishing French literature was now
produced in England. These were the days of the flowering of the
French epic—the *Chanson de Roland* was written at Oxford; *Pelerinage
de Charlmagne à Jerusalem* was composed in the Home Counties as were
the lovely *lais* of *Marie de France* and many of the French popular
fabliaux. Philippe de Thaun's *Bestinaire*, Gaimar's *Lestoire des Engles* and
Wace with his *Roman de Brut* and *Roman de Rou* added to a magnificent
literary tradition. But these great works of literature produced in
England were works of French literature for English 'was banned
from all polite society. . .'.

The English did not take the suppression of their language lightly
and they were aided by the loss of Normandy in 1204 during the reign
of John. The majority of England's nobles and gentry still thought of
Normandy as 'home' while England was merely a colonial possession
in which they held their major domains. Now there was no longer a
'home' for them. The efforts of the Francophile Henry III (1216-72)
to bolster the French language in England by encouraging a new Gallic
influence from Poitou started the awakening of an English nationalism
among the Norman–French. For nearly a century a political and
cultural battle raged between the French-speaking continental
Frenchmen and the Norman–French settlers, marked by such episodes
as the Council of Winchester, the Oxford Provisions and the Baron's
War (1263-7). It was, in fact, the aim of Simon de Montfort, who led
the barons in their struggle for reform against Henry III, to get
English taught in schools. Henry did promise to grant this reform in
1258 to eliminate the strong monoglot French communities in the
country. The promise died with the defeat of de Montfort. Dialectical
differences between the standard Francien of Paris and the Norman–
French of England added to the fires of cultural animosity. Henry's

attempts to replace the Norman–French families in positions of power by Parisian French settlers resulted in pushing the Norman–French influence into the hands of the English.

In 1300 the author of *'Cursor Mundi'* was pleading for status for English. 'If we give everyone their own language, it seems to me we are doing them no injury . . .' But Robert of Gloucester pointed out in the same year, 'unless a man knows French he is thought little of'. Indeed, many English families had Normanised their names during the period when English was synonymous with peasant and Norman with noble. The position was unchanged until the middle of the fourteenth century when Ranulph Higden, a monk from Chester, wrote (1364):[28]

This impairing of the native tongue [English] is because of two things. One is that children in schools, contrary to the usages and customs of all other nations, are compelled to drop their own language and to construe their lessons and their other things in French, and have done so since the Normans first came to England. Also gentlemen's children are taught to speak French from the time they are rocked in their cradle and can talk and play with a child's trinket; and up-country men want to liken themselves to gentlemen, and try with great effort to speak French so as to be thought the more of.

Pressure from the English-speaking community put the French speakers on the defensive and in 1325 a decree was passed ordering that at Oxford 'all conversations be in Latin or French'. In 1332 an Act of Parliament decreed that French must be taught to all children receiving schooling. But advocates for English were becoming more forceful in their demands. The most prominent advocate at this time was John Trevisa who, according to Dr Fowler, was born at Trevessa in the parish of St Enoder.[29] Pei, however, claims that Crocadon in St Mellion was his home. Both agree that he was a Cornish-speaking cleric who was born about 1342 and probably started his education at Glasney before going to Oxford which he left in the 1370s. He died in 1402. It was Trevisa who gave the English the biggest encyclopedia and history of the day in their own vernacular. This was a translation of Ranulph Higden's *Polychronicon*. Dr Fowler thinks that Trevisa was also one of the translators of the Wycliffe Bible. In about 1382 John Wycliffe (1320-84) and his followers, known as Lollards, produced the first English version of the Old and New Testaments.

The preface to the King James Bible of 1611 mentions 'even in our King Richard the Second's days, John Trevisa translated the scriptures into English'. Dr Fowler comments:

> The list of Trevisa's translations is an impressive one. Here is a man who translated an apocryphal gospel, two controversial works of his time, a universal history, an elaborate treatise on the rule of princes, and a complete encyclopaedia. And if, as I have elsewhere suggested, John Trevisa was a translator of the Wycliffite Bible, and an author of Piers the Ploughman, then we clearly have to do with a major figure, perhaps second only to Chaucer in the English literature of the Middle Ages.

Dr Fowler pointed out something that makes Trevisa's work more than a passing interest for students of Cornish. Fowler made the assertion that students 'cannot hope fully to understand *Piers Plowman* [the great English classic contemporary with *The Canterbury Tales*] without a knowledge of the Cornish language and literature'.[30] *The Vision of Piers Plowman* is attributable to William Langland (1332-1400) but Fowler, when working on texts of the work, was 'struck by the fact that most of the source texts existed in English translated by John Trevisa'. Could Trevisa have been an author of the work? Fowler points out that the word *goky* is found in *Piers Plowman* and no other work in English. The *Oxford English Dictionary* confirms this one occurrence of the word in *Piers* but gives no derivation. *Goky* is a Cornish word meaning 'foolish' and it is to be found in the Middle Cornish dramas of the period. It is used in Unified Cornish and survived even in the Cornish dialect of English. Another link, according to Fowler, is the description of the Creation in which the 'list of animals is highly distinctive and unusual, following closely the Cornish *Origo Mundi* (Creation of the World)'. Fowler hopes soon to finish his research into this subject which should be of tremendous importance not only to students of Cornish but to students of English as well.

It was Trevisa who, writing of the re-emergence of English, said:

> Johan Cornwall, a mayster of gramere, chayngede the lore in gramerscole, and construccion of Freynsch into Englysh; and Richard Pencrych lurnede that manere teching of hym, and other men of Pencrych, so that now, the yere of our Lord a thousand, three foure score and fyve . . . in all the grammer-scoles of

England children leaveth Frensch and construeth and lurneth ye
Englysch and habbeth thereby advantage in on syde and
desvayntage yn another. Their avauntage ys that they lurneth
gramer in lesse tyme than children were i-woned to doo;
desavauntage ys that now children of grammer-scole canneth na
more Frensche then can thir lift heale, and that is harme for
them an they schulle passe the see and travaille in straunge
landes.

So Trevisa, the Cornish champion of the English language, claims
that two other Cornishmen, teaching at Oxford in the latter half of
the fourteenth century were responsible for saving the English language.
Basile Cottle cannot resist the comment: 'We are asked to believe,
by a Cornishman, with a Cornish name, that two others from his
Duchy were largely responsible for the redemption of what wasn't
even their native tongue, since all three must have been originally
Celtic speaking.'[31]

Pei suggests that 'it was the Hundred Years War [which started in
1337] with its bitter animosities against the French, and the Black
Death of 1349-1350 leading to a rise in the importance of the labouring
classes and their tongue, that gave the death blow to French in
England'. The establishment of the time would certainly have seen
the necessity to de-Frenchify itself and woo English nationalism in
their efforts to raise armies against France during the war. Philip
Ziegler places more emphasis on the Black Death: 'In England one
important by-product caused in part at least by the shortage of people
qualified to teach in French after the Black Death, was the growth
of education in the vernacular. . . '.[32] The first official step was in
1349 when English was introduced into schools, thanks to Cornish
efforts. As Ziegler says, 'the fruits of Cornwall's reform outweigh
immeasurably the gulf which it placed between this island and mainland
Europe.' In 1362 Edward III was forced by continuing pressure to
agree to a statute directing all pleas in courts to be made in English
and not, as before, in French or Latin. But 'Law French' was not
finally ejected until 1731, despite an effort to oust it by Oliver
Cromwell. In 1362 also the English language was allowed to be
used in parliamentary debate thus giving the language 'official status'.
It was not until 1574 that a decree was passed which introduced the
language into religious life and completed the re-emergence of
English. In 1403 the dean of Windsor wrote a letter to the king

beginning in French but, in mid-sentence, switching to English. The switch was symbolic. By 1413 English had become the language of the royal court. 'The gradual superseding of the French by the English language in the latter half of the 14th Century', writes A. R. Myers, 'is the most important development of the period.'[33]

It had not been an easy struggle and the Francophile backlash had been strong. By the time English was re-established, however, it had undergone profound changes, principally in the simplification of influence and the incorporation of a great deal of Norman–French. Today, 50 per cent of the English vocabulary is of Romance origin, dating largely from this period. The fundamental structure of the language remained English but only 50,000 English words remained in the language which now has a vocabulary of one million words. The language had undergone a change of script, the Norman Conquest being responsible for the change to new Carolingian script which had been developed on the Continent. What had taken place was not simply the re-emergence of the English language but the marriage of English with Norman–French. Wycliffe's Bible, for example, drops many Anglo-Saxon compounds in favour of French and this example began to be followed by others writing in 'new English'. The greatest exponent of the new French–English was Geoffrey Chaucer (1340-1400), a Londoner who used mainly the East Midland dialect of English with a southern admixture. In *The Canterbury Tales* Chaucer uses seventeen French words in the first eighteen lines. His contemporary Langland tried to maintain a purer form of English on which Chaucer poured scorn preferring, he says, the 'sweet rhyme' of French.

Many English language enthusiasts would not accept the new amalgamation of English and French and tried to maintain the battle for the restoration of 'pure' English. Among these men was Bishop Richard Peacock who tried to purify the language in the fifteenth century by using native English word roots rather than derive new words from Latin or French roots. The result was not a success and the new words did not enter the normal vocabulary—for example, words like 'ungothroughsome' instead of the Latin derived 'impenetrable'. It was southern English which held most of the French influence and there was a struggle between the northern and southern dialects but the introduction of printing by William Caxton (1422-91), establishing London as a centre of book publication in 1476 with Malory's *Morte d'Arthur*, won the day for the south. Thomas Cheke produced a New Testament in 'pure English' in 1561 but the battle had been

lost and with the King James I version of the Bible in 1611 the standardisation and triumph of the new English language was assured. Finally, with Dr Samuel Johnson's *The Dictionary of the English Language* in 1755, standardisation was complete.

The story of the fight to revive the English language is important and an understanding of it goes a long way to understanding parallel movements in the Celtic countries today. Cornish language enthusiasts cannot be blamed for viewing the role played by three Cornish-speaking Cornishmen in the English language struggle with a tinge of irony. One wonders what might have happened had John of Cornwall, Richard Pencrych and John Trevisa, applied their mighty intellects and talents to their own native language.

Chapter Three

Tudor Cornwall

It is only from the Tudor period that we begin to get really reliable evidence as to the state of the Cornish language, although Nance points out that the extent of Cornish speaking during the period has been exaggerated.[1] It is also the period which saw the start of an attack on the language that was to be responsible for its eventual extinction. No less than three times during the reign of the Tudors did the Cornish rise in armed insurrection against London government and their defeats had direct and serious consequences on the position of the language in their society. F. W. P. Jago points out that the insurrection of 1549 was 'instigated by the attempt of government to displace the old language'.[2]

The end of the Wars of the Roses (1455-85) saw a short lived era of hope in Cornwall. The ruling classes in Cornwall had, in the main, supported Henry Tudor in his bid for the throne. When Henry was in exile in Brittany the close connections between the two Celtic countries, ties of language and culture, served to strengthen Henry's strategic position. Constant traffic between Cornwall and Brittany kept him in touch with his supporters. Brittany, at this time, was still an independent country. The policies of some of her rulers, such as Yann V 'the Wise', had made her one of the most prosperous countries in Western Europe, mainly because of her powerful merchant fleet. But during the fifteenth century Breton independence was becoming increasingly insecure as French and English power increased. Breton policy was to play off both countries against each other in order to safeguard their own independence. Henry Tudor's bid for the English throne therefore received Breton support. Three years after Henry's succession, in 1488, the Breton armies were defeated by the French at St Aubin du Cormier and the Breton ruler, Francis II, was compelled to accept the treaty of Le Verger, the first step towards total annexation of Brittany by France.

Henry Tudor received tremendous support from the Celts. The Welsh expected Jasper and Henry Tudor to free Wales from English

bondage and poets, such as Dafydd Llwyd, called upon the Tudors to come out of exile and free Wales from her bonds. Henry landed in Wales on 7 August 1485 and unfurled the ancient Red Dragon standard of Wales as his banner. He announced he had come 'to free this our Principality of Wales of such miserable servitude as they have long piteously stood in'. Dr Ceinwen Thomas comments:[3]

All this could have but one meaning for Wales,—that Henry was leading a national war of liberation,—and Henry himself must have known it. As he traversed Wales on his way to Shrewsbury, men flocked to his side and on August 22nd, he won the battle of Bosworth, with a predominantly Welsh army, and slew Richard III of England. His victory was hailed with delirious joy in Wales as the end of the afflictions of the Cymry and the beginning of the freedom of Wales. Gruffydd ab Ieuan ap Llywelyn Fychan wrote confidently of the victorious Henry that he would not permit the old prison and lack of privilege for Wales, and had come to restore to everyone his possessions.

Henry's aim, however, was to be monarch of England and Wales, united in a single, strong kingdom. It is true that on his succession to the throne Henry lavishly rewarded his Welsh and Cornish supporters and the rise of a 'Welsh' king drew many Welshmen and Cornishmen to places of high office at the English court. But they adopted the English language, manners and clothes and many of the Welsh who returned to Wales were nicknamed *Sais* (Englishman).[4] Many Cornishmen, in order to climb the social ladder, began to Anglicise themselves. There was also another pressure on the language; the opening of sea routes, especially to the Americas, which encouraged a large number of Cornishmen to go to sea. Cornish seamen began to see that Cornwall was a small entity in a world mostly dominated by England. Until the fifteenth century, Cornwall had continued to be separate in many ways from England, developing its own national culture and outlook. As late as 1485 certain laws were enacted which were particular to Cornwall.[5] But the rise of the Tudors, with their new laws, taxes and centralist policies, created disaffection among Cornishmen.

The spark which was to lead to the 1497 insurrection was struck in January of that year. Perkin Warbeck, the mysterious young man who claimed to be Richard of York, the rightful king of England, had won the support of the Scottish monarch, James IV, who incidentally

was the last Scottish Gaelic-speaking ruler of Scotland. The Scots had raided across the border in the name of 'Richard of York'. Henry VII decided to strike back. Parliament met in January 1497, and agreed to levy a tax to finance an army to invade Scotland.

In St Keverne, on the east coast of the Lizard peninsula, a black-smith named Michael Joseph spoke out against the tax. Why, he asked, should the millers and miners of Cornwall be ground into powder to pay for a war which was not theirs? In Bodmin a lawyer named Thomas Flamank argued that the defence of England against invasion by the Scots lay with the northern English barons and not with the poor people of Cornwall. William Antron, who had been a Member of Parliament in 1492 for Helston, also spoke against the tax.

The idea to march on London originated in May 1497, when Michael Joseph—known as 'An Gof' (The Smith)—led protesting Cornishmen to Bodmin. They were joined by Flamank and Antron and many people who belonged to prominent Cornish families. Under the leadership of 'An Gof' they took on the semblance of a disciplined army. According to Polwhele: 'the Cornish not being all provided with bows and arrows armed themselves with such tools as belonged to their several trades.'[6] The army, said to be some 15,000 men strong, was so formidable that John Basset of Tehidy, the Sheriff, refused to take out his men-at-arms to disperse them. The insurrectionists, for such had the protest become, marched first to Taunton and on to Wells where they were joined by James Touchet, the seventh Baron Audley. In spite of the recruitment of this aristocrat, who, according to Francis Bacon, was an accomplished soldier and popular man, 'An Gof' remained firmly in command of the Cornish-men, although Flamank and Audley took responsibility with him as 'political leaders'. Before leaving Wells they published a declaration of their grievances. H. A. L. Fisher says, 'the pleadings of Flamank were founded upon a narrow and provincial particularism.'[7] This seems to indicate that, with the survival of the language, the spark of Cornish nationhood had not yet been extinguished.

The Cornish insurgents marched first to Bristol and then to Salisbury and on to Winchester. There seems to have been a question-ing of the purpose of their march across England and it was Flamank who suggested that the insurgents should march to Kent, pointing out that Kent was 'the classic soil of protests'. He was doubtless thinking of Jack Cade's insurrection and of Wat Tyler, John Ball ('the first Socialist') and the Peasant Uprising of 1381.

Worried by the advance of the Cornish army, Henry VII gathered an army at Henley while his lord chamberlain and chief general, Giles, Lord Daubeny, mustered some 10,000 men at Hounslow Heath on 13 June. Daubeny decided to test the strength of the insurgents and sent out a column of 500 mounted men who engaged the Cornish advance guard near Guildford. Daubeny's men were beaten off with several losses. London began to panic. According to Fisher:[8]

> The rebels were 15,000 strong and although they had studiously abstained from pillage on their march they would hardly be so temperate if they were let loose among the opulent thoroughfares of London. For some days the city was in a wild panic but the king returned from Woodstock, as the nobles and gentry of the Home Counties flocked in to defend the capital and as Daubeny, recalled from the north, marched his force on to St. George's Field, the public confidence steadied.

Arriving in Kent the Cornish found the spirit of Jack Cade and Wat Tyler no longer abroad. They gained few recruits to their banner. On Friday, 16 June they pitched their camp on Blackheath while, on the same day, the armies of Henry VII and Daubeny joined together at St George's Field with a total strengh of 25,000 men. During the night a rumour was spread through the Cornish camp that the battle would not begin until Monday morning. The Cornish were lulled into a false sense of security. They did not realise that Henry always considered Saturday his 'lucky day' and was determined to attack the insurgents early that morning. At dawn on 17 June 1497, Henry sent a division under the lords Oxford, Essex and Suffolk, to wheel round the right flank and rear of the Cornishmen. He waited until this force was in the position he had assigned to it and then he gave Daubeny the order to attack. Daubeny was, in fact, over-eager in his attack. He launched his troops at the insurgent position at Deptford Bridge. Here the Cornish were well armed and managed to beat back the royal attack with the skilful use of their bows. Daubeny, himself, was made prisoner by the Cornish but subsequently rescued. The royal army lost 300 men in this attack. But the odds were against 'An Gof' and his army and after some hours they were completely surrounded and in a hopeless situation. What was the use of scythes, billhooks, axes and staves against proper weapons of war held in expert hands? Having lost 2,000 men, 'An Gof' gave the order for surrender.

C

By 2 p.m. on the same day Henry VII had entered London across London Bridge to a victorious acclamation from the people led by the Lord Mayor. He retired to St Paul's to give thanks before joining his wife and son at the Tower of London. 'An Gof' was brought to London in chains but, we are told, 'spake boldly to the people as if had been at his liberty'.[9] On 27 June 'An Gof' and Thomas Flamank were hanged, drawn and quartered. Before his execution, this extraordinary blacksmith from one of the most remote villages in Cornwall, who had nearly toppled one of Europe's greatest monarchs, said he gloried in what he had tried to do and that he would have 'a name perpetual and a fame permanent and immortal'.[10]

The heads of 'An Gof' and Flamank were placed on stakes on London Bridge, while Flamank's quartered body was placed on display in London and 'An Gof's' body was taken to be distributed throughout Cornwall. On 28 June Lord Audley, who had been placed in Newgate, was taken to Tower Hill. He was led through the streets in a paper coat on which his coat-of-arms was painted in reverse and torn to symbolise that he was a traitor. He was beheaded and his head joined those of the two Cornish leaders on London Bridge.

Henry was surprisingly lenient towards the rest of the Cornish insurgents. According to Francis Bacon, 'the king made a great difference between people that did rebel upon wantoness and them who did rebel upon want.'[11] The City Chronicler says that after the battle 'divers of the prisoners were sold, some for 12d. and some for more'.[12] Many of the insurgents escaped back to Cornwall where they immediately joined the banner of Perkin Warbeck. Warbeck, on hearing the news of the Cornish insurrection, seized the opportunity to make his way to Cornwall, via Ireland, which he reached in September. He proclaimed himself Richard IV at Bodmin. Some 6,000 Cornishmen flocked to his banner and followed him to Exeter. Daubeny, marching from London after the fleeing Cornish, was close at hand and Warbeck's courage deserted him. He surrendered and Cornwall was left defenceless. Again Henry was sparing of blood but his commissioners were ruthless in gathering taxation from the brooding Cornish people.

Michael Joseph's prophecy was correct. He did achieve 'a name perpetual and a fame permanent and immortal'. In 1559 an anthology entitled *A Mirror for Magistrates* was published in which a Cornish lawyer, Humphrey Cavell, wrote a versified narrative of the story of the blacksmith from St Keverne. The volume was produced to teach the

orthodox Tudor political doctrines so 'An Gof' is presented in an extremely unfavourable light. The book was immensely popular going from edition to edition between 1559 and 1587. Since the publication of Thomas Wartoun's *A History of English Poetry* in 1781, *A Mirror for Magistrates* has been included in almost every history of English literature. And in the churchyard of St Keverne today there is a memorial which bears the words in Cornish and English:

In memory of Michael Joseph the Smith and Thomas Flamank leaders of the Cornish host who marched to London and suffered vengeance there June 1497. 'They shall have a name perpetual and a fame permanent and immortal.' Erected by Mebyon Kernow. 1966.

The memorial was unveiled on Saturday, 22 October 1966, by Alderman K. G. Foster, the chairman of the Cornwall County Council.

The 1497 insurrection had thrust Cornwall forward into the gaze of the English administration in an unfavourable light. It was the beginning of the end of Cornwall's separate existence. And a new threat was growing; the Reformation, which was to be the main spearhead for the destruction of the language. At the start of the Reformation in 1533, the Cornish language was widely spoken. We have a clear picture of the situation from Andrew Borde's *The Fyrst Boke of the Introduction of Knowledge* which he published in 1542, dedicated to Princess Mary. Borde observed:

In Cornwall is two speches; the one is naughty Englyshe, and the other Cornyshe speche.
And there be many men and women the which cannot speake one worde of Englyshe, but all Cornyshe.

Borde records twenty-five conversational pieces of Cornish and the numerals up to thirty for, according to him:

No Cornysheman doth nomber aboue xxx and is named Deec warnegous. And whan they haue tolde thyrty, they do begyn agayn 'one, two and thre'. And so forth, and whan they haue recounted to a hondred, they saye kans. And if they nomber to a thousand, than they saye myle.

Just prior to the Reformation John Leland (*circa* 1505/6-52) toured Cornwall while preparing his classic *Itinerary*.[13] A graduate of Oxford and Paris he had been made Keeper of the Libraries by Henry VIII sometime before 1530. Leland began a series of journeys throughout the kingdom which extended between 1535 and 1543. Some writers have observed that Leland does not mention the Cornish language in his tour of Cornwall and they reach the conclusion that this was because it was near death and of no importance. But Fortescue Hitchins says: 'Leland passes over the Cornish language in total silence not because it was extinct but because it was universally spoken.'[14] In fact, Leland does not pass over the language in 'total silence' but makes three passing references to Cornish. Referring to Padstow, Leland writes:

From Wade Bridge to Padestow a good quik fischar toun but onclenly kepte, a 4 miles.
This toun is ancient bearing the name of Lodenek in Cornische, and un Englische after the trew and old writings of Adelstow Latine Athelstani Locas.
And the toune there takith King Adelstane for the chief giver of privileges onto it.

He adds: 'the toun of Padestow is ful of Irisch men . . . .'.
Leland also says that 'the name of the toun of Fawey is in Cornisch, Cobwhath', and refers to 'Mousehole, in Cornish Porth Enis, portus insulae'. Such references seem to endorse Hitchins's theory that Leland did not make much of the language simply because it was still so widely spoken in Cornwall that he felt there was no need to explain it. Only later in the century and in the following century did travellers feel the need to explain the 'phenomenon' of the Cornish language because it was so confined and dying that most people had forgotten it.

There are other glimpses of the language before the Reformation. In 1533 the vicar-general, Thomas Cromwell, asked a Cornish landowner, Sir William Godolphin, to send some Cornishmen to London 'for the feat of wrestling'. Cornwall has always been renowned for her particular Celtic wrestling and in 1415 the Cornish fought at Agincourt under a banner showing two wrestlers in a 'hitch'. Geoffrey of Monmouth, Layamon, Spenser and Milton, have all paid tribute to the prowess of Cornish wrestlers. This Celtic form of

wrestling still survives also in Wales, Cumberland and Brittany. François I of France brought Breton wrestlers to his encounter with Henry VIII at Boulogne in 1520 where, on the 'Field of the Cloth of Gold', they indulged in a wrestling match with their fellow Celts of Wales. Another chronicler mentions a contest between Breton and Cornish wrestlers at Chateaubriant in 1551. Replying to Thomas Cromwell's request for wrestlers, Godolphin wrote that he was sending two of his house servants 'who are reckoned the best for the feat' but 'their English is not perfect'.[15] A few years later, in 1538, in answer to another request by Cromwell for tin mining experts, Godolphin writes 'for that work your servants Samson and John Herry have no fellows in Cornwall. You may call Herry to interpret these men's languages for their English is very bad.'[16] In that same year of 1538, John Veysey, bishop of Exeter, was ordering that all or part of the Epistle or Gospel of the day, or else the Paternoster, Ave Maria, Creed and Ten Commandments, should be taught in Cornish where English was not spoken and that chantry priests were to teach children the Seven Works of Mercy in Cornish or in English as required. There are even instances of familiarity with Cornish being stipulated for the appointment of parish priests.[17] Polwhele claims, 'the gentlemen of Cornwall were not unacquainted with the Cornish language at the time of the Reformation.'[18] But the little status the language did have was due solely to the church and the clergy. Dr Rowse comments:[19]

> of the state of the clergy there is no reason to suppose that
> it was very different in Cornwall from elsewhere. Conditions
> differed a little in that the people spoke Cornish but that mattered
> less when the language of the Church was Latin; hence the
> Cornish attachment to it.

But the Cornish attachment was not so much to Latin as it was to the concessions made by the Catholic church to their language. For a time 'beyond all rememberance', as Carew states,[20] the Catholic church had made use of Cornish in church services and this practice, as we have seen, had been endorsed from time to time by the bishops of Exeter. It was under church inspiration that the miracle plays were written and produced. Rowse agrees that: 'Perhaps they may be taken as some evidence of the concession the Catholic Church made to popular feeling, and may help to account for that devotion of the people to

the old faith which led them to rise in rebellion against the Prayer Book in 1549.'[21]

English had been introduced into the religious services in 1540, nine years before the imposition of the English Prayer Book. According to Polwhele, 'Dr John Moreman, a native of Southole and vicar of Menheniot, was the first who taught his parishioners the Lord's Prayer, Creed and Ten Commandments in the English tongue.' Polwhele immediately leaps to the conclusion that 'if the inhabitants of Menheniot in the East of Cornwall, were not acquainted even with the Lord's Prayer in English before they were thus instructed by their vicar, it may well be supposed that, further west, the people had still less knowledge of English'.[22] The statement caused Jago to assert: 'One thing is certain, that when the English service was first used in Cornwall at the end of the reign of that pious king Henry VIII (1509-1547) Cornish was known and spoken from the Tamar to Land's End.'[23]

Nance has pointed out that a wrong conclusion has been reached. The language displaced by English at Menheniot must have been Latin and not Cornish for it was only in monoglot Cornish villages that Cornish was allowed to be used in religious services and one can hardly believe that Menheniot, so near the Devon border, could have been such a village in 1540.

With the death of Henry VIII in 1547, ten-year-old Edward VI came to the throne with the duke of Somerset appointed as Protector. The Reformation proceeded with the appointment of commissioners who made surveys of chantry lands and goods, church plate, jewels, ornaments, bells and vestments. Rowse points out, 'this was already sufficiently disturbing to remote, backward counties like Cornwall which saw in the keeping of parish registers an instrument of increased taxation.' Proclamations were issued directly affecting the superstitions and customs of the people. Candles were not to be borne on Candlemas, nor ashes on Ash Wednesday, nor palms on Palm Sunday. There was to be no more holy water or bread and all images were to be removed from the churches. A zealous supporter of the Reformation in Cornwall was William Body, a layman who had bought the archdeaconry of Cornwall in 1537 with money he had received as a secret agent of Cromwell. Body's zealousness was not out of religious fervour but out of the money to be gained by the expropriation of church property. Pushed beyond endurance a large crowd of Cornish people gathered on 5 April 1548, and attacked the house in Helston

where Body was staying. Body was killed and for months disturbances took place throughout Cornwall.

In January 1549, Parliament passed the First Act of Uniformity which introduced the English language in all church services, not only in England but in Wales and Cornwall. In Wales the Act merely endorsed the Act of Annexation of 1536 (renamed the Act of Union in the nineteenth century) which announced the English government's intention to 'utterly extirpe' the Welsh language. English was to be used in all churches from Whit Sunday, 9 June 1549. Cornwall once again rose in arms led by thirty-six-year-old Humphry Arundell of Helland, who had been named after his grandfather, Humphry Calwodely, a leader of the 'An Gof' insurrection. Several other prominent Cornishmen joined the leadership of the 1549 insurgents, including Nicholas Boyer, the mayor of Bodmin. The insurgents camped around Bodmin in June while Arundell and his fellow leaders drew up articles of supplication to the king. The demands made by the insurgents were entirely conservative, concerned wholly with religious demands such as retention of usage with regard to baptism, confirmation, communion and so on.

There are a number of versions of the petition with the number of articles ranging from eight to sixteen. Perhaps the most important item from the language question was article eight in which it was pointed out 'we, the Cornish men, whereof certain of us understand no English, utterly refuse this new English'.[24] The Lord Protector replied asking why should those who had no English object to English services when they certainly had no Latin? Moreover he was informed, he said, there were few towns in Cornwall 'but you shall find more in them that understand English than understand Latin'. Lake is fairly definite about the part language played in the insurrection. He states: 'The Cornishmen in this rebellion were probably as much instigated by the attempt of the government to displace the old language in the service of the church as by the other innovations made upon their religion.'[25]

The Cornish marched into Devon, receiving a large number of local adherents to their cause, and laid siege to Exeter. On 2 July the city was surrounded and the suburbs taken. Demands were again made to the government; once more it was stressed that few Cornishmen spoke English. Archbishop Cranmer inquired if there were any more who understood Latin. At the end of July the Cornish marched on Honiton and engaged the earl of Bedford's forces, putting

him to flight. Within a few weeks, however, Lord Grey arrived with reinforcements and a terrifying battle was fought. In his *History of Exeter,* John Hooker writes: 'great was the slaughter and cruel was the fight and such was the valour and stoutness of these men [the Cornish insurgents] that the Lord Grey reported himself that he never in all the wars that he had been did know the like.' It took John Russell, Lord Bedford, ten days to regroup his army before pressing on towards Cornwall, with the insurgents retreating but fighting every step of the way. By mid-August Bedford had crossed into Cornwall and a series of defeats and capture of the insurgent leaders completely disheartened the Cornish. Hangings, pillage and burnings followed Bedford's troops across the country. Bedford returned to London taking with him the principal leaders of the insurrection and leaving Sir Anthony Kingston as provost-marshal to carry on the work of execution and reprisals. Kingston left an extremely unsavoury reputation behind him.

With the end of the insurrection the new church services were enforced. English had been introduced into the church services on the principle that people should understand what was being said. Cranmer himself had pointed out how absurd it was holding a service in which 'neither the priest nor his parish wot what they say'. Some intellectuals at the time saw how ridiculous the government policy was with regard to Cornwall and Wales. The playwright Nicholas Udall (author of the first of the classical plays in English, *Ralph Roister Doister*) wrote a pamphlet suggesting that a new service should be translated into Cornish and so enjoyed by the Cornish people.[26] Dr Rowse comments: 'This suggestion was never carried into effect and the Prayer Book became a chief instrument in the spread of the English language in Cornwall.' The introduction of English in religious worship in Cornwall caused two extremist views to be taken by scholars. Dr Borlase writes:[27]

> when the Liturgy at the Reformation was appointed by the authority to take the place of the Mass, the Cornish desired that it should be in the English language, being apprehensive that it might be injoined them in their mother tongue, as it was with regard to Welsh. By this means and the gentry mixing gradually with the English, the Cornish language lost ground in proportion as it lay nearer to Devon.

Whitaker on the other hand maintains:[28]

English too was not desired by the Cornish, as vulgar history
says and as Dr. Borlase avers, but, as the case shows itself plainly
to be, forced upon Cornwall by the tyranny of England at a time
when the English language was yet unknown in Cornwall. This
act of tyranny was at once gross barbarity to the Cornish people
and a death blow to the Cornish language.

Whitaker adds, rather optimistically, 'had the Liturgy been
translated into Cornish as it was in Welsh, the Cornish language
would have been preserved to the present moment.' Both extremist
viewpoints are wrong. Udall's suggestion did have some repercussions.
A conference held in 1560 to study the laws of the Anglican church
moved a resolution entitled 'a punishment for such as cannot say the
Catechism':[29]

Item: that it may be lawful for such Welch or Cornish children
as can speake no English to learne the Praemises in the Welch
tongue or Cornish language.

We find that in the same year, 1560, the bishop of Exeter is directing
that Cornish could be used in the teaching of the Catechism where the
English language was not understood. But it was left to individual
effort while, in 1563, an Act for Translating of the Bible and the
Divine Service into the Welsh Tongue was passed saving Welsh from
a more rapid decay. The motives behind this Act were expediency
rather than humanity. The English government had a lively terror that
Continental Catholics would stir the Welsh into insurrection and
to prevent this the Protestant religion was to be spread in the country.
The government's fears of a Catholic-inspired insurrection among the
subject nations in the British Isles were well founded. While Wales
was accepting the new religion with the help of a Bible, Prayer Book
and services in their language, Cornwall, who was denied these things,
still clung to her language and Catholic religion. This fact was not
lost on Spain, forever seeking allies to help her smash Protestant
England. An Italian agent of Philip II of Spain wrote off a report on
Cornwall to the Spanish ruler. 'Li habitante sono del tutto differenti
di parlare, di costume et di leggi alli Inglesi; usano quali sono in
prospettiva alla Irlanda et sono similmente tenuti la maggior parte
Catholici.'[30] Philip does not appear to have acted on this report
that the Cornish were different in speech, manners and customs from

the English and, like the Irish, were Catholics. Perhaps Philip wondered how much he could trust his agent as the agent assured Philip the River Severn divides Cornwall from England.

The fact that the bishop of Exeter left the translation of the Catechism, Lord's Prayer, Creed and other works in Cornish to individual priests accounts for the variety of translations handed down. So far we know of only one priest who set to work to make translations for his Cornish-speaking flock, John Tregear. But who John Tregear was and what parish he administered to is, as yet, unknown. Tregear's name appears as the translator of a series of sermons by the bishop of London which he transcribed around the year 1560.

In 1555 Edmund Bonner, bishop of London, rejoicing in the accession of Mary Tudor to the throne, the halting of the Reformation and a return to the old Catholic faith, wrote a series of sermons which he called *A profitable and necessarye doctryne, with certayne homelies adioyned therynto, set forth by the reuerende father in God Edmonde byshop of London, for the instruction and enformation of the people beiynge within his Diocesse of London and of his cure and care. Excusum in aedibus Iohannis Cawodi Londini, 1555.* The book was intended to be read in churches throughout the diocese by 'all parsons, vicars and curates, unto the parishioners upon Sundays and Holy Days'. Bonner was to meet his death in the time of Elizabeth. When Elizabeth succeeded her sister on 17 November 1558, religious changes were once more on the way and Acts of Supremacy and Uniformity were passed in 1559. The bishops, led by Bonner, were chief protagonists of the old order and were the first to be brought to the test. All except Kitche of Llandaff refused to have anything to do with the supremacy oath or the Prayer Book. They were immediately deprived of office and, as Elizabeth had no wish to give the old faith martyrs, eight were sent to the Tower of London while the others were given liberty on condition of reporting to the Council from time to time. Bonner, whom Elizabeth disliked intensely, was sent to Marshalsea where he subsequently died.

In about 1560 John Tregear translated twelve of the homilies from Bonner's book. He wrote in a neat, clear hand, heading each page with a holy name as was the custom with Catholics even on legal documents and letters. The title of each homily he translated is given in Latin and he signs each translation. A thirteenth, and last, homily is from an unidentified original twice as long as the others, which average ten pages each, and the translation is made by a different hand. This nameless scribe writes in an untidy fashion and gives a

Cornish title to his homily. The scribe also has a fondness for marginal references. The entire work consists of 130 closely written pages in sixteenth-century Cornish prose and neither the table of contents nor the bishop's foreword have survived, if indeed they were translated with the rest of the work. Only a general heading 'Homelyes XIII in Cornyshe' is given.

Of the translation, Nance writes:[31]

> If any literary value whatsoever attaches to these old homilies this belongs to the English versions, and the interest of John Tregear's translations lies solely in the language in which they are written. Even here we meet with some disappointment, for partly perhaps because he feared to tamper with the exact sense of the English, partly perhaps as falling in with the view of his congregation that high subjects needed loftier and less understandable language than popular Cornish, but chiefly I am afraid out of sheer slackness, Tregear when he came on a long English word like 'incomprehensibility', 'inclynacion', 'uncharitableness' etc. would very often leave it untranslated. He drags in simple English words, too, quite needlessly, such as 'even', 'only', 'not indeed worthy', 'by and by', 'meet', 'due', 'meek', 'lack', 'food', the Cornish of which he, of course, knew very well, and adverbs like 'chiefly', 'finally', 'wholly', 'freely', 'principally'. In one place he starts to write, in English, 'we have thereby' corrected immediately to 'us thynnu drethy': in another he corrected 'truth' to 'gwryoneth' and in another writes only the capital T of 'take' before writing correctly 'kemereugh'. His clerical Cornish is in fact rather like the half French sermon language ridiculed in Brittany as Brezoneg Beleg 'Priests' Breton'. . . .

The Tregear manuscript is the longest piece of Middle Cornish prose writing which has survived to us. Like *Beunans Meriasek* the manuscript was lost and not discovered until April 1949, when John Mackechnie (author of *Gaelic Without Groans*) and a prominent Celtic scholar, discovered it by chance among some papers of the Puleston family of Emral and Worthenbury in Flint, Wales, which had been purchased by the British Museum.[32] Mackechnie immediately contacted Nance.[33] So far there is little known about Tregear although it is thought he was perhaps the priest at Newlyn East. Thomas

Stephyn and Richard Logan have written their names on the manuscript
and this might provide a clue as to its place of origin; similarly a full
study of the Puleston papers may yet tell us more. We have another
shadowy glimpse of Tregear from Dr William Borlase who, in his
vocabulary of the language, quotes words from 'J. T.' or 'John
Tregeare' though only for one or two words which, significantly,
do not come from the 'Homelyes'. This would indicate that Tregear
wrote more work in the language which, although seen by Borlase, has
been lost.

It is a truism that the Reformation was the turning point for the
language. Jenner comments:[34]

> After the Reformation, English came in like a flood: and the fact
> that neither the Book of Common Prayer nor the Bible was
> translated into Cornish shows that, even if Cornish was still in
> use, the people also had a knowledge of English. The chief reason
> for the decay was undoubtedly the failure of Cornwall to produce
> a literature for it is through literature that a language achieves
> permanent form and can struggle successfully with competing
> tongues.

The Reformation had another effect on Cornwall, apart from
forcing the decline of the language. It had the direct effect of stopping
the centuries old intercourse between the Cornish and the Bretons.
Between 1540 and 1560, from the lay subsidy rolls and parish registers,
we find large numbers of Bretons living in Cornwall. Dr Rowse says,
'Bretons constituted much the largest foreign element—if indeed they
are to be considered foreigners in Cornwall, where they spoke the
same language as the people.' He continues, 'but the Reformation,
and the subsequent decline of the Cornish language, cut Cornwall
apart from Brittany, and they ceased to come over.'

Not just the Reformation but the end of Breton independence in
1532 contributed to this cessation. In 1488 the Breton armies had
been defeated by the French and a treaty signed. In 1491 the Breton
ruler Francis II died and his young daughter Anne succeeded him.
In spite of her youth she tried to resume the fight against French
incursions into Brittany but she too was obliged to submit and, in
order to avoid a long war and a disastrous occupation, she was
compelled to marry Charles VIII of France. Following his death she
married his successor Louis XII and tried to secure in her marriage

settlement the independence of her country. She even betrothed her daughter Claude to Charles V of Austria to achieve a power balance. But following Anne's death in 1514 Claude was forced to marry François I of France. Brittany could no longer avoid being united with the French crown and a Treaty of Union was signed in 1532 by which Brittany became an autonomous state within the French kingdom. Brittany retained its own Parliament until 1789 when the new revolutionary French Constituent Assembly suppressed the Breton Parliament and declared Brittany part of France. Brittany, which had supported the French Revolution against the increasing centralist policies of the French monarchy, sent her president M. La Houssaye to protest at the bar of the Constituent Assembly. La Houssaye eventually died in exile in London in 1805. In 1793 a general uprising took place led by La Rouerie and Cadoudal. The Breton War of Independence lasted until 1804 when Georges Cadoudal was beheaded in Paris.

Towards the end of the sixteenth century there is evidence to show that Cornish was still spoken in the east of Cornwall. In a case heard before the Bishop's Consistory Court in 1595 (Elizabeth Trevathock v. Edward John and Petronella John) a girl mentions that while she was weeding a garden she heard two women 'talking together both in Cornish and English'.[35] The village where this incident took place was St Ewe, near St Austell, showing clearly that Cornish survived a long way east of Truro at the end of the Tudor period. On the other hand, however, English was creeping into the everyday speech of people west of Truro for a similar case was heard in 1572 concerning defamatory words uttered before divine service in Lelant church. William Hawsyl gave evidence that upon *dew whallan gwa metton in eglos Lelant* (upon All Hallows' Day in Lelant church) 'the wife of Morrysh David called Agnes Davey "whore and whore bitch" in English and not in Cornowok'.[36]

In the middle of the sixteenth century a play was published entitled *A lyttle treatyse called the Image of Idlenesse conteynunge certeyne matters moued between Walter Wedlocke and Bawdin Bachelor Translated out of the Troyance or Cornyshe tounge by Olyuer Oldwanton and dedicated to the Lady Lust. Imprinted at London by William Seres dwellynge in Powles Church Yard at the signe of the Hedge Hogge.* The cataloguer in the British Museum conjectures the date of publication to be 1550 but Jenner believed the copy to be of a much later date, sometime between 1565 and 1570. A second edition was published in 1574.

The book, which was discovered by A. J. K. Esdaile, a secretary at the British Museum, who showed it to Jenner, is of no literary value. It is a series of moral (or rather immoral) platitudes of a conventional type on love and marriage. According to the author he says he is a Cornishman who found a 'little quire' in the 'Troyance or Cornyshe tongue'. It was commonly thought at this time that the Cornish were descended from Brutus of Troy. He claims he has translated the book from this Cornish version. The only 'local colour' in this scandalous story of a priest, who bears the Cornish name of John Polmarghe and who belongs to a college of 'Penborgh' (Glasney at Penryn?), are the Cornish names, which include Maistur Jewgur and Syr Ogier Penkeyles, and one sentence in Cornish, badly spelt with the words wrongly divided. This occurs in Chapter Seven of the book which is a story of the well-known myth of Pygmalion, the sculptor of Cyprus, who makes a beautiful statue with which he falls in love. He prays to Aphrodite to bring it to life, which she does. The author, ingeniously, adds an invention which is certainly not Ovid's. Pygmalion dies and the wife turns back into alabaster (in Ovid's original the statue was made of ivory); the statue remains in Greece and removes or expels passion and pain of jealousy. There now enters into the story the Princess of Tarant of Ottronto who, finding her husband to have a mistress, is 'warned by a vision to repayre unto this blessed image for help'. She 'did avowe her pylgrymage thyther and receaved the Oracle, *Marsose thees duan guisca ancorne rog hatre arta,* being expounded by the priestess of that Temple to this effect in Englyshe. If to weare the horn thou fynde thy selfe agreeved. Gyve bache agaune and thou salt sone be eased.' The Cornish sentence in the 1574 edition is spelt *Marsoie thees dua guisca ancorne, rog hatre arta.*

The translation given is not precise but fairly well represents the meaning. At this period there seems to have been a perennial joke of obscure origin that married persons whose wives or husbands had lovers or mistresses wore horns. Shakespeare, among other Elizabethan playwrights, did the joke to death but it never failed to produce a roar of laughter from the audience. The proper division of the words in Middle Cornish spelling, according to Jenner, would be *Marsuys thys duen gweska an corn regh a tre arta* (if there is to thee grief to wear the horn, give it home again).[37]

Although the author claims his story was translated from a Cornish manuscript Jenner believes that this was not the case and was simply a trick to promote an interest in the work. However, there seem no

convincing grounds for this assumption. We do know that several manuscripts in Cornish have been lost and it could well be that 'The Image of Idleness' was one such piece. Comparison with some 'bawdy' Irish and Welsh tales shows that such a tale was not alien to Celtic literary tradition. Another piece of evidence to support the theory that a great deal of literature was either mislaid or destroyed during this period is the work of Nicholas Roscarrock. A member of an old Cornish landowning family who, along with his brother Travennor, was imprisoned for his Catholic beliefs in 1583, Nicholas occupied himself with antiquarian studies. He composed a large folio 'Register of British Saints', now in Cambridge University Library. Its particular value is that the folio contains Roscarrock's translation of the lives of Cornish saints from original Cornish manuscripts. Writing to Bishop Camden, in a letter dated 7 August 1607, Roscarrock mentions that he had a Cornish *Life of St Columba* in his possession. The fact that Dr Borlase, in the eighteenth century, must have seen another manuscript by John Tregear, adds to our fragmentary evidence of a lost literature.[38]

At the end of the Tudor period we find many Cornishmen determinedly hanging on to their language. According to Richard Carew many Cornishmen, even when they didn't know the language, would pretend to visitors that they did. Carew says that few Cornishmen, except those beyond Truro, were ignorant of English 'and yet some so affect their own, as to a stranger they will not speak it, for if meeting them by chance you inquire the way or any such matter, your answer shall be *meea navidna cowza sawsneck*—I can speak no Saxonage.'[39]

Chapter Four

Late Cornish

During a state visit to the English college for training Catholic priests at Valladolid, Spain, Philip III and his wife Queen Margaret, listened to a sermon preached in Cornish. Philip and Margaret came to the Spanish throne in 1598 and were very concerned with the training of priests to save England from its 'Protestant heresy'. Philip founded a college for English students at St Omer which his daughter Isabel, who was married to Archduke Albert of Austria, played a part in organising in 1592. The main college for the training of Catholic priests for the British Isles was at Valladolid, a hundred miles to the north of Madrid. On 19 July 1600, the Eve of St Margaret, the Spanish monarch visited the college but the weather on that day was so intensely hot that the reception organised by the priests and students at the college had to be postponed until the Feast of St Bernard on 20 August. At 2 p.m. on that day, their majesties arrived once more at the college and were greeted by the various dignatories and officials. Orations in Spanish, Hebrew, Greek and Latin were delivered. Following these six orators who took verses of Psalm 21 ('The king shall joy in thy strength, O Lord') as their text, spoke in Cornish, English, Welsh, French, Flemish and Italian.

The scene was witnessed by Don Antonio Ortes who recorded what he saw and, later in the year, Andres Sanches of Madrid printed a small quarto volume of 225 pages on the visit entitled *Relation of the visit of the Catholic Kings to the English College of Valladolid in the month of August in the Year 1600. And the reception and feast held in the same college for the Image of Our Lady maltreated by the heretics. Addressed to the most Serene Lady Infanta of Spain Dona Isabel Clara Eugenia by Don Antonio Ortes.* The 'Image of Our Lady maltreated by the heretics' refers to a statue of the Madonna at Cadiz which was knocked down by English sailors led by the earl of Essex when the town was plundered by them in 1596. It was then brought to Valladolid on the Eve of the Nativity of Our Lady, 7 September 1600, and is still there today.

Unfortunately, Don Antonio did not attempt to record any of

the Cornish spoken. Jenner points out, 'it would probably have been dreadfully misprinted, but I think we should have been able to restore the text'.[1] Don Antonio in *Relation of the visit of the Catholic Kings,* describes the Cornish oration in the following manner:

LA LENGUA CORNAICA: THE CORNISH LANGUAGE

'His honour is great in thy salvation: glory and great worship shalt thou lay upon him.' Verse 5.[2]

There spoke in this language a student, a native of that Province of England, whose language is distinct from English, as is in Spain the Biscayan [Basque] from the Castilian; and it has some ways and manner of speaking, with that rapidity of the Basques: and it is the part of England which looks directly towards Biscay and in his manner he spoke it excellently.

INTERPRETE: TRANSLATION

Said the Cornishman: that all men aim at honour and glory, but few find it, because they do not seek it where it is; they seek it in vanity and deceitful splendour of the world and they find themselves deceived and vain: because it is only found in virtue in which the Catholic Kings seek it, and therefore the true honour follows them as the shadows follow the body.

One wonders who the Cornishman was who made this oration. There was only one student in the college register at this time who came from the diocese of Exeter, which covered Cornwall. This was one Richard Pentrey who arrived at the college on 29 April 1600. There had been two students from Exeter before this, a man called Champ who had made a speech to Philip II but had returned to England in 1598 after being ordained; and a man called Bray, described as a Cornishman, who died at the college in 1591. Jenner conjectures that the name Pentrey could be Pentreath or Pendra as the final *th* sound in Cornish tended commonly to drop out. There are two references to Richard Pentrey in the college registers: the first occurs in the *Liber Alumnorium* of the register of students of St Alban's College of Valladolid:

No. 1666 Richard Pentrey, of the Diocese of Exeter, admitted in this College on the 29th day of April in the year 1600. He

previously took the oath according to the custom of the
Seminaries at the College of Seville.

The second reference comes from the *Liber Primi Examinus* of the
same college:

No. 1666 Richard Pentrey, a Cornishman, born of respectable
but heretical parents, at the age of 21 years became a Catholic
at the persuasion of a certain Catholic who is called Mr. Bray,
and was brought from England to these parts beyond the seas.
For five years he lived in the Seminaries, and in that of Seville
he studied rhetoric and philosophy. Then on account of ill health
he was sent here and came to this college on the 29th day of
April in the year 1600, the oath of proceeding to England
according to the custom of the seminaries having previously
been taken in the college of Seville.

Pentrey emerges once more into history in the *Examination by
Sir Harry Vivian of Trelowarren of William Jehoseph of Chechwell in
Dorset, who lately landed in Mount's Bay on return from the English seminary
of Valladolid in Spain*. This took place on 5 October 1600. Jehoseph
told his examiners that 'there were about thirty English scholars there'
(at Valladolid); 'of philosophers there is [amongst them] Richard
Pendrea, a Cornishman'. On being asked where the king of Spain
was when he was there Jehoseph 'saith that the King lay at Madeno
del Campo [Medini del Campo] eight miles from Valladolid and
proposes to be there within a few days after, for they of the English
seminary were providing to entertain him, and of wars he heard
nothing then'.

Jenner suggests that Catholicism lingered on for a long time after
the Reformation among Cornishmen. Those Cornish who kept their
language also kept their religion which gave concessions to it. The
training of Cornish-speaking clerics, such as Richard Pentrey, would
encourage the language. In such circumstances there was a danger of
Catholicism becoming synonymous with language—a situation which
has, unfortunately, to some extent arisen in Ireland. Jenner had even
heard tales of Catholic Cornish speakers meeting in secret in the tin
mines to say their prayers and make their confessions in their native
tongue.[3] There is, at the moment, no evidence to substantiate this
perhaps romantic idea but a careful combing of Catholic libraries

might reveal further fragments of the story. It was only by accident that Canon Michael J. Burns, rector of the English College of Valladolid, discovered Don Antonio Ortes's account of the Cornish oration and forwarded on the material to Henry Jenner in the 1920s.

In 1602 Richard Carew published his famous *Survey of Cornwall*; he had gathered material for this during the last years of the sixteenth century. Thomas Tonkin edited a version of the *Survey* in the early eighteenth century but this was not published until 1811. Carew compares Cornish to Welsh 'but the Cornish is more easy to be pronounced and not so unpleasing in sound with throat letters as the Welsh'. According to Carew:

> The language is stored with sufficient plenty to express the conceit of wit, both in prose and rhyme, yet can they no more give a Cornish word for *tie* than the Greeks for *ineptus,* the French for *stand,* the English for *emulus* or the Irish for *knave.*

In this respect Carew displays a lack of knowledge of the language for *kelmy* is tie; *dhe gelmy,* to tie; *kelmys,* tied, etc. The Irish word for knave is *cneamhaire.* Carew continues: 'Oaths they have not past two or three natural but are fair to borrow of the English, marry the want is relieved with a flood of most bitter curses and spiteful nicknames.' He goes on to list some numerals and to compare ten words with Greek. He comments on the fact that many Cornishmen were refusing to speak to strangers in English, replying *meea navidna cowza sawsneck*; Carew translates this as 'I can't speak Saxonage [English]'. Nance has broken this down into Unified Spelling as *My ny-vynnaf cows Sawsnek.* This, he points out, means 'I won't speak English' with the stress on the word 'I' thus presenting a different and highly significant meaning.[4]

Early in the century, *circa* 1610, John Norden wrote a work entitled *Speculum Magnae Britanniae pars Cornwall,* addressed to King James I. He tell us that:

> the Cornish people for the most part are descended of the British stocke, though muche entermixed since with the Saxon and Norman bloude but until of late yeares retayned the Britishe speche.
> . . . but of late the Cornishe men have muche conformed themselves to the use of the Englyshe tongue; and their Englyshe is equall to the beste, especially in the eastern partes, even from Truro eastwards it is in a manner wholly Englyshe.

In their Weste parte of the countrye as in the hundreds of
Penwith and Kerrier, the Cornishe tongue is most in use amongste
the inhabitants.

In the Cornish-speaking areas of Penwith and Kerrier Norden gives
us an interesting and useful view of the language:

And yet (which is to be marveyled) though the husband and wife,
parents and children, masters and servants, do naturally communicate in their native language; yet there is none of them in a
manner, but is able to converse with a stranger in the English
tongue, unless it be some obscure people who seldom confer
with the better sort. But it seemeth, however, that in a few
years the Cornish will be, little by little, abandoned.

The inference here is clear. Many of the gentry still spoke the
language at this time in order to communicate with their servants.
Under these circumstances it would seem that a fairly substantial
number of monoglots existed who, in the space of the next fifty
years, disappeared entirely. That Cornwall was still regarded as
separate from England, as a country conquered by England, is very
clear in a note of Norden's:

And as they are among themselves litigious [he writes of the
Cornish] so seem they yet to retayn a kind of concealed envy
against the English who they affect with a desire of revenge for
their fathers' sakes by whom their fathers received their repulse.

On 12 August 1611, a William Jordan of Helston finished writing a
composition called 'Gwreans an bys' (The Creation of the World),
another miracle play. It is very unlikely that Jordan was the original
author of this drama for, as Whitley Stokes has pointed out, the way
the stage directions are written indicates a date prior to 1611. 'The
author's mention of limbo, too, may tend to shew that the play was
composed before the Reformation.'[5] Jordan, it would appear, was
merely transcribing from an older manuscript now lost, and possibly
transcribing it for an actual performance. Therefore the assumption
that the cessation of the miracle play performances took place around
1620 is very likely. The state of Cornish in which 'Gwreans an bys' is
written shows the increasing influence of English as the loan words

from English occur in far greater number. Jordan's original manuscript is now in the Bodleian together with a copy.[6]

In 1614 a sometime professor of astronomy at Gresham College, London, Edward Brerewood, published a book entitled *Enquiries touching the diversity of languages and religious through the chief parts of the world*. This became a fairly standard work running to several editions between 1614 and 1674. In Chapter Four, Brerewood comments:

First, therefore, it is certainly observed, that there are at this day 14 Mother Tongues in Europe (beside the Latin) which remain, not only abolished, but little or nothing altered or impaired by the Romans. And those are the 1, Irish, spoken in Ireland and a good part of Scotland; the 2, Brittish in Wales, Cornwale and Britain of France . . .

In a section entitled 'Of the Languages of the People of Europe . . . collected out of Jo. Scaliger', Brerewood remarks: 'There are seven other prime or Mother Tongues but of less worth and dignity than the former . . . the sixth is the Welsh or the ancient Brittish of which Britany or France hath some touch . . .' And speaking of the French 'provincial dialects', he adds: '. . . besides which there are two others, which have no affinity with the Romans or Latin, these are the Brittain, which seems not to differ much from our Cornish, and the Biscay, which is used in the mountainous country, between France and Spain'.

Sir John Doddridge, in his *An Historical Account of the Ancient and Modern State of the Principality of Wales, Duchy of Cornwall and Earldom of Chester*, published in 1630, also comments on the language:

The people inhabiting the same are called Cornish men and are also reputed a remnant of the Britains, the ancient inhabitants of this land. They have a particular language (although now much worn out of use) differing little from the Welsh, and the language of the Britanes in Frances, which argueth their original to have been one nation.

In 1632 a Welsh book appeared on which Cornish versions of the Lord's Prayer and the Creed were given. This was a translation by John Davies, the rector of Mallwyd, of the *Book of Christian Exercise* written by the Jesuit Robert Parsons. Davies called his work *Llyfr y resolution . . . wedi ei gyfiefthu yn Gymraeg* and editions were published

in 1632, 1684, 1711, 1720 and 1802. Among the important works of John Davies was *Y Bibl Cryssegr–lan*, published in 1620. The year 1632 also saw the publication of a play by Richard Brome, a noted actor and playwright who had once been a servant to Ben Jonson, and who persuaded the great English dramatist to write a complementary prologue to the play. The play was entitled: *The Northern Lasse a Comedie, As it hath beene often acted with good Applause at the Globe and Black Fryers by his Maiestes servants. Written by Richard Brome, London. Printed by Aug. Mathevvews and are to be sold by Nicolas Vavasou, dwelling at the little South dore of St. Paul's Church, 1632.*

The play became very popular and eight editions are known to have been published between 1632 and 1714 plus a Dublin edition in 1726. The editions published between 1706 and 1714 had additional songs and music 'composed by Mr. Purcell'. This was not, of course, Henry Purcell who died in 1695 but the great composer's brother Daniel. The play is of interest to the history of Cornish because it contains a line of Cornish. In the play is a character called Master Salmon Nonsense, son and heir to Sir Hercules Nonsense of Cornwall. Nonsense is a suitor to Constance, the Northern Lasse, the heroine of the play. In Act V, scene 8, Sir Percy Squelch, a justice, comes on disguised as a Spaniard who speaks no English. The actors on stage are puzzled at how to make him understand them:

Bullfinch: Alasse what shall wee doe then? Gentlemen, have any of you any Spanish to help me understand this strange stranger?

[They all disclaim knowledge.]

Bullfinch: What shiere of our Nation is next to Spain? Perhaps he may understand that shiere English.

Tridewell: Devonshire or Cornwall, sire.

Nonsense: Never credit me but I will spout some Cornish at him. *Peden bras vidne whee bis creagas.*

Jenner respells the sentence as *Pedn bras a vednough why bos creages* which translates as 'Fat head, will you be hanged?'[7]

Judging by the glimpse of Cornish we get at the beginning of the seventeenth century and also that towards the end of the century we can deduce that the language had gone through a fairly rapid decay.

From a manuscript of William Hals published in Davies Gilbert's history[8] we are told that Cornish was spoken in St Feock until about 1640 and Mr William Jackman, the vicar, who was chaplain at Pendennis Castle during the siege by the Parliamentary army had to administer the sacrament to communicants in Cornish because the aged people did not understand English. Yet within a few years of the ending of the Civil War, the old monoglots were all gone. With the monoglots gone the extinction of the language was inevitable; for it is only while a minority language retains a strong monoglot population that it will exist alongside a major language. Polwhele tells us that in 1650 the Cornish language was still strong in Penwith in the parishes of St Paul and St Just where the fisher and market women and the tinners conversed 'for the most part in the old vernacular tongue'.[9]

When the Civil War came the gentry of Cornwall were split into two fairly even camps. Families such as the Arundells, Vyvyans, Bassetts, Grenvilles, Trelawnys, Godolphins and Killigrews were for the King while the Robartes of Lanhydrock, Sir Richard Fuller, John St Aubyn of Clowance, Nicholas Boscawen and his four sons of Tregothnan and John Trefusis, were for Parliament. Some families split in their allegiance like the Arundells, nine of whom fought for the King and two for Parliament; Sir Francis Godolphin and his poet son Sydney were Royalists while their cousin Francis of Treveneague was a Parliamentarian. After the King had raised his standard at Nottingham on 22 August 1642, the fight began in Cornwall but, following the year 1642-3, life returned to a fairly normal pattern. The average Cornishman had other things to think about than the power struggle at far away Westminster. In fact, Cornish soldiers had to be bribed to serve outside of Cornwall in the respective armies. In 1644, however, the Royalists defeated Essex at Losthwithiel—one of the first major conflicts on Cornish soil. By 1645 Cornwall was beginning to feel the effects of the war. Sir Thomas Fairfax separated the Royalist Cornish army from the other Royalist armies and, in 1646, he drove them back into Cornwall. John Arundell was forced to surrender Pendennis Castle and on Thursday, 12 March, a treaty of surrender was agreed upon. It was not until 1651 that John Grenville and his Royalist garrison were driven out of the Scillies. The downfall of the monarchy entailed the abolition of the duchy of Cornwall as an administrative unit and the sale of the royal estates which were then purchased by the bourgeoisie.[10] According to Nance:[11]

The troubles of the Civil War must have done much to discourage Cornish speaking. Young men who had taken to speaking the English used in either army would be less likely to return to Cornish when the fighting was over. At all events they can have had no great wish to teach it to their families for even in West Penwith John Ray, in 1667, found that few children knew it.

William Scawen, who after the Civil War became the first Cornish-man to attempt to save the dying language, gives us an intriguing picture of the use to which Cornish was put during the hostilities by spies:[12]

In the time of the late unhappy Civil War we began to make some use of it upon the runagates that went from us to the contrary part from our opposite works, and more we should have done if the enemy had not been jealous [suspicious] of them and prevented [forestalled] us. This may be fit to be improved into somewhat of the like occasion happen, for it may be talked freely and aloud to advantage, to which no other tongue hath reference.

The Civil War gives us an interesting glimpse of Cornish through the eyes of a lawyer serving in the Royalist army. Richard Symonds was born at Black Notley, Essex, in June 1617, and joined the Royalist army after the Battle of Alresford, in March 1644, when the Royalists suffered their first big ignominious defeat at the hands of the Parliamentary forces. Symonds was a keen student of topography, genealogy, heraldry and art. When he joined the King's army he took with him his notebook and jotted down much invaluable data.[13] Symonds must have been prepared to meet the difference between the Cornish and the English because, on arrival at Menheniot, he writes with apparent surprise: 'The people speake good and playne English here, hitherto.' More importantly, Symonds lists twenty-four nouns in Cornish and English, gives the Cornish for the numerals one to twenty-one and four conversational pieces. The nouns and phrases seem to have been chosen for their practicality rather than mere antiquarian research. For example, the four conversational pieces are:

God save you	Due ragges blessye
I thank you	Gad marshe
God be with you	Bed me tew thew
I wish you well	Dieu new grace thew gilda

Symonds adds: 'This language is spoken altogether at Goonhilly and about Pendennis and at Land's End they speake no Englishe. All beyond Truro they speake the Cornish language.'

One wonders how much to trust Symonds on this subject as the Royalist army as such did not travel beyond Lostwithiel and Lanhydrock.[14] But Symonds could have been a member of the isolated Royalist garrison at Pendennis Castle, Falmouth, or left the army and journeyed further west by himself. Also he could have picked up the information from a Cornish speaker serving in the Royal army.

The Civil War had a profound effect on the Celtic heritage that survived among the Cornish people. Speaking of Nicholas Boson, who wrote in the latter part of the seventeenth century, Nance comments:[15]

> There are hints in Boson's writings that this Celtic heritage
> still survived to some extent in his day and that tales of Arthur
> at least were more often told then, but the vulgar rivalries of
> English party politics and party religion, had already fastened on
> the minds and thoughts of most Cornish people before the Civil
> War was over. English funny stories and popular songs replaced
> the folk tales and folk songs in Cornish and ever since, instead
> of contributing something first hand to the common stock, it has
> been chiefly second hand English notions of what is amusing,
> interesting or important that the mind of Cornwall has been
> turned.

At the time of the Restoration of the monarch an interesting book on linguistics was published 'at the Sign of the Black Spread Eagle and Windmill in Martins le brad'. The book was entitled *A Battledoor for Teachers and Professors to learn Singular and Plural: wherein is shewed forth by grammar or scripture examples how several nations have made a distinction between singular and plural . . . and in this is set forth examples of the singular and plural about thou and you in several language, Englishe, Latin, Italian, Greek, Hebrew, Caldee Saxon, Welch, Mence (Manx), Cornish, French and Spanish by George Fox, John Stubbs and Benjamin Furley.* It will be noted that George Fox (1624-91) was the founder of the Society of Friends, now popularly known as Quakers. The book contains eighteen examples of the singular and plural in Cornish. Jenner, who makes some interesting comments on the spellings and mutations, also remarks that 'it is interesting that Cornish should have been sufficiently recognised to be thought worth mentioning in 1660'.[16]

But it must be remembered that George Fox spent some time in missionary work in Cornwall during 1655-6 and journeyed at least as far as St Ives and Marazion, so that he had probably heard Cornish spoken and jotted down his examples at the time.

In 1667 the traveller and writer John Ray journeyed to Cornwall and paid particular attention to the language, noting down some phrases and proverbial expressions. He says that 'Mr. Dickon Gywn is the only man we could hear of that now writes the Cornish language' but, Ray adds, that while 'Dickon Gwyn' of St Just was esteemed the most skilful of any man in the Cornish language, he was no grammarian and therefore he supposes that a man called Pendarvis, who was a scholar, must needs have better skill in the tongue. This illustrates the curious prejudice of the time that unless a man knew Greek, Latin, French and perhaps Hebrew as well, he could not be skilled in languages. Poor 'Dickon Gwyn' obviously did not measure up to this standard while Pendarvis did. Ray, incidentally, had copied down the name 'Dickon Gwyn' wrongly from his informants. The man they were speaking of was, in fact, Richard Angwyn or Dick Angwyn of whom we shall learn more shortly. Ray does make one interesting point: 'we met with none here [i.e. near Land's End] but what could speak English and few of the children could speak Cornish so that the language is likely in a short time to be quite lost.'

It was at this time that the last monoglot speakers of the language were dying out. Dr Borlase records that in 1676 a woman called Cheston Marchant of Gwithian, near St Ives, died aged 164 (!) and that she spoke no other language but Cornish.[17] William Scawen also mentions the old lady:[18]

Let not the old woman be forgotten who died about two years since, who was 164! years old, of good memory and healthful at that age, living in the parish of Guithian, by charity mostly of such as came purposely to see her, speaking to them [in default of English] by an interpreter, but partly understanding it. She married a second husband after she was 80 and buried him after he was 80 years of age.

The fact that the death of Cheston Marchant was so recorded indicates that it was now extremely unusual for anyone to be found who spoke Cornish only.

In 1695 Edmund Gibson of Queen's College, Oxford, the lord

bishop of London, edited the first English translation of William Camden's *Britannia or Remaines Concerning Britane* (1614) and in his notes on the Cornish, he observes:

> Their language, too, is English; and (which is something sur-
> prising) observed by travellers to be the most pure and refined
> than that of their neighbours Devonshire and Somersetshire.
> The most probable reason whereof seems to be this, that English
> is to them an introduced, not an original, language, and those
> who brought it in were the gentry and merchants, who imitated
> the dialect of the Court, which is most nice and accurate. Their
> neat way of living and housewifry, upon which they justly value
> themselves above their neighbours, does possibly proceed from
> the same cause.

Gibson adds:

> The old Cornish is almost driven out of the county being spoken
> only by the vulgar in two or three parishes at the Land's End
> and they too understand English. 'Tis a good while since, that
> only two men could write it, and one of them being no scholar or
> grammarian and then blind with age.

Gibson seems to have taken this information from Ray's *Itinerary*. Gibson thought there were only three books in Cornish. One of them was the *Pascon agan Arluth*, or Passion Poem, and 'the other two are translated out of the Bodleian Library, one is translated and the other is now a translating by Mr. Keigwin, the only person perhaps that perfectly understands the tongue'. Gibson does some service by publishing the Lord's Prayer in Cornish, Welsh and Breton and the Creed in Cornish for comparative purposes. He says that the cause of the decay was the Act of Uniformity 'but the Cornish, being in love with the English, to gratify the novelty, desired (it seems) to have the Common Liturgy in that tongue'. Gibson then borrows from William Scawen's essay on the language by saying a cause of the decay was the cessation of the miracle play performances. 'These (with the coming in of Artificers, Trading men, Ministers etc.) may probably have contributed very much to this general neglect of their original language, so that almost nothing now appears of it in their conversation and very little in any old writing.'

It is, however, William Scawen's essay, *Observations on an Ancient Manuscript entitled Passio Christi, written in the Cornish Language, and now preserved in the Bodleian Library; with an account of the Language, Manners and Customs of the People of Cornwall,* which is of great importance from this period and it is, perhaps, the first work in which the problem of the dying language is sympathetically treated. Scawen, a vice warden of the Stannaries, wrote the work about 1680 but it was not published until 1777 from the manuscript which was preserved in the library of Thomas Astle. He was the first Cornishman who expressed a desire to save and restore the language. Of particular interest in his essay are the sixteen reasons he gives for the decay of the language. The first reason he gives is the lack of a distinctive Cornish alphabet. Also high on the list he places the loss of contact between Cornwall and Brittany:

> The great loss of Armorica, near unto us, by friendship, by
> cognition, by interest, by correspondence. Cornwall has received
> princes from thence, and they from us. We had therefore
> mutual interchange, of private families, but as to our speech
> we are alike careless. We can understand words of one another
> but have not the benefit of conferences with one another in our
> ancient tongues. I have met with some Friars born and bred
> there, who, one would think, should be able to discourse in
> their own pristine tongue, and of their birthplace, yet found
> them, though not totally ignorant that such things had been,
> yet insensible and careless of their former condition. They
> could tell me that my name Scawen was in their tongue Elder,
> as here it is; that there are those that bear the same name, and
> one of them a bishop; but when he writ it he changed it to
> Sambucas, shewing thereby a mind to declare to a new rather than
> an inclination to his old name, and relation to his country's speech.

Another important reason was the cessation of the miracle plays, of the 'guirremears' which were performed until the 1620s. Scawen comments:

> These Guirremears which were used at the great conventions of
> the people, at which they had famous interludes with great
> preparations, and not without shows of devotion in them,
> solemnised in great and spacious downs of great capacity,

encompassed about with earthen banks, and some in part stone-
work, of largeness to contain thousands, the shapes which
remain in many places at this day, though the use of them long
since gone . . . this was a great means to keep in use the tongue
with delight and admiration. They had recitation in them poetical
and divine, one of them I may suppose this small relique of
antiquity to be, in which the Passion of Our Saviour and his
Resurrection is described.

Another cause of decay, states Scawen, was 'the loss of the ancient
records which some affirm were burnt and others lost in the ancient
castles of Rostormell and other such'. Restormel lies a mile north
of Lostwithiel. It was destroyed by Richard Grenville in 1644 when
he drove out a Parliamentary garrison under Essex. These records,
Scawen says, were not only of the earldom and duchy of Cornwall
but dated from the time Cornwall was an independent kingdom.
Another reason was the general apathy of the Cornish people towards
the language and, surprisingly enough for the time he was living in,
Scawen says the suppression of the Druids by Christianity led to the
decay of learning among the people. An important reason also is the
one Gibson took up:

The coming in of strangers of all sorts upon us, artificers,
traders, home born and foreigners, who in our great commodities
of tin (more profitable to others than ourselves) and fishing, have
insisted to us to converse with, and often to stay with us; these
all as they could not easily learn our tongue, for which they
could not find any guide or direction, especially in these latter
days, nor the same generally spoken or affected amongst ourselves,
so they were more apt and ready to let loose their own tongue
to be commixed with ours, and such, for the novelty sake thereof,
people were more ready to receive them than to communicate
ours to any improvement in them.

Scawen says that not teaching the Lord's Prayer in Cornish is
another reason plus:

the little or no help, rather discouragement, which the gentry
and other people of our own have given in these latter days,
who have lived in those parts where the tongue hath been in

some use . . . The poorest sort this day, when they speak it as
they come abroad, are laughed at by the rich that understand it
not, which is their own fault not endeavouring after it.

Scawen had attributed one of the reasons for the decay to a lack
of literature in the language. Jenner places a heavy emphasis on this
fact. 'The chief reason for the decay was undoubtedly the failure of
Cornwall to produce a literature for it is through literature that a
language achieves permanent form and can struggle successfully with
competing tongues.'[19] While literature is of considerable importance
it may be pointed out in this respect that a considerable and worthy
literature has not saved the Irish language from a tragic decay. Yet,
as Professor Calvert Watkins has pointed out, 'Irish has the oldest
vernacular literature of Europe.' While, on the other hand, Estonian
which has gone through a successful linguistic revival, was not
written until 1525 and a literature as such was only created in the
nineteenth century. More extreme examples may be found such as
Ostyak, spoken in the Khanti-Mansi area of Omsk, western Siberia,
which only started a written literature in 1931; Gilyak, a Paleo-Siberian
language, not written until 1929; Chukchee or Luoravetian, first
written in 1930 and with the first book appearing in 1932; while
Dorgwa was first written in 1920. All these are healthy linguistic
communities today.[20]

To Scawen, however, the language could only be saved by the
creation of a literature. He appears to be the first Cornishman who
actively sought to preserve the language from death; although Cornish
was only a second language to him he did not consider his knowledge
of it very fluent. His attempts were not met with encouragement
even among his family and friends. He writes:

I have likewise had discouragements amongst ourselves at home.
I have been often told that, besides the difficulty of the attempt,
it would be thought ridiculous for one to go about restoring of
that tongue which he himself could not speak nor understand
truly when spoken to.

Scawen was aware that a number of manuscripts in Cornish did
exist and tried to track them down but with little success. He mentions
a manuscript of 'Anguin', obviously the same Richard Angwyn whom
Ray mentions; also a Cornish Matins, said to have been amongst the

papers of Dr Joseph Maynard, and of a Cornish Accidence (Grammar) compiled by Dr Kennal of Stithians which had been spoiled by children before he could get his hands on it. 'Here I cannot but lament the want of such persons, books, records and papers which were late in being, and not now to be had,' he says, 'and my misfortune in not having translated them, that most unhappily escaped me.'

Nevertheless, Scawen decided that what could not be saved must be created. He prevailed upon several of his contemporary Cornishmen to start writing in Cornish 'which they at first found very hard to be done but after some practise it seemed easier'. This new school of Cornish writing which Scawen inspired, during the period in which the language was near the end of its decline, is termed as Late Cornish. The most prominent name of the new Cornish writers is that of Nicholas Boson of Newlyn, whose work was for some time wrongly attributed to his son John Boson (b. 1653 and d. *circa* 1720-41). Nicholas Boson's parents had brought him up in ignorance of Cornish, 'the reason I conceive to be a nicety of my mother's forbidding the servants and neighbours to talk to me otherwise than in English.' After finishing his schooling and living in France for a while, Boson returned to Cornwall. 'I do not remember that I attain'd to pass in the Cornish Tongue until I came to be concerned in business, and now I do reckon to see into it almost as far as most of my neighbours.' But according to Nance, 'he either wrote his English version first, or at least thought in English rather than in Cornish'; this 'is often suggested by the unCeltic order of his Cornish words and by such unCeltic expressions as *tho bose shoothes war, noriel*—"to be depended on, neither" etc.'[21] The first interesting essay in Cornish that Boson wrote is a short treatise on the language which he called 'Nebbaz Gerriau dro tho Carnoack' (A Few Words About Cornish). The work gives a very interesting light on the attitudes towards Cornish at the time:

NEBBAZ GERRIAU DRO THO CARNOACK

A few words about Cornish[22]

Our Cornish tongue hath been so long in the wane that we can hardly hope to see it increase again, for as the English confine it into this narrow country first, so it presseth on still leaving it no place about ye cliff and sea, it being almost only spoken from ye Land's End to the Mount, and towards St. Ives and Redruth,

and again from the Lizard to Helston, and towards Falmouth, containing about twenty miles in length and [a] quarter [not] or half that breadth, within little extent also there is more of English spoken than of Cornish for there may be some found that can hardly speak or understand Cornish, but scarce any but both understand and speak English, therefore it seems difficult to stay and recover it again, for the old men dying away//* we find the young men to speak it less and less and worse and worse, and so it is like to decay from time to time. Because ye English dialect and pronunciation . . . where in ye land (the Town and Cities only excepted) . . . neither are the old folks to be depended upon, as you will find by ys instance about the Sieur Angwin the greatest and the oldest of the late Professors of ye Cornish Tongue, who being desir'd to interpret *Gevern Anko* concluded that it was 'Goates all'; where as it signified the Bonds of the Hundred of Gevern. He knew it to be the Hundred but forgot that the word *ko* was Cornish for 'remembering'. Something like this I have heard about Mean Omberkarack, therefore if any attempt be made about preserving Cornish, it must be done by such as are perfect natives, and good scholars, scarce to be found, for they are few// but two or three that I know of; whereof one is of more special skill and learning than any that have been this long time before or will come after in all likelihood; so that except it be now done it is never like to be at all hereafter, having so much skill in language, as the Greek, Hebrew etc., of which I heard him say that Cornish carries a very likeness. If that learned wise man should happen to see this, doubtless he would find cause to correct it in orthography etc. However, this may pass for a vulgar essay; for I have never seen any of the antient British writings, the characters on the stately tombstone in Burian Church I know not what to make of, and another stone in Maddon in the Downs of Bosolo, called the written stone to this day bearing letters unknown. What I have met with legible and intelligible is a motto on a Gentleman's coat-of// -arms engraven in silver of above a hundred years old, a knightly family, at present in the west of Devon, and lost 'tis like by his Steward holding court at his manor at Land's End; it was lately found making a hedge and sold; he that brought it sent it unto the first branch of the family now planted at the Mount. The words

* // signifies the ending of pages on the original.

1 'The Bodmin Gospels', ninth/tenth century

Dubo kp... ...gor

Vocabula
Angel

Os omps. Buy chefindoc. Celū. nef. Angls. ail. Archangls. archail. Scella
stereu. Sol. heuul. Luna. luir. firmamentū. firmament. Cursus. rede
gua. oiund. L Cosni. enbrē. Tellus. tir. terra. doer. huni. gueter. oiare
mor. Equor. spaneu mor. pelag. mordiseid. Occeanū. mortor. homo. den
onas. L oiasels. gurruid. femina. beneurid. Seruus. antromer. membrū. esel.
Capud. pen. vertex. dipuleuuit. Cerebrū. impinon. Cerux. chil. Collū.
cōna. frons. tal. nasus. trein. Haris. fruc. Capillus. bleuynpeu. Cesaries.
gols. Coma. eudin. Auris. scouarn. maxilla. grud. Timp. ereu. facies.
enuoch. Superliū. abrans. palpebre. bleuenlagat. Ocls. lagat. ul ocli. legeit.
pupilla. biuenlagat. Os. genau. Oss. ascorn. Deus. dans. Denores. dannet.
Lingua. tauot. palatū. stefenic. labia. gueus. Guttur. briansen. men
tum. elgeth. Barba. bars. Barbā. bares. Collū. guar. pectus. eluitdiuu
ron. Cor. colon. pulmo. seeuens. lectir. aiu. fel. bisdel. Stomac. glas.
Splen. lepillor. Adeps. blonec. Aruina. suif. viseus. eulurionem.
Crstū. enederen. Sanguis. guit. Caro. chic. Cutis. he. pellis. eroin. Sea
pula. scuid. Dorsum. chein. Ueuter. tor. L talon. Brachiū. brech.
Vlna. elin. man. lau. L lof. Digit. bis. Digiti. bess. Digitū. bes. Vngs.
euuin. palma. palf. Artus. chefals. Lat. tenepen. Costa. asen. Renes.
diuglun. Heruus. goiu en. vena. guid. feuuir L Cora. morbot. Clun.
peuclun. Genu. penclin. Vulua. cheber. Sura. logodeuter. Crus. fer.
Tibia. elescher. Talus. tufern. pes. truit. planta. godeutruit. Allgr. bis
truit. vngla. epincarn. patriarcha. hupeltat. propha. profut. Apls. apostol.
Archieps. archescop. Cps. escop. Regnū. ruisanaid. Abbas. abat. prebit
hebren chiat pluit. oferiat. sacerdos. punder. Clericus. Cloireg. Diacoñ.
L leuita. diagon. monac. manach. monacha. L oiomalus. manaes. Ana
choita. ancar. hermita. eruut. Honna. laines. Cantor. cheniat.
Cantrix. canoiet. Lector. redior. Lectrix. rediores. Laic. leic. Comux.
chespar. Castus. guas. Incest. sqeuip. pulcher. teg. formosus. faidus.
Speciosus. L Decorus. Carder. Deformis. disliu. Pater. tat. oiater. oiam.
Auus. hendat. Abauus. hengog. proauus. dipog. Atrauus. gurthhog. Fili.
mab. filia. oiuch. Liberi. flecher. Soboles. ach. familia. goscoipi teilu.
frater. broder. L braud. Soror. puir. victric. altrou. Honerca. altruan
priuign. els. filiaster. elses. Hepos. noi. Hepeis. noit. Altou. L Hutto.
tatyat. Altic. L Hutic. oiamaid. Alūpil. oabmeidrin. patruus. eurt
abartat. Auuncls. abarh. mam. oiatercera. moderch abarhma. Amita.
abarh tat. Ocskyi. Impoc. L euissin. Basiū. poceuil. propine. nestheuin.
guessin

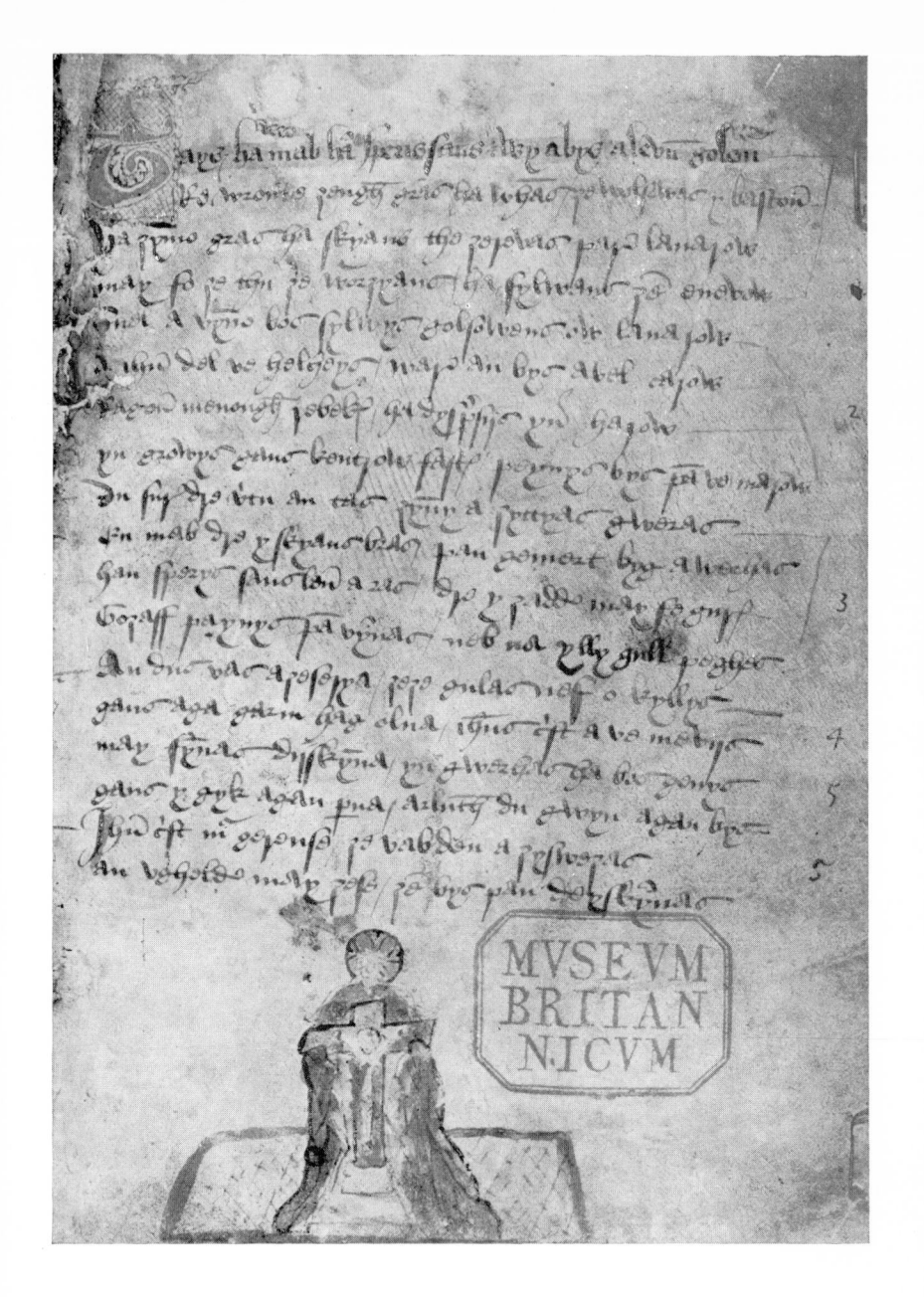

3 The first page of the fifteenth-century *Pascon agan Arluth* or Passion Poem

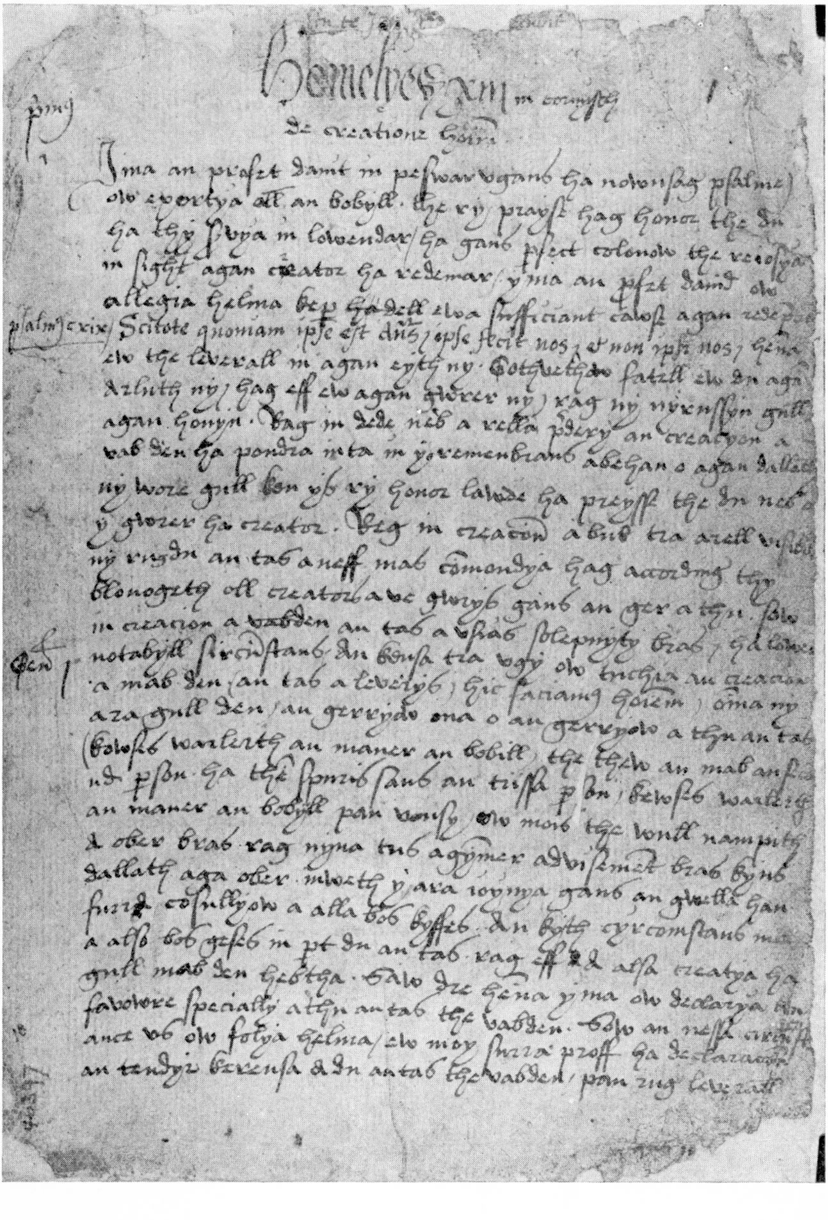

Homelyes xiij in cornysch

De creatione [...]

(A handwritten page of early modern Cornish cursive script, largely illegible)

4 A page from the Cornish version of Bishop Bonner's sixteenth-century *Homilies*

5 A page from *Bewnans Meriasek*, the Life of St Meriasek, dated A.D. 1504

6 (above) *Gelrlyfr Kyrnweig*: pages from Edward Lhuyd's Cornish vocabulary, dated A.D. 1702

7 (opposite above) *The Ordinale*: transcript with an English translation and Latin preface by John Keigwin, *circa* A.D. 1707

8 (opposite below) *The Ordinale*: transcript by John Keigwin, *circa* A.D. 1707

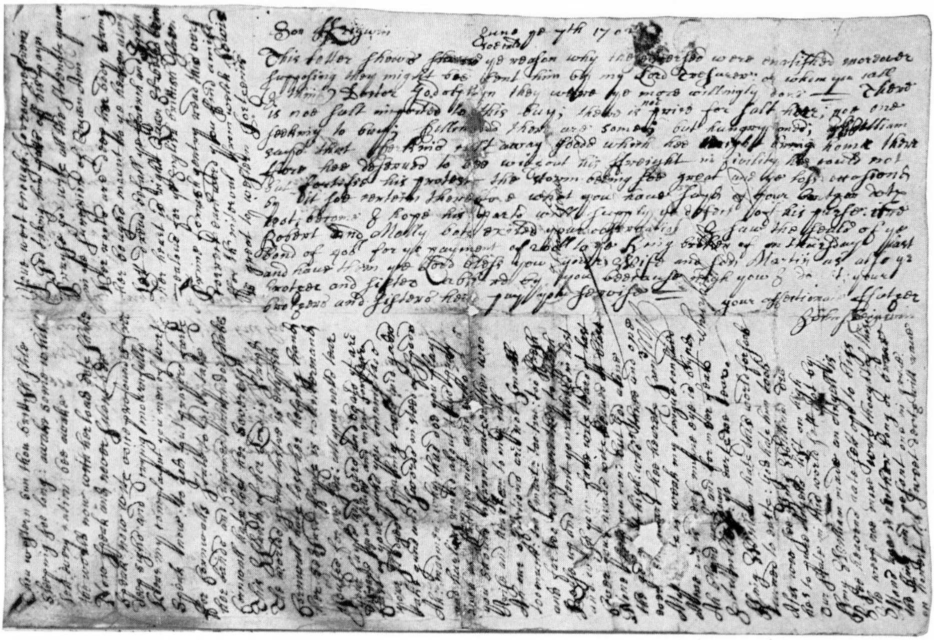

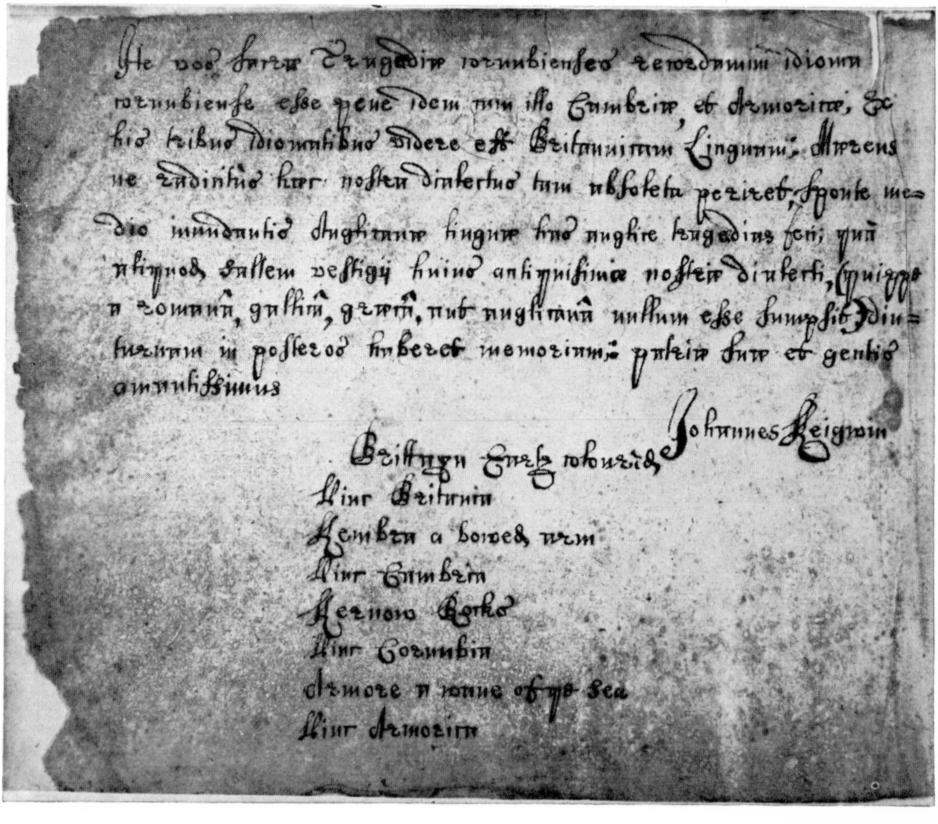

Dr Keigwin   June ye 7th 170_

This letter showes ye reason why the [...] were [...]
supposeing they might bee sent then by my Lord [...]
of [...] God al[...]yn they [...] he more willingly done —
[...] is no salt [...] this bay; [...] it [...] for salt [...]
[...] to buy [...] that are [...]

[...] your affectionate [...]
[...] John Keigwin

[The lower half of the upper sheet consists of additional closely-written lines that are illegible.]

He vos Saxae Brigadiae corinbienses rewordamini idioma
corinbiense esse pene idem cum illo Cumbriae et Armoricae, Et
hic tribus idiomatibus videre est Britannicum Linguarum. Mircens
ne radinius hic nostri dinlertus tum absoleta perires, sponte me-
dio inundantis Anglicanae linguae hud nuphir tragedius sori, quin
utinrod, saltem vestigy huius antiquissimae nostri dinlerti, squippe
in romanu, gallum, garum, nud nuphranu unilum esse humphib idin-
turinam in posteros haberet memoriam; patriae suae et gentis
amantissimus

                                                    Johannes Keigwin

            Brittyn Enez rowrith,
    Miur Britanin
    Hembra a bowed urm
    Miur Cumbra
    Hernow Corho
    Miur Corunbia
    Armore is name of ye sea
    Miur Armorin

DHE COF A
MYCHAL JOSEP
AN COF
HA
THOMAS FLAMANK
HEMBRYNKYSY AN LU KERNEWEK
A GESKERDHAS BYS DHE LOUNDRES
HA GODHEVEL ENA DYALANS
METHEVEN 1497
"Y A'S TEVYTH HANOW A
BES VYNYTHA HA BRY A DHUR
HEP MERWEL"
DREHEVYS GANS MEBYON KERNOW.
1966

IN MEMORY OF
MICHAEL JOSEPH
THE SMITH
AND
THOMAS FLAMANK
LEADERS OF THE CORNISH HOST
WHO MARCHED TO LONDON
AND SUFFERED VENGEANCE THERE
JUNE 1497
"THEY SHALL HAVE A NAME
PERPETUAL AND A FAME PERMANENT
AND IMMORTAL"
ERECTED BY MEBYON KERNOW.
1966

9 The memorial in Cornish and English in St Keverne to Michael Joseph and Thomas Flamank, leaders of the 1497 Cornish uprising

HERE LIETH INTERRED
DOROTHY PENTREATH
WHO DIED IN
1777.
SAID TO HAVE BEEN THE
LAST PERSON WHO CONVERSED
IN THE ANCIENT CORNISH
THE PECULIAR LANGUAGE OF
THIS COUNTY FROM THE
EARLIEST RECORDS
TILL IT EXPIRED IN THE
EIGHTEENTH CENTURY
IN THIS PARISH OF
SAINT PAUL
THIS STONE IS ERECTED BY
THE PRINCE
LOUIS LUCIEN BONAPARTE
IN UNION WITH
THE REV? JOHN GARRETT
VICAR OF ST PAUL
JUNE 1860.
HONOUR THY FATHER AND THY MOTHER:
THAT THY DAYS MAY BE LONG UPON
THE LAND WHICH THE LORD THY GOD
GIVETH THEE.   EXOD. XX.12.
GWRA PERTHI DE TAZ HA DE MAM:
MAL DE DYTHIOW BETHENZ HYR WAR
AN TYR NEB AN ARLETH DE DEW
RYES DEES.   EXOD. XX.-12.

MARTIN TEAGUE

10 The memorial to Dolly Pentreath, 'the last speaker of Cornish', at Paul Church

on it are 'The great God giver of all things' which some what
varies from the present speech, so late (it seems) Cornish was in
use in that county, and now is almost disused in this; which to me
confirms the conclusions of its discontinuance for myself being a
native in the very heart of this country where the Cornish is
most spoken, yet I do remember that being about half a dozen
years of age, I could neither speak nor understand it, the reason
I conceive to be a nicety of my mother's forbidding the servants
and neighbours to talk to me otherwise than in English. A like
case I have sometime met withall of the Lord Montague in his
Essays about learning Latin. And here if I may be allow'd to
allude into ye Great and Ancient Ansonius

Parvum Hoerediolum Majorum Regna Meorum Quod Proarus,
quod Arus quod Pater excoluit.
A little heritage of home race,
My father's, grandfather's, great grandfather's place.

When going abroad to School and afterwards over to France,
I do not remember that I attain'd to pass in the Cornish Tongue
until I came to be concerned in business, and now I do reckon
to see into it almost as far as most of my neighbours, and do
much esteem it, but I cannot ascribe to it more than is meet, for
it appears to be imperfect in many words, which must be supplied
from the Latin, or the English: and it is uncertain whether//
this loss did befall it at first by the Romans intermixing with the
Britains, or afterwards by the Saxons; probably by both. But I
do here avoid (as much as I can) such likeness of sound, as
discovers our language to be beholden to others; and having by
me a little *Fancy of the Dutchess of Cornwall,* written for my
children some years past, about the thirtieth page, I have given
my Observations of the Cornish Tongue, how it came to be
divided amongst the Britains, Welsh and Cornish amongst whom
it is not like to abide long, by [something omitted] it dye away
and come to nothing; I do presume so at least, for the Britains
and ye Cornish, because of the finer French taking the place upon
the one, and the nobler English upon the other. I know not
what// the Welsh may attempt for the preservation of their tongue
but I know this by her sister Cornish, that it is but coarse and
insignificant in comparison of the English, which is read to give
it advantage by exchange; and yet the Angles might be as blunt

D

as they found the old Britains in speech and language, when they first came over, until our better clime and the traffick of our island improved it to this pass. But if any will contend that the British tongue may attaind the like improvement, as their fortune succeeded, I am so far from opposing the reputation of my mother tongue, and country, that for their sake I will willingly consent, and the rather least of it, the *Dutchess of Cornwall's Progress* should hereafter be seen in the hands of my children, some might take occasion to object that I slighted Cornish . . . because I would make myself a Transmarine, but therein appears with what respect I carry the whole matter of Cornish; and it must be envy itself that will think I do believe what I therein have fained about the particular. 'Vis animo, nec tauta. Superbia Victic.' However, seeing it is now come to my mind I will conclude this scribble with the last line of Horace's first Ode:

Quod si Me lyricis Vatibus inseres
Sublimi feriam Sydera [sic] vertice.

There are several extremely interesting references in this work. Firstly, Boson mentions 'Sieur Angwin' as 'the greatest and the oldest of the late Professors of ye Cornish Tongue'. Again the shadowy figure of Richard Angwyn stretches across the historical canvas. Although we have no written Cornish remains from his pen his name keeps on appearing. John Ray had stated that he was 'the only man we could hear of that now writes the Cornish language'. While this is clearly inaccurate, it indicates that Angwyn certainly had a reputation in the language. Scawen tells us that on the death of Angwyn he was promised his papers and manuscripts but the relatives had torn them all up. If only Scawen had managed to save one Cornish manuscript! Little is known about Angwyn and nothing, unfortunately, of his knowledge of the language except that he was highly thought of. He was the son of Martyn Angwyn of St Just, to whom Nicholas Boson sold his lands in Keigwin in 1663. The following year Nicholas sold some land in Parke-an-Chappell in Bosuyn to Richard, also of St Just. Richard is further mentioned in a deed dated 1670. His will was dated 4 October 1671 and probate of the will was granted on 16 June 1675, which gives us a rough date of death.[23]

One may feel that Boson is, perhaps, harsh on Cornish in describing it as 'coarse and insignificant'. Nance comments on this:[24]

In coming to modern Cornish, however, one feels that Nicholas Boson's low opinion of its capabilities was a natural result of his attempt in *Nebbaz Gerriau* to make the language do something of which it was no longer capable. He was no disparager of Cornish things, but on the contrary the 'Old Cornwall' pioneer of his day: learning Cornish because it was Cornish, and passing on to his children by means of stories as much of this and of the tradition of Cornwall as he knew.

Boson also mentions 'a little *Fancy of the Dutchess of Cornwall*, written for my children some years past'. Boson had three children, John, Thomas and Katherine; the two former have left written proof in verse and prose that they learnt Cornish. The tale, however, entitled *The Dutchess of Cornwall's Progresse to see ye Land's End and to visit ye Mount* was wrongly attributed to John Boson. It was not until the historian A. K. Hamilton Jenkin, was researching in the 1920s in the Bodleian Library and found a manuscript belonging to Lhuyd which included full extracts from the tale, that the authorship was correctly attributed to Nicholas.[25] Lhuyd had noted *Alhan o chwedl o waith Mr. Nicholas Boson o Newlyn, yn ei ieuenktyd* (from a tale of the work of Mr Nicholas Boson of Newlyn in his youth).[26] Nance places the authorship between the years 1660 and 1670.

The tale, which is basically a survey of West Penwith folklore, was written in English but owes its escape from total obscurity by the inclusion of three couplets and a short prose passage in Cornish. The story ranges through the district with its legends, mermaids, stone circles and witches. Nance points out, 'Nicholas Boson was evidently not afraid to joke about witchcraft, but he had been educated in France. . .'. Nicholas lived in the time of the great persecution of witches, so perhaps, by receiving his education in France, he did not feel the suspicions and become prey to the fearful atmosphere that most country people felt when the subject of witches was mentioned. Nance comments: 'If only for this flood of light that it throws upon witchcraft as practised at Tol Pedn and the Chair Ladder, *The Dutchess of Cornwall's Progresse* must take a foremost place amongst these relics of older Cornish folk-lore.'[27]

A third important piece of Cornish literature we must ascribe to the pen of Nicholas Boson is the story of *Jowan Chy an Hor* (John of Chyanhor or John of St Levan). Nance writes:[28]

Our one Cornish folk-tale *Jowan Chy an Hor*, written says Lhuyd, who first printed it, between 1660 and 1670, might seem to have been one that survived in English, for, as Tom of Chyannor Bottrell gives an expanded version of it in his *Traditions and Hearthside Stories of West Cornwall*. Here and there, however, he betrays his source for it by using the exact wording of Tonkin's inaccurate translation of Lhuyd's Cornish, as given by Pryce, a quite decisive point being his use of *nackan*, handkerchief, where Tonkin indeed blundered, not recognising a 'mutation' and misled by Welsh *moled*, into translating *pollat* as 'handkerchief' but where the original, like Lhuyd's Welsh translation of it, means something as different as 'young fellow' or 'sweetheart'. Hunt, *Popular Romances*, gives a feeble version of the tale as 'The Tinner of Chyannor' in which most of the hero's adventures are left out, and its 'three points of wisdom' or 'advices', the essentials of the story as told all over Europe, reduced to one: but this, too, was given to Hunt by Bottrell, doubtless in a more complete form, so that, but for Lhuyd's printed respelling of it, and a portion of the original version in John Boson's hand, in the Gwavas MSS at the British Museum, this tale would have been lost, and this in spite of it being not peculiarly Celtic, but merely told in Cornish. It is, of course, far too long to quote here, running to several pages of print, but as the best example of Cornish narrative prose, it has far more than a folklore value to learners of Cornish with whom, in Mr. Jenner's respelt form, it has become a first text book.

The medieval tale of *Jowan Chy an Hor* has appeared in other Celtic literatures. A similar tale was collected by John Campbell (Ian Óg Ile) which appeared in *Popular Tales of the West Highlands*, a four volume work of tales orally collected with translations from Scottish Gaelic by John F. Campbell and published in 1860-2. The tale was reprinted as '*Na Tri Chomhairlean*' (The Three Counsels) in *More Tales of the West Highlands*, published in 1940. There is also a Breton version of the tale which was published, for comparative reasons, by Roparz Hermon (author of *Précis Grammaire de Bretonne,* etc.) in the magazine *Gwalarn*.[29] The Celtic scholar Professor Ludwig Mulhausen (Muelhausen) made a study of this tale which he published in 1938 as *Die Kornishe Geschichte von der drei guten ratschwägen*. In 'Nebbaz Gerriau dro tho Carnoack', Boson mentions that he knows

of two or three good scholars in the Cornish language. 'Whereof one is of more special skill and learning than any that have been this long time before or will come after in all likelihood.' The man, whom Boson does not name, is supposed to have 'so much skill in languages, as the Greek, Hebrew etc.' It seems that there could only be one person to whom Boson was referring and that is John Keigwin of Mousehole (b. 1641 and d. *circa* 1710-16). Keigwin was a reputed master of Latin, Greek, Hebrew, French and Cornish. Keigwin did much work on the language although Nance says his Cornish is not a good Cornish to follow.[30] But E. G. Retallack Hooper says:[31]

> It has been averred that Keigwin could not read easily the old
> script, but it was Davies Gilbert, President of the Royal Society,
> who could not read John Keigwin's handwriting and did not
> understand Cornish, and indeed who glorified in its decline,
> who published the Passion Poem in 1826 and the Creation
> in 1827. Consequently, although Keigwin had a great reputation
> in Cornwall, his work lay forgotten until the next revival
> of interest brought by the work of Edwin Norris and Whitley
> Stokes.

Keigwin was the nephew of William Scawen and it was he who translated the bulk of Middle Cornish literature into English. According to Gilbert Davies, Keigwin was attending the assizes for Cornwall in 1678 when he was requested by the lord chief justice, Sir Francis North, to undertake a translation of *Pascon agan Arluth* (The Passion Poem). Jordan's *Gwreans an bys* (Creation of the World) was translated into English at the request of Jonathan Tewlawney, lord bishop of Exeter in 1693. Among the Keigwin manuscripts[32] is a copy of the 'Ordinalia' written about 1707 containing transcriptions of the three plays, the Creation, the Passion and the Resurrection, with an English translation and Latin preface.[33] Another version of this, from the Sebright collection which originally must have belonged to Lhuyd has the name Izabel Keigwin on the cover.[34]

One of the peculiar Cornish remains left by Keigwin was the translation of a letter of thanks sent from Sudley Castle by Charles I on 1 September 1643, acknowledging the help given his cause by the Cornish people. As Nance remarks: 'This in 1643 would no doubt have been welcome in many West Cornwall parishes, but coming more than sixty years later on it was too late . . .'. The letter is

headed *An Woolok da disquethys an Pow Kernow ganz y brosterath an kensa Mightern Charles el boz gweethes is disquethyans es umma sywya dewelas* (The good regard that was shown to the County of Cornwall by His Majesty the First King Charles may be known by the declaration that is here following. . .). In this Keigwin makes a slip and uses the Hebrew word *milchamath* for war instead of the Cornish word *bresel*.

Another prominent member of the group which sought to revive Cornish as a literary medium was William Rowe of Hendra in Sancreed who also wrote during this period. To the fragile pile of written Cornish he contributed translations of Genesis 3, St Matthew 2: 1-20, and St Matthew 4. Rowe was knowledgeable about the language spoken in Sancreed in 1650-90 but his spelling varies from the other writers in that he sticks closely to English phonetics. His translations were first published in the *Revue Celtique* in 1908.[35] There were other members of the group like John Tonkin, a St Just tailor, who composed a song about James II and William of Orange which began *Menja tiz Kernuak buz gazowas* (If Cornish folk would but hearken).[36] This expressed his Jacobite views in a nation of Whigs and there are fourteen four-line stanzas. The song dates from about 1695. There were other, more shadowy members of the group such as Oliver Pendar, the Rev. Henry Ustick, vicar of Breage, and James Jenkins of Alverton, with whom we shall deal more fully in the following chapter. It is thanks to this group of 'amateur philologists' that we have some folk songs noted down in Cornish. In 1698 Captain Noel Carter of St Agnes wrote down one for the collector Thomas Tonkin of Trevaunance. This song is also a riddle as well as a folk song:

Ha mî ow môs en gûn lâs
Mî a-glowas trôs an buscas mines
Mes mî a-droucias ün pesk brâs, naw ê lostiow;
Ol an bôbel en Porthîa ha Marghas Jowan
Nerva na wôr dh 'ê gensenjy—

As I went on a green plain (sea)
I heard the sound of little fishes,
But I found one great fish, with nine tails:
All the people in St Ives and Marazion [here the Market of John]
Could never get hold of it.

Nance says:[37]

This is the only genuinely home-grown Cornish folk-song that we
have, for *Delkiow Sevy,* 'Strawberry Leaves', is but a translation
from a vulgar variant of the old English favourite, 'Dabbling in
the Dew', still better known as 'Where are you going to, my
pretty maid?' of which there are too many versions to allow a
claim that this, sung in Cornish by Edward Chirgwin in 1698,
could have been the original. As a 'three men's song', *Ha mî
ow môs,* remains unsung, for lack of a tune that fits, but as a
riddle I would solve it as 'answer, an octopus', his body counted
as one 'tail' and his eight arms as the rest of the nine. Tonkin
suggests 'a ray' but this is the Cornish *trŷ lost,* 'three tails', and
besides lacking six of the required tails, it never in Cornwall
rivals the giant rays of the West Indies in size, while an octopus
may occasionally be met with, from its size and pulpiness
difficult to handle, even with the *gwelenhîg,* 'hook rod', that is
made to catch the *padalenken,* 'ink pot' or cuttle fish.

The song that Nance mentions, *'Delkiow Sevy',* was also recorded
by Thomas Tonkin of Trevaunance, who notes 'this was the first song
that I ever heard in Cornwall: it was sung at Carclew in 1698 by one
Chyrgwyn, brother-in-law to Mr John Grose (the old Mr Grose) of
Penzance'. In the Gwavas MSS. in the British Museum there remains
the original version written by Edward Chirgwin who spaces out the
syllables for singing.[38] Nance says the song is not original but a
translation of an English song. Professor Jackson, who includes the
song in his *Celtic Miscellany*, agrees with this opinion.[39] The song
begins:

Pela era why moaz, moes fettow teag,
  Gen ackas pedden dew ha ackas blew mellen?
Moas than ventan, sarra weage,
  Rag delkiow seue gwra moesse teag.

Where are you going, my little fair maid,
  With your rosy cheeks and your yellow hair?
I am going a-milking, kind sir, she said,
  For strawberry leaves make the maidens fair!

Nance points out:[40]

> that anyone who wished to sing in Cornish in 1698 should have
> gone to the trouble of translating an English folk-song seems to
> show that then already, Cornish folk-songs, if sung at all, were
> hard to come by. It will always remain one of Cornwall's
> mysteries, when and why our native notes were all thrown aside.

As Nance demonstrates in 'Folk lore recorded in the Cornish language', the few scraps of original Cornish folk-lore and sayings—such as the
unique Peter Piperism *Ês kês? Ês, pô nag ês? Mar ês kês, drô kês; a pô nag
ês kês, drô 'n peth ês!* (Is there, cheese? Is there, or isn't there? If there's
cheese, bring cheese; if it be that there's no cheese, bring what there
is!)—would be entirely lost but for the efforts of the Late Cornish
writers. The importance of this new, almost feverish, burst of literary
activity during the last phase of the spoken language is therefore of
paramount importance in the history of the language.

Chapter Five

The Death of the Language

With the loss of the monoglots in the seventeenth century and the rapid decline of the Cornish-speaking areas, despite the gentlemen antiquarians and their efforts to recreate a literature in the language, the days of Cornish were clearly numbered. Scawen's hope of 'the restoring of that tongue' was now a forlorn one but still the little group worked on. During the first decade of the eighteenth century they were joined by William Gwavas of Paul whose manuscript remains have left us the most important collection of Late Cornish writings.[1] Gwavas was born in 1676, the son of William Gwavas Senior who owned the fishing tithes for the village of Paul. Gwavas Senior had achieved some notoriety in Paul where a dispute had arisen because of the increase in the practice of catching pilchards by drift nets. The fishermen of Paul refused to pay tithes when they caught fish in this manner and so Gwavas Senior had sued them for non-payment. It was a test case in which some thirty fishermen represented the whole fishing community and the legal costs were borne by all. Gwavas won the day. Although he forced the ordinary fishermen to pay the tithes he still encountered dissent from the wealthier fishermen with interests in drift net fishing. In 1684 he brought a case before the court of the exchequer against six men including merchants Nicholas Boson, Noell Tonkin and John Keigwin.[2] John Freeman, the agent of Gwavas, alleged that Keigwin was supervising the unloading of pilchards from one of his boats when he, Freeman, asked him about the payment of tithes due to Gwavas. Keigwin's reply was 'Sirra, I will pay none.' Gwavas again won the ensuing court case. It was not an auspicious liaison between families who had a common interest in the dying language of the community. The decision rankled among fishermen even when William Gwavas Junior took over the ownership of the tithes on his father's death. Antagonism between the local fishermen and Gwavas continued to grow until, in the summer of 1724, the antagonism became open revolt when Martin Matthews of Penzance 'sett up the Red Flagg on his Boate in opposition or Defyance to the

payment of the Tythes on Pilchards'. The fishermen were taken to court by Gwavas. However, Gwavas took pains to justify his position and published the entire case in book form in 1730 as justification for his actions.[3] Nance, researching in Penzance Library, found a dozen Gwavas documents dated 1732-5 relating to the dispute about the payment of tithes. On the back of one of them was the sentence *Rag Ennos—ha Ennis ew Dalh a Mount ha porth Ennis* (Ragennis and Enys are opposite the Mount and Mousehole).

Gwavas became a barrister of the Middle Temple, London, where he lived for some time in Brick Court. He was also lay vicar of his native parish of Paul. It is hard to say exactly when Gwavas started his passionate interest in the language—John Keigwin was writing to him on the subject as early as 1693. It appears that Gwavas looked upon John Boson, the son of Nicholas, as his tutor in the language but John's Cornish does not seem to have been as good as his father's and in his manuscripts John is trying to use the spellings that Edward Lhuyd introduced. As late as 1710 we have letters from Gwavas to Boson asking his advice and stating he knew little of the language:

An tiz na vaze en plew Germo, en Pow Kernow, pa Triga dadn
doar, en wheliow Sten, vedn towl avez Gurhall da, nighies en
Mor, heb own gwir, an Dew po an Laha gerriow remma an tiz
an Loundrez a credgi boz gwir, mez tho ve gawas gobaith
hedna drok-ober ve gawas rag an Pow ma.
   Yu hemma screpha Kernuak da: rag ve adzhan me mez nebes
an Tavas ma.

The men that are no good in Germoe Parish, in the land of
Cornwall, or living underground in the tin works, will cast
away a good ship, floated in the sea, without any fear of God,
or of the law, and the words of these that the men in London
believe to be true, but I have hope that they will not be found
a crime for this country (or that the crime will not be found
henceforth in this land).
   Is this good Cornish writing? For I know but little of this
tongue.

The reference to the men of Germoe, a village halfway between Porthleven and Marazion, who appear to have an unsavoury reputation as wreckers, is certainly intriguing. To this letter Boson replied:[4]

                              Miz Ebral pempas dydh
                                sitak canz ha deg.

Kar Ves . . .
 Ma Goz screfa compaz Den fir o vi,
 Ha skienz lyk en tavaz Pou gen ni,
 Na re-an gouas koler, va screfa vaze
 Gen ol ou kolan ve, ma ve goz guas
    Dhuan Boson
An tiz Germo criez stynnorian dhens tiz mescieok heb oun Deu,
ha an Bez, na ell'am lavar idn gear da vorthan. JB
 . . . Dhens Karembma dhe'u.
    Ma gi Kerembma dha i

                              April month, fifth day,
                              seventeen hundred and ten.

Dear friend . . .
 Your writing is correct, wise man of mine,
 and knowledge sufficient in the tongue of our country,
 do not have choler, for you write well,
 with all my heart, am I your servant,
    John Boson.
The men of Germoe, called tinners, they are crazy folk, without
fear of God and the world: I cannot say one good word for
them. JB.
 For this time, God be with you

The Gwavas collection of verses, proverbs and words is of tremendous importance to Cornish students. One of the most interesting
items in the collection is a letter from a Newlyn man who, unfortunately, does not sign his name, but writes to Gwavas in Cornish
sending him a copy of Psalm 100 in the language. He says:

Ma an mablecan ni e gana terwitheyaw war an Zeel—ema agan
mablyen ny orth ê gana trewithiow war an sul—ow clerk.

This information, that ministers sometimes sung Psalm 100 in
Cornish in the church of Paul, shows that Cornish in church use had
not died out with the last sermons in Cornish reputedly preached by
the vicar of Landewednack in 1667. If we are to believe Polwhele,
Cornish was used on a number of monuments in Cornwall. He claimed

to have collected a great many of these epitaphs although the only Cornish epitaph to survive comes from a monument in Paul church and dates from the period in question:

> In memory of Captain Stephen Hutchins
> of this parish who departed life at
> Port Royall in Jamaica the 24th Day of
> August 1709 and was buried by the Communion
> Table in Kingstown Church in the one
> and 40th year of his age.
> Bounas heb dueth eu poes karens wei
> Tha pobl bohadzak Paull han egles nei.

> [Life eternal is the reward of your kindness
> towards the poor folk of Paul and our church.]

Perhaps the epitaph was written by Gwavas himself? Gwavas also notes another interesting use of the language in the religious context. He lists a copy of a certificate of the banns of a couple who were married in Sennen and which had been read out in St Just church. The certificate, if authentic, must have originated between 1582 and 1636, when William Drake Senior and William Drake Junior were vicars at St Just. The copy of the certificate in the Gwavas collection is signed by Thomas Drake, the son of William Drake Junior, who was not a parson. Thomas must have either copied the certificate from his father or grandfather's papers or, perhaps, wrote it from memory. The Gwavas version, which differs slightly from a version given by Tonkin which was published in Pryce's *Archaeologia,* reads:[5]

Tubmas Trythal, Proanter Sennen	Thomas Trythal, parson of Sennen
Demythys Juanan Dean ha	Marry John the man and
Agnys an Bennen	Agnes the woman
Bannes an wy	banned together
Diziel (alias Zylvath) tri	Sundays three
En Plu East Egles nei.	In St Just our Church.
Th. Drake	Th. Drake

Cornish folklorists owe a debt of gratitude to Gwavas for jotting down many Cornish proverbs which give glimpses into the wit, wisdom and philosophy of the Cornish people. Proverbs such as

Cabmdhavas e metten glaw yu etn (A rainbow in the morning, rain is in it).
About 1704 he jotted down a number of folk rhymes from William
Allen of St Agnes:

Na reugh eva re	Do not drink too much
Mez eva ra guz zehaz:	But drink for your thirst
Ha hedna, muy po le,	And that, more or less
Vedn gwitha, corf en ehaz.	Will keep you today in health.

It is William Allen who presents us with a problem. John Ray,
a few years after his tour of Cornwall, published a collection of
proverbs in 1670 which contained a rhyme on married life:

First month, smick smack!
Second month, hither thither!
Third month, thwick-thwack!
Fourth month: the devil take them that brought thee and I
together.

In 1704 William Allen gave Gwavas's friend Thomas Tonkin this
version:

Kensa blethan, byrla a' baye:
Nessa blethan, lull a' laye:
Tridgya blethan, hanna drubba,
Peswarra blethan, mola Dew war ef weeg dry hy uppa.

Tonkin translates this as:

The first year, hug and kiss:
The next year, lull and laye;
The third year, take and bring:
The fourth year, the curse of God on him that brought us
together.

Did John Ray, on his visit to Cornwall, pick up the verse and have
it translated into English? Or did William Allen translate it from the
English of Ray? Is this a genuine piece of Cornish folklore?[6] A further
complication appears in O'Neill Lane's *English–Irish Dictionary*

of 1907. Under the word 'thwack' (*buailim*) there occurs what appears to be a close translation of Ray's verse:

An tan postar dis go go nuadh bhionn an chead mhi 'na gealaigh mheala agus 'na poga milse, an dara mi anonn is anall, an treas mu na builli, agus an ceathramhadh mi go mbeiridh an diabhal leis an drong do cur tusa mise le cheile.

When a couple are newly married the first month is all honeymoon and sweet kisses, the second shoving, third thwack, thwack, and the fourth, the devil take them that brought you and me together.

One proverb Gwavas and his colleagues did collect finds many parallels in Celtic thought—*Houl sooth, Tor leabm paravy an gwaynten* (South sun, full belly, brings on pleasures of spring). Another piece collected from James Harry, described as a sixty-five-year-old mason of Ludgvan, gives an indication of the subtle humour of the Cornish:

Me a pew an deau Enouz	I do own the two islands
Marhazow, Rode Wavas,	Marketjew, Gwavas Rode,
Newlyn ha Porth Ennis,	Newlyn and Mousehole,
Ha an Castel Broas es en or Widnack	And the great castle which is in whitish earth
Ol rinna me a pew	All these I own
Pa angy heb Peren idnack.	When they are without any owner.

Another interesting aspect of Gwavas's correspondence in Cornish is his letters to someone in America dated 1710 in which he enclosed a copy of the Apostles' Creed. It may well be that these letters were just examples of the language sent to interested scholars or letters sent to exiled Cornishmen who had taken their knowledge of the language with them. Perhaps the original letters are now tucked away in some American library.[7]

The most significant development in the study of the Cornish language was the arrival in Cornwall of Edward Lhuyd at the beginning of the eighteenth century. Lhuyd was the Keeper of the Ashmolean Museum, Oxford, and according to Sir John Rhys, who became the first professor of Celtic studies at Oxford in 1876, Lhuyd was 'in many respects the greatest Celtic philologist the world has ever seen'.

Lhuyd was the first qualified scholar to make a serious study of the Cornish language, along with the other Celtic languages with the exception of Manx. Until this time the scholastic attitude to the Celts floundered in numerous legends, many of them incredibly impossible, all of them taken seriously. Among the ideas put forward by serious scholars of the day on the origin of the Celtic peoples were that they had descended from the Trojans who had fled to Britain after the fall of Troy, or from the Phoenicians, or that they were one of the lost tribes of Israel, or that they were ancient Egyptians and, more popular still, was the theory that they were the descendants of Noah and Japhet. Even after Lhuyd's time this theory was popular. In 1716 Theophilus Evans published his *Drych y Prif Oesoedd* (The mirror of the first ages), which became the only widely read history of Wales until the middle nineteenth century. In this book Evans traced the origin of the British Celts back to the Tower of Babel and the Welsh language to Gomer, the grandson of Noah. From Gomer, it was reasoned, came Gomeri, Cimbri and Cymry. Such ideas were supported by Henry Rowlands, a friend and correspondent of Lhuyd, who supported the idea of the descent from Japhet in his *Mona Antiqua Restaurata*, published in 1723 in Dublin and in 1766 in London. The theory that the British Celts descended from Gomer and the Tower of Babel was also current in Cornwall as may be seen from a letter written by John Boson on 5 April 1710:

Sera ve rag lavar dhem Gomar mab Japhet mab Noah ve an Den rig clapia Kernuak termen an Tur Babel ve devevalz ha rag hedna ni el guelas ha adzhan an Tavaz Kernuak dha boz Tavaz koth ha truadh eu dha boz kellaz, boz oun dha ve na vedn an tavaz ma beska boz kavaz arta en uz ni na bounaz heb diuadh (po nerra po na moy).

My father did tell me Gomer, son of Japhet, son of Noah, was the man who did speak Cornish in the time that the Tower of Babel was raised, and therefore we can see and know the Cornish language to be an ancient language, and pity it is to be lost, but fear to me that the language will not ever be found again in our age, not life without (or 'ever' or 'any more').

There was one notable exception to the scholars who supported the various legendary theories on the origin of the Celts. This was a Scottish scholar named George Buchanan who published a history of

Scotland in 1589. In this he dismissed the attempts to trace the origin of the Celts back to Japhet and in an excellent piece of scientific work he showed, with reference to Greek and Latin sources, that the Gaelic peoples of Ireland, the Isle of Man and Scotland, and the Britons of Wales, Cornwall and Brittany, were branches of the ancient Celtic peoples of the Continent. Lhuyd was a lone subscriber to Buchanan's work and in the late seventeenth century and early eighteenth century he travelled through all the Celtic countries studying their philology and history. Lhuyd actually spent four months in Cornwall learning the language, not such a difficult task for a Welsh speaker who had a considerable knowledge of the other Celtic languages. Lhuyd wrote:

> The way I took to get some knowledge of the Cornish language was, partly by writing some down from the mouths of the people in the West of Cornwall, in particular the parish of St. Just; and partly by the like help of four gentlemen, who wrote out for me many Cornish words; in particular, Mr. John Keigwin of the Lower House in Mousehole, Mr. Eustick in the aforesaid parish of St. Just, Mr. James Jenkins of Alverton by Penzance and Mr. Nicholas Boson of Newlyn in the parish of Paul.

On 10 March 1701, Lhuyd wrote to his friend Henry Rowlands listing the places where the language was spoken and he repeated this in the first volume of his work on the Celts, *Archaeologia Britannica,* which was in the hands of the subscribers by 1707:

> The places in Cornwall that this day retain the Ancient Language are the Parishes of St. Just, St. Paul, Burrian, Sunnin, St. Laven, St. Krad, Marva, Maddern, Sunner, Tewednock, St. Ives, Lelant, Leigian, Gyval; and all along the sea shore from the Land's End to St. Keverne near the Lizard Point. But a great many of the inhabitants of these parishes, especially the gentry, do not understand it, there being no necessity thereof in regard there's no Cornishman but speaks good English.

The extent of Lhuyd's knowledge of Cornish has been criticised. He had learnt mainly from Keigwin, Ustick, Jenkins and Nicholas Boson. Nance says 'Had that other great man, Edward Lhuyd, trusted to unlearned but habitual Cornish speakers more than to amateur

philologers like John Keigwin, his four months in Cornwall might have been spent to even better purpose.'[8] But it would appear that Lhuyd realised his limitations and writing to Jenkins at St Piran in the Sands (Perranzabuloe) on 16 March 1702, he says of a poem he has written in Cornish:

> the Cornish verses (since you must have them) are here sent
> to you: though they are not worth the trouble of reading, much
> less sending so far. I aimed at imitating the Book Cornish
> rather than the Cornish now spoken, for, as you'll find when you
> receive your mss. it has been much corrupted this last age or two.

Lhuyd refers to a nineteen-verse elegy on the death of William III which, apart from the opening lines, he had written after the form of a three-line metre per stanza known in Welsh as the *Triban Milwr* or Warrior's Triplets. This form, the englyn, can be found in Welsh poetry as early as Llywarch Hen's '*Marwnad Gereaint ap Erbin*' (Lament for Geraint) and for the death of Cynddylan in the sixth century. The englyn is the most widely used of Welsh poetic forms and corresponds in many ways to the Greek epigram. It is quite difficult to translate because, according to Anthony Conran, 'Englynion, far more than other forms, seem to belong to the language itself; more so, in fact, than they belong to their authors.'[9] Of this form of poetry there seems only one genuine survival in Cornish which was taken down by Lhuyd. There are two versions:

An lavar coth yu lavar guîr
Bedh darn nêver, dhan tavaz rê hîr
Mez dên neb dawaz a gallaz i dîr.

What's said of old, will always stand:
Too long a tongue, too short a hand,
But he that had no tongue, lost his land.

An lavar goth ewe lavar gwîr
Ne vedn nevera doas vâs a tavas re hîr
Bes den heb tavas a gollas e dîr.

The old saying is a true saying
never will come good from tongue too long
but a man without a tongue shall lose his land.

This can be described as the only original Celtic poem in Cornish for the prosody of the rest of the poetry in Cornish is basically English in concept, although the seven- and four-syllabled metres of the verses of Middle Cornish are close to that of Middle Breton. Lhuyd tried to construct his elegy in the englyn style in contrast to the epigrams of Gwavas and Boson who used eight-syllabled lines based on English rhythms. However, Lhuyd's Cornish poem is more a product of a Welsh speaker than a Cornishman. Likewise, Lhuyd's introduction to the Cornish section of his work *Archaeologia Britannica*, written in Cornish and entitled *Dhan Tiz Hergaraz ha Pednzhivik pou Kernou—annerh, ehaz hag eyrsder viskvethek* . . . (To the courteous and noble inhabitants of the country of Cornwall, honour, health and happiness everlasting . . .) is also a product of a Welsh speaker. Oliver Pender, writing to Gwavas on 22 August 1711, criticises Lhuyd for this and explains:

Rag na algia en clappia na screffa Curnoack peccara why. Thera moy Gembrack peath rig ea gweele.

For he could neither talk nor write Cornish like you. It was more Welsh, what he did.

Nevertheless, Lhuyd's work was of tremendous value not only for Cornish but Celtic studies in general. Using the science of philology Lhuyd began to clear up many of the popular misconceptions about the Celts. He showed the relationship of the Celtic languages dividing them into Brythonic, characterised by the transformation of the original Indo-European *qu* sound into *P*, and Goidelic, characterised by the retention of the original *qu* sound as *c*. Hence Lhuyd spoke of the P Celts and the Q Celts. The first volume of Lhuyd's projected work was a Glossography which was published in 1707. It was entirely philological and questions of antiquities and natural history were postponed to the succeeding volume which never appeared due to Lhuyd's tragic death in the Ashmolean in 1709. The *Archaeologia* contained an introduction in Cornish only to the Cornish section, a Cornish grammar and the story of *Jowan Chy an Hor* or John Chyanhor in Cornish. Lhyud explained:

A Cornish–English Vocabulary (as is mentioned in the Cornish Grammar) was at first intended to have been included in this

volume, besides the Cornish words of the comparative Etymology and those of the Second Title, as also an account of the British and Celtic proper names, but the book being otherwise improved to a bulk beyond what was at first designed, they are left the next. And I was the more willing to omit for the present that vocabulary, partly in regard to the Armoric, differing but little from the Cornish, supplies in a great measure the defect, and partly because I have been for some time informed of a Cornish Vocabulary composed by a gentleman who lives near Truro in that county, who may probably have some thoughts of publishing it.

Writing to Gwavas from Pol Gorran on 19 July 1738, Thomas Tonkin bemoans the fact that he had told Lhuyd that a Mr William Hals was compiling a Cornish vocabulary called 'An Lhadymer ay Kernou' (The Interpreter of Cornwall) and was thereby instrumental in stopping Lhuyd publishing his own vocabulary. According to Tonkin, William Hals (1655-1737?) of Fenton Gymps, was not very fluent in the language:

I have not corresponded with him for these many years and shall only give this friendly admonition, that, if he still entertains thoughts of publishing his An Ladymer ay Kernow and (what he calls) his Parochial Antiquities of Cornwall, he would do well to have them carefully revised by some learned discreet persons, especially the latter.

Tonkin later wrote an introduction to an edition of Carew's Survey of Cornwall, dated at Pol Gorran on 9 July 1733, but which was not published until 1811. In this he says:

But since I am now upon Cornish I ought not leave another gentleman unmentioned, Mr. William Hals of St. Wren who has been for at least fifty years past, labouring on that language, and the history of this county, the first by way of a dictionary which he calls An Latimer ay Kernou and the other Parochial Antiquities of Cornwall. It is between 25 and 30 years since I have seen any of his collection and I believe at least 20 years since I have seen him. I am told that he has greatly improved and polished them since that time. . .

Tonkin therefore did not think much of Hals's scholarship while Pryce describes Hals's work as 'a most strange hodge podge of Hebrew, Greek etc. and British words'. It was not until after his death that the first part of his work was published by his nephew in Truro in 1750. This was published under the title *The Compleat History of Cornwall—general and parochial, written by William Hals, Gentleman, deceas'd, a native of that county, perfect master of the Cornish and very well versed in the British and Saxon as well as the learned languages.* The first part of this work was actually part two, the part which contained the parochial history, while a promised 'Etymological Cornish Vocabulary' never saw the light of day. Part of '*An Lhadymer ay Kernou*', however, has been recovered, the manuscript running from A to BRIGH and is in the National Library of Wales.[10]

At this time a Cornish vocabulary was badly needed and Lhuyd's own vocabulary, having been deferred to the second volume of his work which was not published due to his death, also became lost for a while. William Wynne, a contemporary of Lhuyd's at Oxford, and a medieval scholar, had quarrelled with Lhuyd and felt a bitterness towards him which manifested itself even after Lhuyd's death in 1709. Glyn E. Daniel writes: 'It was William Wynne who, to his eternal shame, and the perpetual loss of Celtic studies, persuaded Jesus College, Oxford, not to purchase Lhuyd's manuscripts and books after his death.'[11] The loss to Cornish studies was immense for all Lhuyd's Cornish manuscripts, letters, notes and the vocabulary disappeared. Part of Lhuyd's papers were purchased by Sir Thomas Sebright of Beechwood in Hertfordshire but he died on 11 April 1736. The Beechwood manuscripts, as they were called, were sold in three separate lots and each was lost. Many years later, however, Lhuyd's vocabulary, entitled '*Geirlyfr Kyrnweig*' (Cornish Vocabulary) and containing Lhuyd's elegy on the death of William III, dated 1702, was discovered in the National Library of Wales.[12]

Before his death Lhuyd made one extremely important discovery. A Mr John Antis (d. 1745) had discovered an ancient manuscript containing a vocabulary which was classified as Old Welsh. He did not think the classification was accurate and contacted Lhuyd. Lhuyd wrote:

Mr. Antis found in the Cottonian Library of London a British Vocabulary written many years ago and wrote to me about it. When I had seen the book I knew very well that it was not a

Welsh Vocabulary as it appeared by the Latin title 'Vocabularium Wallicum' written at the end of it, but a Cornish vocabulary.

The 'Cottonian Vocabulary', now in the British Museum,[13] is the most important piece of Old Cornish surviving from the twelfth century, containing nearly all we know of the Old Cornish period. Copies of the manuscript were made by Lhuyd's assistant, the Rev. Moses Williams M.A., F.R.S. (1686-1742) who was a sub-librarian of the Ashmolean Museum.

The arrival of Lhuyd into the field of Cornish studies was highly important but it is only in retrospect that Lhuyd's work has really come to be appreciated. Pryce wrote nearly ninety years after Lhuyd's death that it 'must have been the greatest loss to this pursuit that it ever had, or ever will meet with, on account of his profound learning and singular attachment to the recovery of our primitive language'.[41]

The gentlemen antiquarians in Cornwall had tried, since the 1660s when Scawen prevailed on his friends to write in Cornish, to build up a literature in Late Cornish. Their writings, sadly enough, have little literary merit and merely serve to show us the state of the language in its last stage before its death. Also their knowledge of the language in which they were writing could have been vastly improved as Nance indicated:[15]

It is very tantalising, too, to realise, as one must after a little study of the facts, how narrowly we have missed several chances of adding to our Cornish Vocabulary, or even possibly of keeping the language alive. Had John Ray, for instance, been willing to learn from Dickon Angwyn of St. Just and to disregard his lack of scholarship, he might have been the means of preserving 17th Century Cornish, that, grammarian or not, Angwin clearly wrote and spoke. Had that other great man, Edward Lhuyd, trusted to unlearned but habitual Cornish speakers more than to amateur philologers like John Keigwin, his four months in Cornwall might have been spent to even better purpose. But more than this, as I hope to show, had Dr. Borlase or Dr. Pryce even been willing to learn from those who had no Latin, it was probably not too late for either of them to have gathered in words and sentences, the whole language in its latest phase. It maddens one to think of these learned laborious Cornishmen, misprinting earlier collections, misreading ancient manuscripts,

fumbling their few Celtic or West Country English words with an indiscriminate hurling together of Cornish, Welsh, Breton and Irish from Lhuyd's *Archaeologia Britannica*, compiling dictionaries and making cryptograms for Cornish students that take ten times as long to unravel as they did to write, while all the time the language itself was being spoken by the poor old 'backjowster' bringing fish round to the back door, or even by the bent old gardener mowing the grass from whom—alas!—it would be infra dig to learn.

As the amateur antiquarians began to die there were no enthusiasts to replace them and interest in the language began to die also. During the first decade of the century perhaps the most prominent loss was that of James Jenkins of Alverton, near Penzance, who had helped Lhuyd study the language and whom John Boson describes as 'our Cornish bard'. Jenner refers to Jenkins as 'the last poet of the language'.[16] Lhuyd paid Jenkins the compliment of sending him, for approval, a copy of his Cornish elegy on William III 'as if he accepted him', says Nance, 'as the best judge of Cornish verse and John Boson implies that Jenkins was esteemed as then the most learned of Cornish writers'.[17] Alas, we have only a few verses by which to judge Jenkins:

Ma leeaz Greage. Lacka vel Zeage.
Gwell gerres. Vell commerez.
Ha ma leeaz Bennen. Pocare an Gwennen.
Eye vedn gwrrez de gu Teez. Dandle peath an beaz.
Fleaz hep skeeanz. Vedn gweel gu Seeaznz.
Bur mor crown gy pedery. Pan dall gu gwary.
Ha madra ta. Pandrigg Seera ha Damah.
Narehanz moaz dan Cooz. Do cuntle gu booz.
Buz gen nebbes lavirrians. Eye venjah dendel gu booz dillaz.

There are many wives. Worse than draff [useless].
Better left. Than taken.
And there are many women. Like the bees.
They will help their men. In earning worldly wealth.
Children without understanding. Will act according to their caprice.
But if they consider. What their play is worth.

And mark well. What Father and Mother did.
They would not go to the wood. To gather their food.
But with a little labour. They would earn their food and clothing.

The other poem by Jenkins is longer:

Cousow do ve che dean mor ferre
De leba es meare a peath ha lease Teer
Ha me reeg clowaz an poble compla
Fa Ethreaz do chee Eithick gwreage dah
Hye oare gwell padn dah gen hy glane
Ha et eye ollas hye dalveha gowas tane
Na dalle deez perna Kinnis war an Sawe
Na moase cuntle an drize dro dan Keaw
Rag hedna vedn boaz couzese dro dan pow
Gwell eye veeha perna nebas glow
Ha hedna vedn gus tubma a theller e aragg
Ha whye ell evah cor gwella mor sease du bragg
Na dale deiw gwell treaven war an treath
Dreath hedna why vedn kelly meare a peath
Buz mor mennow dereval worbidn an pow yeine
Why dalveha gowas an brossa amine
Ha ryny vedn diria bidn moar ha gwenz
Nagez drog vyth gwres lebben na kenz.

Listen to me, you man so wise
That has much wealth and many lands
Yet I have heard the people remarking
That to you is given a terribly good wife
She can make good cloth with her wool
And in her hearth she deserves a fire
You ought not to buy firewood by the horseload
Nor go gathering the brambles about the hedges
For that will be tattled around the countryside
It would be better to buy some coal
And that will warm you behind and before
And you may drink best beer if you have malt
You ought not to build houses on the sand
But that you will lose much substance
But if you want to build against the cold country

You ought to procure the largest stones
And those will last against sea and wind
There is not any harm done, now or before.

Jenner says the verses of Jenkins 'seem to show indications of a
feeling for internal rhymes and something like a rudimentary *cynghanedd*
but there is not enough of it to reduce to any definite rules. . .'.[18]
Jenkins died in 1710 and John Boson composed an elegy on him which
is dated 17 February 1711. The elegy, significantly, is written in
three-line stanzas on the pattern of the Welsh *Triban Milwr* and seems
a conscious attempt at following Lhuyd's example:[19]

En Levra coth pa vo Tour Babel gwres
scriffas Gomar mab basket vo en bras
ha dotha tavaz Karnoack vo kes.

Lebbon duath tavas coth by en Kernow
Rag kar my Jenkins gelles durt an Pow
Vor hanow taz my en Eue tha Canow.

Descans ony gen hemma an Brossa es
Desces en Tavasow ha dotha Bres.
Ha Pedn Feerha ha Moy Skeeans Res.

Ancho vedn gweel an Dean eu wella
Cotha dadn Daor pokare an ecella
Meera a kol ry termen them tha hoola

At building Babel's Tower as books do tell
Did Gomar grandson unto Noah dwell
To whom the ancient Cornish language fell.

Cornwall now mourns thy tongue just lost and gone
Jenkins our Cornish bard is fled among
the saints to sing his everlasting song.

Learn we hence the finest flight of wit
Well skilled in language, with judgement fit.
A thoughtful head, much knowledge joy'd to it.

Must yield to sweeping death that levels all
The oaks and cedars tall, the suburbs withal
Great is the loss. Permitting tears to fall.

Gwavas also felt moved to write an epitaph for Jenkins:

Padn an mean, ma Deskes broaz Dean,
En tavaz Kernuak gelles.
Termen vedn doaz rag an Corfe tha thoras
Mes Tavas coth Kernow ew kelleys.

Beneath this fair stone the remains lay of one
in Cornish tongue skilled above all
The day shall arrive when his bones shall revive
But the language is gone past recall.

Between the years 1710 and 1716 John Keigwin, whom E. G. R. Hooper regards as one of the most important and sadly maligned figures of the revivalist group, died. Boson also wrote his epitaph which is dated 20 April 1716:

En tavas Greka, Lathen h'an Hebra
En Frenkock ha Carnoack deskes dha
Gen oll un Gormola Brez be dotha
Garres eu nei, ha Noadgez e wortha.

In tongue Greek, Latin and Hebrew
In French and Cornish, learned well
With all the Glory of Mind was to him
Has left us, and fled is he on high.

As Gwavas had been a pupil of John Boson, so Thomas Tonkin became a disciple to Gwavas. In his edition of Carew's *Survey of Cornwall*, Tonkin describes his mentor as:

William Gwavas Esq., perhaps the only gentleman now living
who hath a perfect knowledge of the tongue. He has been so
kind as to lend me his helping hand, to look over, and amend my
Cornish Vocabulary, and to furnish me with several pieces in
the said language, which are inserted in my said Archaeologia
with his name prefixed to them.

In 1735 Gwavas and Tonkin made a study of the places where the language was still spoken 'and the language they found was a most

irregular jargon, the chief peculiarity of which was a striking un-certainty of the speaker as to where one word left off and another began'.[20] Gwavas and Tonkin found that the language had now confined itself to an area from Penzance to Land's End. Tonkin, in a letter to Gwavas dated at Pol Gorran on 19 July 1736, says:

> And as for the Vulgar Cornish now spoken (except what I have taken out of Mr. Lhuyd's *Archaeologia*) it is reduced to such a small nook of the country, and those ancient persons that still speak it, are even there so few, the language itself corrupted, and they too for the most part such illiterate people that I cannot sufficiently commend your great industry in gathering together so much of it, and that so correct, as you have now enabled me to set forth; since what it has been my fortune to collect myself has been so little in comparison as not to deserve the naming separately.

Tonkin decided, with Gwavas's help, that he would publish a vocabulary and grammar although, he points out to Gwavas, that he would not publish if there was 'the least prospect left of the recovery of Mr. Lhuyd's papers, especially his Cornish Vocabulary'. But Sir Thomas Sebright, who had bought Lhuyd's manuscripts, had just died and the manuscripts had been split up and lost. Tonkin had not found the work easy as he explained to Gwavas:

> I may add that very few of those that speak the language can give any tolerable account of the orthography, much less of the etymology, or derivation of those words which they make use of and are many times apt to jumble two or three words together, making but one of them all, tho' they pronounce them rightly enough. Of this you were pleased to give me lately some instances —as in *merastadu,* which they pronounce in one breath as if it had been but one word, whereas it is a contraction of four *mear 'ras tha Dew,* much thanks to God, and anciently written *maer gras tha Deu* and *merastawhy,* much thanks to you, a con-traction of *meor 'raz tha why.*

Tonkin's projected vocabulary and explanatory notes were not published in his lifetime. They were discovered a generation later by Dr William Pryce and published, without acknowledgment, as part

of his work *Archaeologia Cornu-Britannica* in 1790. The work that Gwavas and Tonkin were doing on the language received attention from the famous Exeter printer Andrew Brice (1692-1773). Writing an introduction to a dialect play called 'The Exmoor Scolding' in *Brice's Weekly Journal*, Andrew Brice commented:[21]

> As it's natural and full of Honour to love one's Country so it's
> as natural (and why not as praise-worthy?) to love its language.
> And I hear of a Gentleman in Cornwall (in Antique Age Renowned
> for Love to Saints and Shipwrecks!) who has taken noble mighty
> pains in translating the Bible into Cornish or Cornubian Welch.

This is probably a reference to Gwavas although we have no evidence at all that Gwavas or any of the Late Cornish writers undertook the task, much less completed it, of translating the entire Bible into Cornish. They had, however, translated many chapters from the Bible. Gwavas, after a lifetime's study and devotion to the language, died in Paul on 9 January 1741. He had tried to follow a mode of life he summarised in a Cornish verse:

Che Dean Crêv, leb es war Tîr,
Inthow grâ, gen skians fîr,
ha'n Dew euthella, vedn-ri,
peth ew gwella ull, rag whi.

Thou strong man who on earth dost dwell
today with prudence act thou well
And God supreme, for thee will do
what He thinks best is good for you.

The language attracted the attention of another antiquarian William Borlase. Borlase was born on 2 February 1695/6, the second of thirteen children, and was ordained as a minister in 1720. In 1722 he became the rector of Ludgvan and ten years later received the incumbency of St Just. He has come down in history as a 'crazed old bigot'[22] who unmercifully persecuted the Wesley brothers when they began to preach Methodism in Cornwall. John Wesley's first visit to Cornwall was in 1743 and his last visit in 1789 during which time he succeeded in converting the majority of Cornishmen to his creed. But the persecution of the Wesleys and their converts, so popularly ascribed

to William Borlase, was, in fact, the work of his brother the Rev. Dr Walter Borlase of Castle Horneck, near Penzance, vicar of Madron and Kenwyn, and also vicewarden of the Stannaries. Reference is made to the persecution of the Wesleys by one 'Dr. Borlase' and William did not receive his doctorate until after this time so that the only Dr Borlase in Cornwall at the time of the persecutions was William's brother.[23] Borlase became a Fellow of the Royal Society in 1750 and four years later published *The Antiquities of Cornwall* 'with a Vocabulary of the Cornu-British language'. This comprised of fifty pages 'drawn from all available sources expressly to preserve as much as possible of the old language'.[24] As well as the vocabulary, is a section entitled *Natali Solo*, in which Borlase prints a contraction of Lhuyd's Cornish grammar. Borlase also set out the reason for publishing the work:

> The sooner therefore such a work was under taken, the greater likelihood there was that more of the language might be preserved, than if the attempt was deferred: and some who had a regard for their country lamented that it should utterly lose its ancient language and those who were curious had a mind to understand something of it, I found the work was much desired and I was willing to do something towards restoring the Cornish language, though I might not be able to do all that fewer avocation would have permitted.
>
> As incomplete as the following vocabulary is, I am persuaded that it will be of some use. In the present language of my countrymen there are many words which are neither English nor derived from the learned languages and therefore thought improprieties by strangers, and ridiculed as if they had no meaning: but they are remnants of their ancient language, esteemed equal in purity and age to any language in Europe.

Before his death in 1772 Borlase published some other important works: *Observations on the Ancient and Present State of the Isles of Scilly and their importance to the Trade of Great Britain* (1756); *Natural History of Cornwall* (1758); *Concerning the Creation and the Deluge* (1769), etc. Borlase had collected nine volumes of material for compiling his *Natural History*, seven volumes of which have been lost and only two volumes were recovered by his great-great-grandson, the historian William Copeland Borlase, from a Bristol bookseller named Kerslake

in the late nineteenth century.[25] Among the Borlase manuscripts were copies in his handwriting of manuscripts by Lhuyd, Gwavas, Tonkin, Ustick, Scawen and Boson. It is obvious from the manuscripts and the notes, dated 5 June 1748, and headed 'Mems. of Cornish Tongue' that Borlase intended to publish a much more comprehensive treatise on the language.[26] These particular manuscripts were purchased on behalf of the Institution by John Davies Rhys, president of the Royal Institution of Cornwall 1893-5 and 1912, when William Copeland Borlase died.

What was the state of the living Cornish language in the mid-eighteenth century? Indeed, was the language alive at all? Dr Borlase did not seem to think so. In his *Natural History of Cornwall* he comments: 'That we may attend it to the grave: this language is now altogether ceased, so as not to be spoken anywhere in conversation.' Had the people who, in 1735, still spoke the language in the Penzance–Land's End area died out? Two years before Dr Borlase declared the language dead, a book was published in London entitled *Youth's Philosophical Entertainer, or the Natural Beauties of Cornwall, Devonshire and Somersetshire, with Additional Remarks by Various Hands*. The book was in the form of questions and answers between P for Pupil and T for Teacher. A passage read:

P. What language is spoken by the inhabitants of this county [Cornwall]?
T. In some far parishes, indeed, near the Land's End, there is a corrupt dialect of the Cornish tongue even still retained: but the gentry and other people of fashion talk as pure English as the natives of London.

Was the 'Teacher' merely behind the times or was the author of this book better informed than Borlase himself as to the state of the language? In retrospect it would seem the latter was the case for a mere four miles away from Dr Borlase there lived an old 'fish jowster' who was to live in history as Dolly Pentreath, the last speaker of the language. But, as we shall see, she was merely one of a group of people who could still speak the language from a native knowledge.

In 1742 Captain (later Admiral) the Hon. Samuel Barrington took a Cornish sailor from Mount's Bay on a trip to Brittany. To his astonishment he found that the sailor, speaking Cornish, made himself easily understood by the Bretons. Intrigued by this, Samuel Barrington

wrote to his brother Daines, who was then aged nineteen. Daines was to become a highly regarded historian and member of the Society of Antiquities. It was over twenty years later that Daines paid a visit to Cornwall and, bearing in mind his brother's story, made a search for speakers of the Cornish language. He discovered one fluent speaker, Dolly Pentreath of Mousehole, near Penzance, and wrote an account of an interview he had with her. Unwittingly this account gave foundation to the popular myth that Dolly Pentreath was the last speaker of the language. In fact, in his account, Daines Barrington mentions two other women who understood Dolly Pentreath's language 'which implies a certain knowledge of the Cornish tongue'. Barrington sent his account to John Lloyd F.S.A. who read it at a meeting of the Society of Antiquities on 6 May 1775, and it was later published in the Society's journal *Archaeologia*:[27]

On the Expiration of the Cornish Language

I myself made a very complete tour of Cornwall in 1768, and recollecting what I had heard from my brother, I mentioned to several persons of that county, that I did not think it impossible I might meet with some remains of the language who, however, considered it entirely lost. I set out from Penzance, however, with the landlord of the principal inn for my guide, towards Sennan, or most western point; and when I approached the village, I said, that there must probably be some remains of the language in those parts, if anywhere, as the village was in the road to no place whatsoever; and the only alehouse announced itself to be the last in England. My guide, however, told me that I should be disappointed, but that if I would ride ten miles about in my return to Penzance he would carry me to a village called Mousehole, on the western side of Mount's Bay, where there was an old woman called Dolly Pentreath, who could speak Cornish very fluently. Whilst we were travelling together towards Mousehole, I enquired how he knew that this woman spoke Cornish: when he informed me that he frequently went from Penzance to Mousehole to buy fish, which was sold by her, and that when he did not offer a price which was satisfactory, she grumbled to some other old women in an unknown tongue which he concluded therefore to be the Cornish. When we reached Mousehole I desired to be introduced as a person who had laid a wager that there was no one who could converse in

Cornish, upon which Dolly Pentreath spoke in an angry tone of voice for two or three minutes, and in a language which sounded very much like Welsh. The hut in which she lived was in a narrow lane, opposite to two rather better cottages at the doors of which two other women stood, who were advanced in years, and who, I observed, were laughing at what Dolly Pentreath said to me. Upon this I asked them whether she had not been abusing me, to which they answered 'Very heartily and because I had supposed she could not speak Cornish'. I then said that they must be able to talk the language: to which they answered, that they could not speak it readily, but understood it, being only 10 or 12 years younger than Dolly Pentreath.

I continued nine or ten days in Cornwall after this, but found that my friends, whom I had left to eastwards, continued as incredulous almost as they were before, about these last remains of the Cornish language, because (amongst other reasons) Dr. Borlase had supposed, in his *Natural History of Cornwall*, that it had entirely ceased to be spoken. It was also urged, that as he lived within four or five miles of the old woman at Mousehole, he consequently must have heard of no singular a thing as her continuing to use the vernacular tongue. I had scarcely said or thought anything more on the matter, till last summer having mentioned it to some Cornish people I found they could not credit that any person had existed within these five years who could speak their native language; and therefore, though I imagined there was but a small chance of Dolly Pentreath continuing to live, yet I wrote to the President, then in Devonshire, to desire that he would make some enquiry with regard to her: and he was so obliging as to procure me information from a gentleman whose house was within three miles of Mousehole, a considerable part of whose letter I shall subjoin.

'Dolly Pentreath is short of stature, and bends very much with old age, being in her eighty seventh year, so lusty, however, as to walk hither (viz. Castle Horneck) above three miles in bad weather, in the morning, and back again. She is somewhat deaf, but her intellect seemingly unimpaired, has a good memory, so good that she remembers perfectly well that about four or five years ago, at Mousehole, where she lives, she was sent for to a gentleman, who, being a stranger had a curiosity to hear the Cornish language, which she was famed for retaining and speaking

fluently, and that the inn keeper, where the gentleman came
from, attended him.'

This gentleman was myself, however, I did not presume to
send for her, but waited upon her.

'She does indeed, at this time, talk Cornish as readily as
others do English, being bred up from a child to know no other
language; nor could she (if we may believe her) talk a word of
English before she was twenty years of age; as her father being
a fisherman, she was sent with fish to Penzance at twelve years
old, and sold them in the Cornish language, which the inhabitants
in general (even the gentry) did then well understand. She is
positive, however, that there is neither in Mousehole, nor in any
part of the country, any person who knows anything of it, or at
least can converse in it. She is poor and maintained mostly by the
parish, and partly by fortune telling and gabbling Cornish.'

I have thus thought it right to lay before the Society this
account of the last spoken Cornish tongue, and cannot but think,
that a linguist (who understands Welsh) might still pick up a
more complete vocabulary of the Cornish than any we are as yet
possessed of, especially as the two neighbours of this old woman,
whom I have had occasion to mention, are not above 77 or 78
years of age, and were very healthy when I saw them; so that the
whole does not depend on the life of this Cornish Sybil, as she
is willing to insinuate. If it is said, that I have stated that they
cannot converse so readily in it as she does, because I mentioned
that they comprehended her abuse upon me, which implies a
certain knowledge of the Cornish tongue. Thus, the most
learned of men of this country cannot speak Latin fluently, for
want of practise, yet it would be very easy to form a Latin
vocabulary from them. It is also much to be wished, that such
a linguist would go into the Isle of Man and report to the
Society in what state that expiring language may be at present.
As for the Welsh, I do not see the least probability of its being
lost in the more mountainous parts; for as there are no valuable
mines in several of the parishes thus situated, I do not conceive,
that it is possible to introduce the use of English. The present
inhabitants, therefore, will continue to speak their native
language in those districts, for the Welsh cannot settle in England
because they cannot speak our tongue, nor will English servants
for husbandry live with the Welsh because they would not

understand their masters. I am, dear sir, your most faithful, humble servant.

Daines Barrington.

It is likely that the gentleman from Castle Horneck who supplied Barrington with further details about Dolly was, in fact, Dr Borlase himself, though one wonders why, if this is so, Barrington doesn't acknowledge him and, indeed, the interview must have taken place a short time before Dr Borlase's death. As Nance has stated, it is a sad fact that nobody took Barrington's advice and no linguist bothered to visit Dolly Pentreath or her neighbours to pick up what remained of their knowledge of the language. The only response Barrington's letter had, in fact, was a letter written in Cornish and English by a Mousehole fisherman called William Bodener being sent to Barrington who published it in *Archaeologia*.[28] Bodener shows that he, too, had a knowledge of the language and claims that four or five other people in Mousehole could speak Cornish, one of whom must have been Dolly. E. G. R. Hooper says: 'What strikes one here is the good grammatical Cornish of Bodener.'[29]

Bluth vee ewe try egence ha pemp. Thearra vee dean broadjack an poscas, me rig desky Cornoack termen me vee maw. Me vee de more gen carra vee a pemp dean moy en cock, me rig scantlower clowes eden ger Sowsnack cowes en cock rag sythen war ebar. No rig a vee biscath gwellas lever Cornoack. Me deskey Cornoack mous da mor gen tees coath. Nag es moye vel pager pe pemp en dreav nye ell clappia Cornish leben, poble coath pager egence blouth. Cornoack ewe all neceaves yen poble younk.

William Bodener

My age is three score and five. I am a poor fisherman. I did learn Cornish when I was a boy. I was at sea with my father and five men in a boat. I did scarcely hear one word of English spoken in the boat for a week together. I have not ever seen a Cornish book. I learnt Cornish going to sea with the old folk. There are not more than four or five of us in our town can speak Cornish now, old people of fourscore years. Cornish is all forgotten by the young people.

William Bodener

E

This time someone was provoked into going to Cornwall to try to record some Cornish from the mouths of the last speakers. A writer, signing himself 'Alphabeta' of Berkeley Square, London, wrote a letter to the *Universal Magazine*, dated December 1780, saying that the previous summer he had sought out William Bodener but failed to find him as he was 'upon the water in the way of his employment'. It is a great pity that 'Alphabeta' did not try harder in his efforts. A Mousehole fisherman informed Polwhele that Bodener and Dolly Pentreath would talk together for hours in Cornish. It is with a touch of melancholy that one hazards a guess as to what those conversations were about. The world they had known as children had disappeared. The language they had learnt and played in was gone. Dolly herself died in December 1777, and was buried in Paul on 27 December. The parish register says Dorothy Jeffrey was buried on that day and a note claims that this was, in fact, Dolly Pentreath. Lake says that Pentreath was Dolly's maiden name and she was the daughter of a Nicholas Pentreath and was baptised at Paul on 17 May 1714.[30] But if this were so the age given by Barrington and his informant at Castle Horneck of eighty-seven cannot be right. One cannot think they made such a mistake as to be twenty-four years out. The trouble is that the name Dorothy Pentreath was a very common one in the area. It has been argued by W. Treffry Hoblyn that Dolly was probably 'Doaryte, daughter of Nicholas Pentreath, baptysed at Paul Church, 16 May 1692'.[31] But whatever the mysteries of her birth, Dolly Pentreath died in 1777 and with her death one of the few remaining repositories of the language vanished without anyone noting down one word of her knowledge.

When Dolly died a man named Thomson, a native of Truro, who made engines for the mines, composed an epitaph for her, showing there were still people around who could write the language:

Coll Doll Pentreath cans ha deau
Marrow ha kledyz ed Paul pleû,
Na ed en Egloz, gan pobel braz
Bes ed Egloz-hay, coth Dolly es.

Old Dolly Pentreath, aged 102,
Deceased and buried in Paul parish too,
Not in the Church with people great and high,
But in the churchyard doth old Dolly lie.

The sadness of her death, especially the personal loss to the few remaining speakers such as Bodener, was lost on most people. Rather it was a subject of amusement. In 1785 the *Universal Magazine* published a portrait of her by R. Scaddon while Peter Pindar (Dr Wolcot) wrote an ode:

Hail Mousehole! birth place of old Doll Pentreath
　the last who gabber'd Cornish—so says Daines
Who bat-like haunted ruins, lane and heath,
　With Will o' Wisp to brighten up his brains
Daines! who a thousand miles unweary trots
For bones, brass farthings, ashes and old pots
To prove that folks of old, like us were made,
With head, eyes, hands, and toes, to drive a trade.

Polwhele even casts doubt on Dolly's ability to speak Cornish and, with the usual prejudice of the time, which prevented Borlase learning the still living language, dismissed her and refused to believe that an old 'fish jowster' could have anything to say to men of culture.[32] He met Thomson, the engineer who composed Dolly's epitaph, at Plymouth Docks in 1789 and said he 'knows more, I believe, of the Cornish language than the old lady whom he celebrated, ever knew'.

In view of the evidence regarding the last speakers of the language one cannot help but agree with Whitaker's conclusions:[33]

Mr. Barrington, let me here observe, in 1773, pretendedly sung the death song of the Cornish language and committed it to the grave with Dolly Pentreath, the fisherwoman of Mousehole. But in this he appears to have been mistaken, as Dr. Borlase was before him; when the Doctor, a native and a resident, an antiquarian and a linguist, so early as 1758, declared it to have altogether ceased, so as not to be heard anywhere in conversation, at that very time, as Mr. Barrington has observed, to the disgrace of his attention, an old woman was lying 'within four miles of him' and talking the language fluently. Nor can we convict Mr. Barrington of similar inattention. He was merely a stranger and a visitant in the country. But the language survived its last speaker. In 1790 William Pryce MD of Redruth, Cornwall, published his *Archaeologia Cornu-Britannica or an Essay . . .* In the preface to this publication he gives us such information as showed the

language had not expired with Mr. Barrington's fisherwoman, to have been still continuing in existence and to have had its last struggle for life, if it is even yet dead, at or about this very prominence of the Land's End.

There is still scope for research on 'the last speakers', for Jenner, in his address to the Philological Society, stated: 'Some time ago I came upon a letter in the British Museum addressed to Sir Joseph Banks, dated 1791, in which the writer mentions his own father as the only living man who could speak it (Cornish).'[34] Unfortunately, as Jenner later explained, 'reference to this letter has been lost, and there is so much Banks correspondence in the British Museum that it is almost impossible to find it again'.[35] One gets a sense of frustration from this period that, despite antiquarian curiosity, not one linguist felt the compelling need to track down these few remaining speakers and jot down their knowledge. The frustration is somewhat heightened when we learn that in 1793 a young Breton, who had escaped the guillotine in Brest during the suppression of Brittany's autonomy, sought refuge with friends in Penzance, and failed to note the similarity of Cornish to his native Breton. The young Breton, who stayed a year in Cornwall, within a mile or so of where the last remains of the language still lingered, was La Gonidec, who compiled the great Breton dictionary.

The end of the century, however, did see the publication of a major work on the language, albeit a controversial one. This was *Archaeologia Cornu-Britannica* by Dr William Pryce, published in 1790. Pryce had discovered the unpublished vocabulary and notes of Gwavas and Tonkin, had taken the grammar of Lhuyd, and published the whole thing, without acknowledgments, as his own work. An example of the closeness to which Pryce kept to the original may be seen by a comparison of the following extract to the letter of Tonkin to Gwavas quoted earlier in this chapter:

As for the Vulgar Cornish now spoken, it is so confined to the extremist corner of the country, and those ancient people who still pretend to jabber it, are even there so few; the speech itself is so corrupted; and the people too, for the most part, are so illiterate, that I cannot but wonder at my patience, and assume some merit to myself, for my singular industry, in collecting words which I have accumulated from oral intelligence; especially

as hardly any of the persons, whom I have consulted, could give
a tolerable account of the orthography, much less the etymology
or derivation of those words, which they use, for they often
join, or rather run, two or three words together, making but
one of them all, though their pronunciation is generally correct;
as for instance *merastadu*, which they pronounce in one breath,
as if it were a single word, whereas it is four *meor 'ras tha Dew*,
many thanks to God, anciently written *maur gras tha Dew*: and
merastawhy, many thanks to you, a contraction of *maur 'ras tha why*.

Pryce's plagiarism was not revealed until the linguist Prince Louis
Lucien Bonaparte discovered the original manuscripts in the 1860s.
But Pryce had made an excellent contribution to the study of the
language in publishing, albeit without acknowledgment, the important
work of Gwavas and Tonkin.

If old Dolly Pentreath was not the last speaker of the Cornish
language, who was then? We shall never know for a language does not
die suddenly, snuffed out with one last remaining speaker. As we shall
see in the following chapter, it lingers on for many years after it has
ceased as a form of communication between people, many people still
retaining enough knowledge from their childhood to embark on
conversations if they were ever lucky enough to come across a person
with a similar knowledge. We can trace several people who survived
Dolly who would have been a boon to interested philologists, had
there been some at the time. In 1777 John Nancarrow of Market Jew,
who was not more than forty years old at the time, spoke the language
having learnt it in his youth and claimed he could converse readily
in it as could 'an inhabitant of Truro'. This latter reference seems to be
the engineer Thomson. Two other old women of Mousehole named
Jane Cock and Jane Woolcock have also been identified as having
spoken the language with Nancarrow and Bodener. Bodener himself
lived on until 1794 but his two sons had no spoken knowledge of the
language. Dr William Pryce, making perhaps his only original contribution to his book, states:

I have heard from a very old man, now living at Mousehole,
near Penzance, who I believe is, at this time, the only person
capable of holding half an hour's conversation on common
subjects in the Cornish tongue. He tells me that above three
score years ago, being at Morlaix on board a smuggling cutter

and the only time he was ever there, he was ordered on shore, with another young man, to buy some greens, not knowing a word of French, as he thought, he was much surprised to find that he understood a great part of the conversation of some boys at play in the street, and upon further enquiry, he found he could make known all his wants in Cornish, and be better understood than he could be at home, when he used that dialect.

This seems to be a reference to William Bodener and, of course, Morlaix, in Brittany, was Breton speaking at this time. In August 1779, the rector of Ruan Lanihorne, the historian John Whitaker, made a visit to Land's End in search of Cornish speakers. He wrote:[36]

I have heard in my visit to the west of two persons still alive that could speak the Cornish language. On my offer of English money for Cornish words to the men at Land's End they referred me to an old man living about three miles off towards the south at St. Levan (I think) a second chapelry with St. Sennan in the parish of St. Buryan; and intimated that I might have as many words as I would choose to purchase.

Again the same tragedy appears. Whitaker did not follow up the knowledge he gained, did not track down 'the old man living about three miles off' or make any attempt to take down his knowledge of the language. By the end of the eighteenth century one thing was definite as John Bannister commented: 'The close of the 18th Century witnessed the final extinction, as spoken language, of the old Celtic vernacular of Cornwall.'[37]

Chapter Six

The Embers

To what extent did the Cornish language linger on in the speech of the Cornish people after it had ceased to be a common means of communication? There are various examples of survivals. Some Cornish people retained a knowledge of the entire Lord's Prayer and Creed in the language, while others memorised verses or retained sentences, lines of Cornish which, as the language faded from memory, became jumbled pieces of nonsense. Many Cornish people, in the hundreds of Penwith and Kerrier, retained the knowledge of how to count in the language. But a great deal of Cornish lingered on in the Cornish dialect of English and, indeed, Cornish words still linger on in such use today. A Cornishman explaining that his cows had been fed would say 'The cows is quaffed.' In Cornish the word *quoffy* means to swell or overeat, while *quoff* means distension or repletion. Likewise, 'We got into a fore-end-all!' has been the comment when a Cornishman has been led into a 'blind alley'. The Cornish *forth hens dall* means, literally, a blind way road.

Jenner says that he had heard, but did not vouch for the accuracy of the statement[1]

> that there were old people in the early nineteenth century who
> habitually recited the Lord's Prayer and Creed in Cornish at
> their private prayers as they had been taught to do as children.
> Be this as it may, there were people who could have done so,
> and one instance came under my observation. My own mother-
> in-law (the late Mrs. Rawlings of Hayle) when she was a child,
> that is to say sometime before 1830, had learned to say those
> things in Cornish.

Edwin Norris records that he heard an old man recite the Creed in Cornish just prior to 1860. When, in 1925, W. D. Watson was searching for people who retained any traditional pieces of Cornish, he came across Edmund Matthews in Redruth, who had been born in

Paul, whose mother Mrs Betsy Matthews, who died in Paul in 1887, had known a great deal of Cornish, including the Lord's Prayer, the names of the months and numerals. Edmund Matthews, himself, had retained nothing but a few numerals while his brother Robert Matthews had memorised all the numerals up to twenty.[2] There were certainly a large number of Cornish people who had retained a knowledge of Cornish numerals. According to Jenner:[3]

> Now it is easy to see that those who learned English as a new language would find it easier to count in Cornish and would count their fish in that tongue, and their children would hear them do so, and would do so themselves, and so for that purpose the numerals as far as twenty would survive long after the death of the rest of the language.

In September 1865, J. H. Nankivell of Penzance, wrote to the *Gentleman's Magazine* on what he described as 'Vestiges of the Celtic and Anglo-Saxon Tongues':

> When wandering by the lovely shores of the Mount's Bay one may often hear the fisher boys shouting to each other 'Jack, where did you get your breel?' (Mackerel) and on board the mackerel boat when the nets are taken up, the men exclaim: 'Breel! mata! idn! deaw, try, pedwar, pymp, whea, all scawd!' (A mackerel! His fellow, 1,2,3,4,5,6 all the shoal!) A few years ago the hearth or fireplace used in these boats was a piece of granite hollowed out, and it was called 'myn olla'; the same kind of simple hearth is still used by the Breton fishermen and they call it by the same name 'myn olla'.

Nance points out that Nankivell has incorrectly recorded this occupation chant: *Brí'el mâta; treja, peswara; pempes; wethes!*[4] While presenting us with a brief, exciting glimpse of the survival of Cornish, Nankivell states:

> it is not much, but I believe that there is more to be found. The great district of the Lizard or Meneage peninsula has not yet been searched, but there are several workers in the field, and before long we shall perhaps know for certain how much tradition remains.

If there were 'several workers in the field' not much of their work in collecting traditional Cornish, unfortunately, remains, although we are told by the Rev. W. S. Lach-Szyrma that, in 1864, a list of 404 Cornish words in common use was compiled by a Mr Couch and published and soon after a Mr Thomas Garland added a further 248 words to the list.[5] In the article, the Rev. Lach-Szyrma, the vicar of Newlyn, comments:

The memory of the Cornish language as a past tradition lingers
to a greater degree in certain families than is commonly suspected.
I have found some half dozen persons (mostly, I own, belonging
in one family) who can recite the Cornish numerals up to 20.
All these persons now reside in the old parish of St. Paul, in
which Dolly Pentreath lived, and in which Mousehole is, the last
stronghold of the Cornish language.

Lach-Szyrma gives a word list and compares the numerals he had obtained from traditional sources to those Norris published from the Middle Cornish literature. A Mr William Noy (or Noyes) of 38 Sutherland Square, London, S.E., replied in the *Academy* claiming that Lach-Szyrma was wrong in many of the words he listed. The writer added that he was preparing to publish a Cornish vocabulary.[6] Soon afterwards, Lach-Szyrma wrote to Henry Jenner informing him that he had found some old people who could repeat the numerals and knew other words of Cornish. In July 1875, Jenner went to West Cornwall and, in the company of Lach-Szyrma, visited these old people in Newlyn and later in Mousehole. Jenner divided his findings into three classes: A, the numerals; B, detached words; C, three complete sentences.[7] Jenner compared the complete numerals recorded by his informants with those given by Pryce and Norris. In this case Jenner's information came from John Kelynack, a Newlyn fisherman; his wife, who had learnt the words from her father, John Tremethack who died in 1852 aged eighty-seven; Mrs Soady, a widow about eighty years old who had also learnt from her father; Stephen Richards of Newlyn, a captain in the merchant navy service, aged seventy; Bernard Victor of Mousehole, a fisherman, aged seventy and Mrs Tregarthen of Newlyn, aged sixty. Jenner reported his findings to the Philological Society while Lach-Szyrma contributed a paper to the *Revue Celtique*.[8]

The traditional knowledge of numerals outlasted even the nineteenth century and in the early years of the twentieth century Nance made a

E*

tour copying down numbers remembered traditionally by Cornishmen and women. He took numbers from Miss J. Kelynack, the daughter of the Newlyn Kelynacks; J. Lawnery of Mawnan gave a similar version of the numbers up to twenty and told Nance he had learnt them from his mother, a Quick of Wicca, Zennor, who had also taught him the Cornish names of the days. R. D. Daniel of Austell learnt the numerals from a man called Daniel at Rosemergy in Morvah while Richard Hall of St Just learnt them from W. J. Vingoe in 1914. Vingoe had learnt them, in his turn, from his mother, Mrs Elizabeth Vingoe of Boswarva, Madron. William Symons of St Ives also taught his grand-daughter, Mrs Hodge, in 1875, the numerals up to twenty.[9]

A few years after Nance recorded his traditional counting, W. D. Watson was told by A. D. Jenkin of Trewirgie (in 1925) of people in Mullion who could still count in Cornish. Watson found that Mr Albert Harvey, a native of Paul, had learnt the numerals when he was young and claimed the knowledge was widespread. Albert's brother, William, recalled that he and his brother and other boys in Paul had learnt to count in Cornish. Another man, John George, could only remember the numerals one to six and fourteen but he also knew a few words of Cornish. G. S. Barry of Lanner learnt the numerals from William Cooke, who originally came from Gweek but died at Lanner in 1883. Numerals were also taken from Edmund and Robert Matthews.[10] The recording of the numerals was an important piece of research for those interested in seeing the later stages of the language's development. But as well as numerals, whole sentences had been retained by people who, losing the very memory of the language, retained the words as pieces of 'nonsense' or even 'magical sayings'. Such a sentence was retained by R. J. Noall of Hellesvean in the early part of the twentieth century. He had been taught it by his brother, who in turn was taught it by a cousin who had learnt it from his grandparents. It was represented as a queer piece of nonsense jabbered by an old Ludgvan character and came down as *Jeé an jee wóppen, ha gessa boo átter*. Nance respelt this as: *Ajy hens yu open, he geses ow bugh ater* or, in Unified Cornish, *Ajy an yu oppen, ha gesys ow bugh ater*. Translated thus the sentence would be 'the road gap (gate) is open and my cow let out!'[11] Strange that a moment of stress, a cow leaving its field because some unthinking person had left the gate open, excited an old man to revert to his childhood language and for that exclamation to be preserved by word of mouth over one hundred years—its meaning lost. But with numerals here, sentences and

individual words there, was there anyone left in the nineteenth century who retained a more complete knowledge of the language?

According to the St Ives historian J. Hobson Matthews, John Davey of Boswednack, Zennor, 'could converse on a few simple topics in the ancient language.' John Davey was born in 1812, in St Just, and died in Boswednack in 1891. He was a farmer, although for a time he had kept a school at Zennor. Nance says:[12]

> Had not the whole history of the language prepared us for such neglect, it would seem far less credible that as recently as 1891, the year of his death, John Davey's Cornish, like that of Dolly Pentreath or William Bodener a century earlier, was allowed to perish unrecorded that at so late a date a man still lived who could recite some traditional Cornish, less astonishing, but even more sad, is it that not one word of all his store is known to his descendants today, although it is well remembered that he possessed it.

J. Hobson Matthews published his *History of St. Ives* in 1892, the year after Davey died. To what extent did Davey know Cornish and did Hobson Matthews ever meet Davey? Davey's father was a schoolmaster in St Just. He had been born in Boswednack in 1770 and died in St Just in 1844. Among the books he left his son John was a copy of Pryce's *Archaeologia Cornu-Britannica*. Had Davey merely committed Pryce to memory, or learnt Cornish from the work? We have only one piece of traditional Cornish recorded from John Davey's lips by Hobson Matthews, a short verse which is to be found nowhere else, thus indicating that Davey knew some 'original' Cornish. The verse as Hobson Matthews records it is:

A Grankan, a grankan,
a mean ow gowaz o vean
ondez Parc an Venton
pub trelowza vean
Far Penzans a Maragow
Githack Macrow
a mac trelowza varrack.

To Hobson Matthews this was 'a mere jumble of place names' but Nance respells the verse with an English translation:[13]

A Grankan! A Grankan!
E'mên a-gawes saw bighan
Hunj es Park an Venten
A-dêf trŷ lous a vên
For' Pensans ha Marghaj-Yow
Yû uthek moy crî, hag üthek moy crow
Ha mâk trŷ lous a varghak!

O Crankan! O Crankan!
On the rock thou hast but little
Further than the Well Field
That will grow three sprouts to each stone
The Penzance and Market Jew road
Is vastly more green and vastly more fresh
And will nourish three sprouts to each rider.

According to Nance:

Crankan still has its 'Well Field' and its 'Lower Park Venton'
and that Market Jew road was proverbially the accepted word for
barrenness is proved also by an uncomplimentary name, 'Market
Jew Street Stitch' given to a field on Trythal, not far from
Crankan. This in Cornish was Lean For' Marghas Yow, we may
be sure 'street' replaced 'road' in its English translation.

As Nance laments, what knowledge would have been forthcoming if
say, Jenner, had spent some time with a notebook and John Davey
before the latter's death in 1891.

Individual words, and even phrases, did linger on, however, in
the Cornish dialect of English. As Lach-Szyrma pointed out:

The question of 'utter extinction' hangs, as many such enquiries
must do, on the definition of the term. There may be no person
living who can, without reference to a dictionary, speak a series
of sentences on common topics in pure Cornish, and yet the
words of the language may have a lingering, or more than lingering
existence—a real vitality, mingled with English!

Lach-Szyrma maintained that he sent 200 examples of Cornish
words which had survived in dialect to the Philological Society of

London. One such example was the term of endearment 'piggy-whidden' (little white one) used to a child at Tredavoe. He pointed out:[14]

a good deal of old Cornish still lingers among our mining and fisherfolk, not only in their ancient pronounciation and structure of sentences, and idiomatic expressions, but even in their actual words. Of these I have endeavoured to pick out those that seem to me to be bona fide Cornu-British words, and with the aid of philological friends, weeding them out, I hope ultimately to have a list of the real survivals of Cornu-British.

However, it was left to Nance to publish a survey of the Cornish words in dialect. An example of a phrase used in the first decade of the twentieth century was one rescued by a Miss Millicent Vivian at Gwinear. This was a term of endearment: 'Tai baree!' or 'Tai baree! sha winnet!' said to crying children. Jenner spelt this as *'Taw warre: Zeh enep!'* and in Unified Cornish it would be *'Taw whare! Segh dha enep'* or 'Hush now, dry your face!' Nance overheard several Cornish words when children were playing games. At Redruth, when playing marbles, a child would take 'gridlance' and move his marble to a more favourable position. In Cornish *gruthylans* is a doing or a making. Likewise a shout of 'Na custance!' is made when a player strikes a marble by accident and does not wish to be penalised for it. In Cornish *na cryssythyans* means 'no punishment'. At Polperro when a child wishes to stop the game, he shouts 'Sens!' literally, in Cornish, 'Hold!'[15] In Camborne still to say 'Taw tavas' means 'Shut up!', literally 'Silent tongue!' The examples of such word survivals in dialect are numerous. And not just Cornish words have survived in this fashion but Cornish grammar. This is inevitable in language transference. A well-known Irish example is 'I am after going down the road'. This is merely a rendering of Irish grammar with English words and means 'I have gone down the road.' So, in Cornish, 'Goin' home are 'ee?' is English in wording but Cornish in word order. Similarly 'I do say' for 'I say' and 'I do do' for 'I do' is a literal rendering of *my a wra a gül*.

In the academic fields a number of histories of Cornwall were issued during the first decades of the nineteenth century and these touched on the language, repeating most of the well-known myths and misconceptions. Polwhele's seven volume *History of Cornwall*, published

in London in 1816, proved to be the most authoritative of these even though he, too, was prone to prejudice and several inaccuracies. The remains of the language were briefly raked over by Davies Gilbert, one-time president of the Royal Academy who, in 1826, published John Keigwin's version of *Pascon agan Arluth*, which Gilbert re-named 'The Poem of Mount Calvary'. In 1828 he also published Keigwin's translation of *Gwreans an bys*. Gilbert obviously had no knowledge of the language at all for his two books were riddled with errors from beginning to end and there was not even a pretence at editing the work. The Celtic scholar Zeuss, who published his *Grammatica Celtica* some thirty years later, mildly commented on the fact. Edwin, in his *Ancient Cornish Drama,* was more emphatic: 'I would go still further than Zeuss and say that the person who prepared the manuscript for the printer was quite unable to read the work he was copying, moderately speaking, there are eight errors in every stanza.' Dr Whitley Stokes observes: 'Zeuss might well have extended his censure to the translation by Keigwin (interpaged in Mr. Gilbert's edition) which betrays great ignorance of the Cornish language.' E. G. R. Hooper, however, who accuses Norris of 'making use of Keigwin's works without mentioning their existence', says: 'It has been averred that Keigwin could not read easily the old script, but it was Davies Gilbert, President of the Royal Society, who could not read John Keigwin's handwriting and did not understand Cornish . . .'.

One certainly doubts Davies Gilbert's knowledge of Cornish from a contribution he made to the *Cornish Magazine* in 1828 of a 'Cornish Cantata'.[16] This consisted of nine verses of place names which he had published 'to convince the world of the euphony of our ancient tongue'. The place names were produced in alternative rhyme and readers were assured that 'when pronounced according to our provincial orthography, they cannot fail to affect a Cornish heart with that peculiar sort of pleasing melancholy which is excited by the portrait of a dear, departed friend'. But Gilbert had no melancholy yearnings for the Cornish language. According to his introduction to 'The Poem of Mount Calvary': 'No one more sincerely rejoices than does the editor of this ancient mystery that the Cornish dialect of the Celtic or Gaelic languages has ceased altogether from being used by the inhabitants of Cornwall.' After the disastrous attempt of Davies Gilbert at editing the Cornish texts, it seemed that the language was entirely forgotten for a generation.

Achievements in the scholastic field outside of Cornwall were

opening new doors to knowledge of the Celtic languages and, indeed, all European languages. An English judge of the high court of Bengal, Sir William Jones, observed that Sanskrit, the ancient language of the Vedic scripts in north-west India which had been fixed as a literary medium as early as the fourth century B.C., showed remarkable resemblance to European languages, notably Greek and Latin. A new science was established, the study of comparative grammar, and by the nineteenth century the theory of an Indo-European family of languages had emerged. This presupposes the existence at some time in remote antiquity of a unified primitive Indo-European parent language which had its homeland somewhere between the Baltic and the Black Sea, possibly already differentiated into dialects before succeeding waves of migrants spread the languages westwards to the Atlantic and eastward to Asia. The Indo-European language cannot be assigned to any datable period or described in detail. Indo-European is the parent tongue of all the European languages with the exception of Basque, Hungarian, Finnish and Estonian (with their Utalian relatives) and the Caucasian languages. The Indo-European, or Indo-Aryan, is parent to 300 languages and dialects in India. Philologists began to make new, exciting discoveries. In 1905 at Boghazkoy, in Asia Minor, many old tablets were found bearing inscriptions in Hittite, the language of the Hittite Empire which flourished in Asia Minor in the nineteenth to fourteenth centuries B.C. before it was overcome by the Phrygian invasion of 1200 B.C. The tablets, written in an Akkadian cuneiform syllabary, containing tracts on political, religious and legal matters, were deciphered in 1916 by a Hungarian named Hronzy and Hittite was established as an Indo-European language but representing an earlier offshoot than any other known branch, pushing the hypothetical Indo-European parent language further back into the mists of antiquity.

In 1838 Franz Bopp, a German scholar, proved that the Celtic group of languages were part of the Indo-European family. Scholars, comparing the Celtic group with other Indo-European groups, found that in Celtic changes took place at the beginning of words in the form of aspirations and ellipsis, whereas in Latin and Greek, the changes took place at the ending of the words. Bopp demonstrated that these changes, far from being evidence against the Indo-European character of Celtic, were a proof that Celtic formerly had similar endings to Latin and Greek. Through the mists of myth and legend, which had been so thoroughly spread in the eighteenth century, scientific scholarship

began to break down barriers. But it was a slow process and sometimes scholars leapt to wrong conclusions. For example, Tokharian was for many years thought to be a branch of Celtic because of its similarity. In 1906 Sir Aurel Stein and Sven Hedin, exploring the deserts of Chinese Turkestan, came on a sealed chamber in a Buddhist temple, which revealed many ancient manuscripts in various languages, some of them unknown to Stein and Hedin. According to Stein[17] the layers of manuscripts rose to a height of ten feet above the floor of the temple and filled a space of 500 cubic feet. Scholars began to study the manuscripts and by 1908 a hitherto unknown language, which they named Tokharian, was discovered. From the manuscripts it was thought there were two varieties of this language—Agnaean and Kuchean. The texts dated from the eighth to ninth centuries A.D. and it was an important discovery for, although in the eastern Indo-European area, the language had more similarities with the western Indo-European area. The similarities with Celtic were remarkable. According to Myles Dillon, one of the greatest experts on the Irish language:[18]

some scholars supposed that these Tokharians away on the border of China were Celts who had wandered far beyond the limits of the Indo-European area, rather as the gypsies wandered west from India. When I was a student in Heidelberg in 1924 that was the doctrine there.

Soon after Franz Bopp had completed his identification of the Celtic languages as Indo-European, a schoolmaster living in the town of Bamberg, Bavaria, decided to make a study of early Celtic literary remains. His name was Johann Casper Zeuss. He did invaluable work for Irish, gathering collections in libraries of the great Irish foundations abroad, such as Wurzburg, St Gall and Milan, where the manuscripts of Bobbio were known to be preserved. He put the study of Irish on a completely new footing, setting up a system of grammatical forms from early manuscripts and glosses, comparing them with Gaullish remains and Ogham inscriptions. He published his work in Leipzig in 1853 under the title of *Grammatica Celtica*. Reference to his findings enabled scholars to date texts and, indeed, to interpret texts which had hitherto been untranslatable. Zeuss did not confine his studies to the Irish branch of Celtic but worked on all the Celtic languages including Cornish. Although he mistakenly published some Old Cornish glosses as Old Welsh, Edwin Norris describes Zeuss's essay into

Cornish as 'the only work which furnishes a good scientific view of the language'.

In Cornwall, itself, there had been a growing interest in local antiquities leading to the foundation, in 1818, of the Cornwall Philosophical Institution which, in 1821, changed its name to the Royal Institution of Cornwall. In 1833 a Royal Cornwall Polytechnic Society was founded in Falmouth but the scholars who read annual papers on diverse Cornish subjects to these learned societies entirely ignored the old Cornish language. It was therefore left to a non-Cornishman to revive an interest in the language. Prince Louis Lucien Bonaparte arrived in Cornwall in the late 1850s in search of relics of the language. A philologist, he had made investigations into several minority languages in Europe, including Basque and Breton. Bonaparte tracked down the village of Mousehole where Dolly Pentreath was buried and decided, with the aid of the Rev. John Garrett, the Irish vicar of St Paul, to erect a memorial over her resting place. Apparently, despite the interest of the time and Thomson's epitaph, no one knew exactly where Dolly Pentreath was buried but the Rev. Garrett came across some descendants of William Bodener who directed him to the spot. An obelisk was erected with an inscription which read:

Here lieth interred Dorothy Pentreath, who died in 1778, said
to have been the last person who conversed in the ancient
Cornish, the peculiar language of this country from the earliest
records till it expired in the eighteenth century, in this parish
of St. Paul. This stone is erected by the Prince Louis Lucien
Bonaparte in union with the Rev. John Garrett vicar of St. Paul,
June, 1860.
Honour thy father and thy mother, that thy days may be long
in the land which the Lord thy God giveth thee. Exod. xx. 12.
Gwra pethi de taz ha de mam: mal de Dythiow bethenz hyr
war an tyr neb an arleth de dew ryes dees. Exod. xx. 12.

According to a Mousehole fisherman writing to Dr Jago, author of an *English–Cornish Dictionary*, in 1881/2, the memorial to Dolly had been placed in the wrong spot. Dolly, he also pointed out, had died in 1777 and not in 1778. The fisherman was named Bernard Victor who had been born in Mousehole on 21 August 1817. His grandfather had been George Badcock, who died in July 1834, aged

eighty-four and, in 1777, had been the undertaker who had interred Dolly. Victor, who afterwards wrote a prize winning essay on Cornish, said that no memorial had been erected to Dolly at the time of her death and that eight chosen fishermen from the village had taken her to her last resting place. In May 1882, Dr W. T. A. Pattison, a colleague of Jago, visited Victor to pinpoint the site of the grave. Pattison and Jago carefully checked all sources concerning the location and annoyed Victor by not simply taking his word for it. In a sharp note to Jago dated 22 May 1882, Victor wrote: 'It is not to be said that the monument is in the right place because it was put there by the order of Prince Louis Lucien Bonaparte or by the Rev. John Garrett— the one a Frenchman and the other an Irishman!' On 26 May Jago had to placate Victor by pointing out:[19]

> I had no doubt of your statements and only wrote you again to obtain the fullest information possible. Such information coming from one so well acquainted with many words and even phrases of the ancient Cornish language, and this apart from books, renders it peculiarly interesting, and I am much indebted to you for your letters.

While in Cornwall Bonaparte bought some Cornish manuscripts from a bookseller called Rodda of Penzance for the sum of 8s. 6d. On careful scrutiny he found that the manuscripts were original letters of Gwavas and Tonkin and not only letters but Tonkin's projected book on the language 'the same', wrote an indignant Bonaparte, 'that Pryce unscrupulously printed at Sherborne in 1790 under his own name'.[20] Robert Williams in his Lexicon Cornu-Britannicum, which was published in 1865, dismisses Pryce's work entirely:

> This is so full of errors that the editor soon felt satisfied that Pryce was entirely ignorant of the Cornish language and had no acquaintance whatever with Welsh. The discovery of the original manuscript now in possession of Prince Louis Lucien Bonaparte shews the work to have been compiled in 1730 by Tonkin or Gwavas and disingenuously published by Pryce as his own.

Bonaparte, however, comments that Williams's criticism of Pryce would have to apply to Gwavas and Tonkin since Pryce only published

their manuscript. He did not feel the criticism valid, therefore, that Gwavas and Tonkin were 'entirely ignorant of the Cornish language'.[21] Despite the criticism of Pryce's effort, his careful editing did do Cornish a great service for it enabled nineteenth century scholars to gain sufficient knowledge of the language to bring out scholastic translations of Cornish words. The original manuscripts of Gwavas and Tonkin became lost when Bonaparte's library was broken up after his death. They were rediscovered purely by chance when Edward S. Dodgson, an authority on Basque, was working in the Biblioteca de la Diputación de la Provincia de Vizcaya in Bilbao. Dodgson informed Jenner who, in 1909, travelled to Spain to investigate the manuscripts and subsequently wrote a paper on them.[22] Several overtures to purchase the manuscripts have been made by the Royal Institution of Cornwall without success.

Bonaparte's trip to Cornwall had succeeded in publicising the language and now scholars outside Cornwall were beginning to take an interest. Edwin Norris edited a two volume work entitled *The Ancient Cornish Drama*, published in 1859.[23] This contained the text of the *Ordinalia* with a translation as well as a grammar. Through Zeuss and other Continental Celtic scholars, a knowledge of Cornish was spreading to the most unlikely places. A German linguist named Sauerwein wrote two poetical epistles in Cornish to Norris, who was a friend of his, in 1859 and 1861.[24] These were perhaps the first Cornish poems composed in over a hundred years. More significantly, in scholastic circles, the great English Celtic scholar, Dr Whitley Stokes, one of the most prominent of nineteenth century Celtic philologists, edited and translated *Pascon agan Arluth* from the original manuscript[25] and published it as an appendix to the 1860-1 volume of the *Transactions of the Philological Society*. Serious academic scholarship had finally brought Cornish to the notice of Cornish scholars and in the same year, 1861, John Bellow read a paper 'On the Cornish Language' to the Royal Cornwall Polytechnic Society urging more scholastic research on the language.[26] Bellow told the Society:

> it may perhaps be said that as Cornish is no longer spoken and
> contains no literature worth mention, there is not sufficient
> inducement to learn it. This is true. So far as regards its use as a
> medium of communication. But there is another aspect in which
> a language may have claim on our attention, besides this, viz., the
> aid it is capable of affording in tracing the roots of words in

other tongues—the light it may cast on the relationship of some of those tongues to each other. Even a dead language will thus furnish us at times with links in a chain that must otherwise remain imperfect. In this, then, lies the present value of Cornish to us; and if the language is suffered to disappear entirely the science of philology will sustain some loss by its doing so.

He added:

The ancient Cornish language lies like a buried city under our feet—we pass to and fro above it, but heed it not in the hustle of everyday life. Yet in its words there is as much reality as ever there was in sculptural obelisks of Egypt or marble slabs of Nineveh, for they hide treasures of history, never recorded by pen, but not the less true or accessible to diligent research. It is for Cornishmen to say whether this search shall be made or not: and it is but reasonable to hope that a language, which has proved so interesting to a foreign prince, as to bring him to our shores for the purpose of investigating it, may also excite some interest among the descendants of the men who spoke it.

One Cornishman had been interested enough to work on the language. Charles Rogers of Stonehouse had compiled a vocabulary covering 992 pages plus 36 pages of introduction, on $9\frac{3}{4}$ in. by 8 in. paper, and entitled 'Vocabulary of the Cornish Language compiled with additions by Charles Rogers. Stonehouse, 1861, with introductory remarks'. It is not recorded whether Mr Rogers attempted to publish his work but the manuscript was left to his son Owen Rogers M.D. who bequeathed it to Bodleian Library on 29 December 1898.[27] Another Cornishman, the famous traveller and writer, George Borrow (1803-81) also displayed a knowledge of the language. Borrow, who learnt Welsh, Irish, Latin, Greek, Hebrew, Danish, French, Italian, Spanish and Portuguese—before he was eighteen years old!—made a tour of Wales in 1854 which he recounts in a book called *Wild Wales*, first published in 1862 and still in print today. In this book he recounts an occasion when travelling over the Welsh mountains with a guide who asks him which of the two roads he wished to take. Borrow replied: 'There is a proverb in the Gerniweg, which was the language of my forefathers, saying "Never leave the old road for the new": we will therefore go by the hen fordd, that is to

say, the old path.' Borrow had obviously read *Jowan Chy an Hor* in which the proverb *Na reys gara an vor goth rag an vor noweth* (Do not leave the way old for the way new) occurs. He must have been either conversant with Pryce's book, or more probably, Lhuyd's work.

Following the interest shown by the Royal Cornwall Polytechnic Society in the language, Thomas Quiller-Couch read a paper on 'The Cornish language' to the Royal Institution of Cornwall in 1864.[28] The same year Dr Whitley Stokes published an edited version and translation of '*Gwreans an bys*' (Creation of the World) which he had prepared in August 1862.[29] In the following year the first comprehensive Cornish dictionary was published. Its author was a Welsh speaker, the Rev. Robert Williams of Rhydycroesau, and his work, *Lexicon Cornu-Britannicum*, subtitled *Gerlyvr Gernewec*, was a very thorough presentation of the language. Dr Whitley Stokes, however, did not think highly of Williams's work and complained: 'Mr. Williams has throughout his *Lexicon* been misled by Welsh analogy.'[30] Bonaparte also criticised Williams's work as did the famous Celtic scholar Professor Joseph Loth.[31] But Williams's *Lexicon* is still used as the standard Cornish dictionary by academics today for reasons we shall deal with in Chapter Eight.

In 1869 W. W. E. Wynne of Penarth Library found a small quarto volume, size 8½ in. by 6 in., in old brown leather binding, consisting of ninety leaves, augmented with pencil notes. The manuscript had been finished by Dominus Rad. Ton in 1504 and its title was *Beunans Meriasek* (The Life of St Meriasek). Although it had been found among the Hengwrt manuscripts, Mr Wynne did not think the language was Welsh and so he consulted the Rev. Williams. On 1 March 1869, Williams confirmed his suspicions:

I congratulate you on the possession of a treasure, which you are not aware of. The Ordinale of St. Meriadoc . . . is a genuine Cornish Mystery, the existence of which has hitherto been unknown. There are only five different Mysteries known and printed, which furnished me with the materials for my Cornish Dictionary. None of us who have studied this branch ever heard of such a drama, so that it is of great value for philological purposes.

It was, indeed, of value. Williams published the first thirty-six lines of the drama in the *Archaeologia Cambrensis* for 1869.[32] A great many

new Cornish words were discovered and it was Whitley Stokes who published them as *A Cornish Glossary*, which ran to 2,000 new words of Cornish, in 1868-9.[33]

In Cornwall, Cornishmen had been slow in studying the language. The first serious study on the language was presented to the Royal Institution of Cornwall in 1866 by William Copeland Borlase entitled 'A collection of hitherto unpublished proverbs and rhymes in the ancient Cornish language from the MSS. of Dr. Borlase'. But the study which was intriguing Cornishmen, which was directly connected with the language, was the study of place names. With the death of the language, and even the vague memory of its existence forgotten, Cornwall was left with a countless number of place names which, in the eyes of most people, were merely gibberish. With the cessation of the language the Cornish people had become cut off from their past. Even the most serious scholars began to give credit to the most peculiar fantasies about the Cornish. The most popular theory was that of the 'Lost Tribe of Israel'. From place names such as Marazion and Market Jew scholars concocted the idea that the Jews had emigrated to Cornwall in vast numbers after the fall of Jerusalem, or even that Jews were taken to work as slaves in Cornish mines. Old tin works were locally called 'Jew's Houses' and legends, starting with Joseph of Arimathea landing in Looe with the young Jesus Christ, abounded. Some people even professed to see Jewish features in Cornish faces. Marazion, it was pointed out, would be Hebrew— *Marah Zion* meaning 'bitter harvest', a reflection of their flight after the fall of Jerusalem. It was left to a professor of comparative philology at Oxford, Max Müller (Rt Hon. Friedrich Max Müller) to debunk these erroneous ideas completely in a paper on the language entitled 'Are there Jews in Cornwall?'[34] From the earliest record of Marazion, in 1308,—Maragasiou—T. F. G. Dexter maintains the name means Jou or John's Market (i.e. *marghas*—market).[35] Other scholars point out that it could equally well mean Thursday Market or Two Markets if one reads Carew's Marchas Diow. But according to P. A. S. Pool:[36]

As a further example, the name Marazion is derived from *marghas byghan*, small market, the name of one of the two settlements comprising the town; the other was called *marghas Yow*, Thursday market, whence the name Market Jew, given formerly to the town and still to Market Jew Street in Penzance which leads to it. The name has thus no connection with Jews or with Zion.

The 'revelations' of Max Müller inspired the Rev. John Bannister to address the thirty-seventh annual meeting of the Royal Cornwall Polytechnic Society, meeting in Falmouth in 1867, on 'Cornish names'. He pointed out that 'Cornwall has exhibited, during the past 100 years, a remarkable phenomenon, the final extinction, as a spoken language, of its old vernacular . . .'. By so doing it was also losing the meaning of its place names. Bannister published a list of 20,000 Cornish names and their meanings in 1871 under the title of *Glossary of Cornish Names*. According to Jenner, Bannister's work was worse than useless because it was misinformed.[37] Dexter points out that 'many of the derivations must be most carefully considered before adoption'. Another work on Cornish names was produced in 1870 by R. S. Charnock who gave a fairly exhaustive list of Cornish names but whose derivations, according to Dexter, must be received with caution.[38]

An event which, in retrospect, was of great significance to the study of the language, took place in 1873. Henry Jenner, born in St Columb Major in 1848, then a young assistant keeper of manuscripts at the British Museum, read a paper to the Philological Society on 'The Cornish language'.[39] Jenner's scholarship brought a new impetus to Cornish studies and, by the time he died in 1934, he became known as the 'Father of the Cornish Language Revival'. In his first paper on the subject Jenner presented most of the then known facts about the language and concluded:

This, then, is all that can be found at present on the subject of the Cornish language. I have done much more in the way of compiling than of originating anything, for the subject has been pretty well exhausted by other writers; and unless some new book should turn up, very little of any importance remains to be done.

Jenner was to prove himself wrong.

In 1875 Lach-Szyrma had contacted him and together they had visited old people taking down the last traditional scraps of the language. The two men's search for people with any traditional knowledge of the language is uncomfortably like Islwyn Ffowc Elis's novel *Wythnos Yng Nghymru Fydd* (A Week in Future Wales) where the hero, Ifan Powell, goes on two journeys into the Wales of the future. In one visit he comes on a happy, independent, bilingual Wales. In

the other visit he encounters an Anglicised, terrorised West England, a forest reserve peopled with the aged and ruins. He meets a man who has learnt Welsh from books and the two men travel through the country searching for anyone with any traditional knowledge of the language. They reach Bala and are sent to see a senile old woman. The following passage, in which italics represent Welsh actually used in the conversation, is taken from Gerald Morgan's translation:[40]

Richards sat in front of the old woman and said in Welsh, *'How are you? Are you feeling fairly well?'*
The old woman opened her eyes and looked at him lifelessly.
'Mm. Who are you?' she asked.
'I am talking Welsh to you, old lady,' said Richards. *'Can you speak Welsh?'*
Richards made several more attempts, but in vain. Then I asked if I might try. Richards changed places with me, and I took the old woman's hand. More than anything in the world I wanted to hear her speaking a word of Welsh, someone who had lived in my own time, and had spoken my language. I wanted to hear her say anything that would show that the vandals had not completely obliterated my Wales for ever, especially in Bala . . .
'Old woman,' I said, *'Do you know this? Try to remember.'* And I recited slowly: *'The Lord is my shepherd. I shall not want. He maketh me to lie down in green pastures . . .'* The old woman's eyes closed. That's it, I thought, but I went on. *'He restoreth my soul. He leadeth me . . .'* Suddenly I realised that the old woman's lips were moving. She was reciting the words with me. Her eyes opened, and her voice grew stronger and stronger . . . *'Yea, though I walk through the valley of the shadow of death, I will fear no evil . . .'* And when she came to the last words of the psalm, she spoke them with a strength in her voice and a light in her eyes whose like I have never seen before or since.
'And I will dwell in the house of the Lord for ever . . . Who are you my boy?' She turned her bright eyes on me. *'Are you Mary Jones' boy? They've moved Thomas Charles' memorial from the chapel, you know . . . those English . . .'* She gripped the arms of the chair and sat bolt upright. *'They did it, with their noise and their forestry and their rules and regulations . . . they . . . .'* But I don't know you, do I?' She sank back, and her eyes misted. 'I don't know anything now . . .'

I got up and left the room. I had seen with my own eyes the death of the Welsh language.

Perhaps the death of the Welsh language will not, at least, be as ignominious as that thanks to the efforts of Cymdeithas yr Iaith Gymraeg. However, Welsh is by no means secure yet, but the lessons from the death of their sister language, Cornish, have been taken very much to heart.

On 14 August 1876, the British Archaeological Association held a 'Cornwall Congress' at Bodmin with the Rt Hon. Earl of Mount Edgcumbe presiding. All the papers read before the congress were on various aspects of Cornish antiquities. Jenner delivered a paper on 'The history and literature of the ancient Cornish language'.[41] He was thanked on behalf of the congress by Lach-Szyrma who said that 'the Association had that day passed over the sepulchre of a recently deceased Cornish language'. There was scarcely another case of a death of a language in modern times to be cited, and he mentioned that there were '. . . still old people who could count up to about twenty in Cornish. The old man who he had found to know most of the old tongue had just died.'

The paper created considerable interest and Lord Mount Edgcumbe suggested that a society be formed for the publication of such remains of the Cornish language as had not already been printed. He was supported by William Copeland Borlase and it was agreed[42]

there is sufficient on this subject to form a fair sized volume in the Gwavas collection and among the MSS of Dr. W. Borlase, the Cornish historian, preserved at Castle Horneck. Should its philological publications be successful, the society would probably extend its operation to other local literary antiquities.

A prospectus will be issued before long.

Soon afterwards the congress announced that membership of the society would cost one guinea and interested parties should contact Jenner or Borlase. But lack of money and probably a hostile reception from the Royal Institution of Cornwall and the Royal Cornwall Polytechnic Society, which probably felt such projects were their province, killed the idea.

Publication of manuscripts did go on, however. In 1872 Whitley Stokes edited and translated *Beunans Meriasek* for the Philological

Society.[43] He added to this a 'Glossary to *Beunans Meriasek*' in *Archives für celtische Lexicographie* and a short paper on Norris's *Ancient Cornish Drama*.[44] In the same volume Professor Loth examined aspects of the language. The columns of the *Revue Celtique* also carried numerous papers by Whitley Stokes, Professor Loth, Jenner and Lach-Szyrma. It was Stokes who pointed out the existence of 'The Prophecy of Merlin' manuscript and the former existence of a Cornish *Life of St Columba*.[45] Still little was published in Cornish journals except for a paper read by W. C. Borlase in 1878 to the Royal Institution of Cornwall on 'The Gatley collection of Cornish MSS deposited in the Muniment Room'. John Gatley had collected and recorded all sorts of out of the way Cornish information and the principal item of the collection was a copy of Keigwin's translation of *Gwreans an bys*, dated 1698, with a commonplace book kept by William Gwavas.

Towards the end of 1877 Jenner decided to try to stir up some public interest in the language among Cornish people. It had been an important year for him. First, he had married a Miss Rawlings, better known as the Cornish novelist Kitty Lee.[46] Secondly, it was the year he had discovered the famous 'Charter Fragment' described as 'probably the oldest existing piece of Cornish literature'.[47] Jenner was working in the British Museum cataloguing Additional and Egerton MSS and Charters which had been acquired by the Museum in 1854-75. His job was to draw up a very compressed description of the Additional Charters among which were thirty-seven grants of land in Cornwall, chiefly in St Stephen's parish in Brannell. These had been presented in 1872 by Sir Charles Trevelyan and were given under the reigns of Edward III to Edward IV. On the back of one charter Jenner saw some verses in Cornish. He first published them in *Athenaeum* in 1877 and sent a copy to Whitley Stokes who published a version in *Revue Celtique*. The year 1877 was also the centenary of the death of Dolly Pentreath. With Lach-Szyrma, Jenner organised a special commemoration service and messages were received from H. Gaidoz, founder and editor of *Revue Celtique,* and from the bishop of Truro who, to Jenner's puzzlement, sent the following message: '*kymmer dhe vytour, ha bydh yn dhe servys len*' (take thy mitre and be loyal in thy service).

It was, in fact, a message which had been sent to the bishop on his inauguration when Cornwall once more became an independent diocese (after 800 years) in 1876. Although they wished to publicise the language, at this stage both Jenner and Lach-Szyrma stood where

Davies Gilbert had done fifty years before them. They both 'rejoiced' in the death of Cornish as a vernacular and their interest in it was as a subject of historical and philological study. Nevertheless, the publicity surrounding the centenary became the main sparking point of the revivalist movement.

In 1879 the *Cornishman* newspaper offered a prize for an essay, written by a layman, on the language. Two essays were forthcoming both with glossaries, and both by Mousehole residents. The first essay was by the cantankerous Mousehole fisherman, Bernard Victor; the second was by W. P. Pentreath of Loon Bennett, Mousehole, then a student at the Wesleyan College at Westminster. The essays were sent by the newspaper to Professor John Rhys, who had just been appointed (in 1877) the first professor of Celtic at Merton College, Oxford. Rhys replied: 'On the whole, the writers show a great deal of enthusiasm for their subject and I find myself unable to decide on their merits as they are so nearly equal. I would suggest the prize be divided equally between them.' The essays were also sent to Jenner who endorsed the decision and the *Cornishman* published the essays.[48] The essays stirred up some controversy from a correspondent who signed himself 'W.N.' This turned out to be the same William Noy or Noyes who had clashed with Lach-Szyrma in the columns of the *Academy* a few years previously. Of the essays, he said, 'of course there is nothing new in them—nothing but what has been said over and over again'. Of Victor's 140 words only sixty to seventy were Cornish.[49] In the same issue W. J. P. Jago wrote enclosing a list of twenty-seven words which were in use in St Austell when he was a boy and which he maintained were Cornish. He subsequently supplied a lengthier word list which was published over three issues.[50] Hot words were penned over which were genuine Cornish words and which were not. On 12 June Mr J. Edwyn Pentreath wrote to suggest: 'Surely it should be the aim of Messrs. Victor, Pentreath, W. N. and Rev. Lach-Szyrma inter alia to unite in all researches as to bona fide remnants of Cornish philology, rather than bickering whether this or that word is a very exact Cornish?' The correspondence finally ended in August with Victor supplying a version of the Lord's Prayer in Cornish[51] and a correspondent 'A.T.' supplying a version of the Lord's Prayer in Breton for comparison.[52] The publication of lists of words thought to be Cornish and used in the Cornish dialect led to the publication of a *Glossary of Words in Use in Cornwall* by Miss M. A. Courtney and T. Quiller-Couch in 1880.

Two years later, Frederick W. P. Jago, who had supplied such long word lists to the *Cornishman*, published a book entitled *The Ancient Language and Dialect of Cornwall* in which he maintained:[53]

> that even now the Cornish people are speaking a large number of Celtic or ancient Cornish words without being very aware of it.
> The Cornish dialect may well be called the shadow, or penumbra, of the ancient language, the link between the old and new tongue, between Celtic and English.

From London, in 1887, he published an *English–Cornish Dictionary*. It was a compilation which was the result of many years of research; unfortunately, for the student, it was not a good work because it contained a lot of pseudo-Cornish and slang words.

But now interest in the language was growing and was not confined merely to scholars. In 1890 Lach-Szyrma published a small book from Truro entitled *The Last Lost Language of Europe*. It contained some first lessons in Cornish and although very elementary, they provided a means of learning the basis of the language. Throughout the century the Cornish language had been reduced to a few faintly glowing embers; but by the end of the century, sparks were beginning to be seen. It was the next century that saw the rekindling of a fire.

Chapter Seven

The Revivalists

In 1901 a group of Cornishmen formed a movement which aimed at the revival of Cornish as a spoken language, the 're-establishment' of a Gorsedd, along Welsh lines, and the encouragement of Cornish sports such as hurling and wrestling. The movement, which they called Cowethas Kelto–Kernuak (The Celtic–Cornish Society), was the brainchild of L. C. Duncombe Jewell who became its honorary secretary. Sir W. L. Salusbury Trelawny Bart. was elected president and Henry Jenner became one of three vice-presidents. It was a significant development. In 1877 Jenner, together with Lach-Szyrma and other language enthusiasts, had been echoing Davies Gilbert's 'rejoicing' that the Cornish language had died. Their interest in the language had been merely that of antiquarians and philologists. What had happened by 1901 to change Jenner's views and, indeed, the views of a sufficient proportion of interested persons that they formed a language revivalist movement?

The development in Cornwall must be seen in the context of the Celtic renaissance of the late nineteenth century. Celtic studies had, for the first time, become 'respectable' in English academic eyes mainly due to the work and influence of the great Continental Celtic scholars such as Hermann Ebel, Caspar Zeuss, Holger Pedersen, Kuno Meyer, Joseph Loth, Joseph Vendryes and E. Bachellery. Matthew Arnold, with his lectures on Celtic literature[1] was instrumental in getting the first professor of Celtic, John Rhys, appointed at Oxford in 1877. With this 'establishment' of Celtic studies came the sweeping away of the old myths which had sprung up about the Celtic peoples and their linguistic relationship to each other. Five years after his appointment Professor Rhys published *Early Britain: Celtic Britain* in which he set forth his views on Celtic origins. Rhys was to pick up, after very nearly two centuries, the work begun by Lhuyd in his *Archaeologia Britannica*. According to Glyn E. Daniel, '. . . in a welter of ten centuries of speculation and guesswork, Lhuyd and Rhys stand out as about the only people who

really sought an answer to our questions by serious means of scholarship'.[2]

Coupled with this scholastic enthusiasm for things Celtic, there came a popular reaction from the people of the Celtic countries against increasing Anglicisation and Frenchification. In Wales, the Education Act of 1870 contained no provision for teaching Welsh and all the schools established under the Act were English. It was in these schools that the notorious 'Welsh Not' was used; a stick hung round a child's neck with which he was beaten at the ending of the school day, was used as a punishment for speaking Welsh in or out of class. Welsh opinion, angered by such cruel monoglot methods in schools, reacted and this led to the formation of the Society for Utilizing the Welsh Language in 1885. Its aim was 'to see established in Wales a sound system of bilingual education such as that which exists in Switzerland, in the Flemish parts of Belgium and in several divisions of the Austrian Empire'. The movement was led by Dan Isaac Jones who, unfortunately, died in 1887 having fought a vigorous campaign to get the teaching of Welsh into the school curriculum in schools in those areas where Welsh was spoken. At this time (1901) there were 929,824 Welsh speakers, 49·9 per cent of the population, of which 15·1 per cent spoke Welsh only. The move for Welsh political independence, which had manifested itself in the 1860s when Welsh immigrants had tried to establish a Welsh-speaking state in Patagonia, called Y Wladfa, now consolidated itself into a political movement called Cymru Fydd (Future Wales) which was established about 1886. One of the most prominent Cymru Fydd leaders was David Lloyd George.[3]

In Scotland, where 230,806 people spoke Scottish Gaelic (only 5·57 per cent of the population of which 0·68 per cent were monoglot Gaelic speakers), there was a tremendous upsurge of interest in the Celtic revival, not only manifesting itself in Gaelic literature and the history of the Celtic peoples but in Celtic music, art, dress and sports. The lead in this was taken by a language movement called An Comunn Gaidhealach, formed in 1891, which pressed for the teaching of the language in schools in areas where it was spoken; its wider use; and the cultivation of literature, history and music art. Politically the Scots consolidated their movements for independence and a Scottish Home Rule Association was formed in Edinburgh in 1886. Between 1883 and 1895 a movement called Comunn An Fhearain (Highland Land League) was active in demanding the establishment of a radical Scottish state. It was moribund between 1895 and the turn of

the century when Dr Gavin Brown Clark (1840-1925), a Scottish Member of Parliament who had been associated with Marx's First International, revived it. Dr Clark was involved in presenting numerous Self Government for Scotland Bills in the early years of the century. An Fhearain tried hard to prevent the decay of the language.

The Celtic revival touched the smallest of the Celtic nations, the Isle of Man, where, in 1901, only 4,419 people spoke Manx, 8·1 per cent of the population. The decline of Manx speakers had been extremely rapid since 1866 when the Manx Parliament, Tynwald, had been reconstituted. In fact, Henry Jenner, who took an interest in Manx, conducted a survey in 1874 and found that there were then 12,350 Manx speakers, well over 25 per cent of the population.[4] On 22 March 1899, the Manx enthusiasts formed Yn Cheshaght Ghailckagh (The Gaelic League) to preserve Manx as the national language and to study and publish existing Manx literature and cultivate modern literature in the language.

In Ireland there had been a rapid decline of Irish speakers following the Great Famine. In 1851 there were 1,524,286 Irish speakers of whom 319,602 spoke no English. This represented 23·3 per cent of the population. By 1891 the population of Ireland had dropped by two million and Irish speakers had dropped to 680,245 of which 38,192 spoke no English—this represented 14·5 per cent of the population. Had the so called 'National School' system, introduced in Ireland in 1831, been what its title (an utter misnomer) suggested it was, then the language might have been safeguarded. By 1901, however, the rapid decrease had been in part halted. At this time there were 641,145 Irish speakers of whom 20,953 were Irish monoglots, representing 14·4 per cent of the population. The foundation of the Society for the Preservation of the Irish Language in 1876 and the Gaelic Union in 1878 showed the growing consciousness of the people towards the importance of the language. But the real revivalist movement began when the Irish scholar, Dr Douglas Hyde, gave his lecture on 'The Necessity for De-Anglicising Ireland in 1892'. This led to the foundation of Conradh na Gaeilge (The Gaelic League) on 31 July 1893 'to preserve Irish as the national language of Ireland and to spread its use as a spoken language'. According to Brian Ó Cuív: 'by 1901 the effects of the Gaelic Revival were reflected in the Census Returns, for although the number of Irish speakers continued to fall in the Gaeltacht [Irish speaking] areas elsewhere in the country increases were recorded.' From 1879 Irish had been allowed as an extra subject to be taught

outside school hours but Conradh na Gaeilge pressure forced the authorities to let Irish be taught in school hours from 1901 onwards. It was not until 1906-7 that Irish was allowed as a teaching medium in Gaeltacht schools. The Irish language movement, initially, achieved the most success in the fight against Anglicisation. The language movement can be said to have been the great inspiring force behind the 1916 uprising in Ireland.

The Celtic revival also made its presence felt in Brittany but the French did not look on the renaissance with the superficial liberality which England displayed. Since the smashing of Breton autonomy, the destruction of the Breton Parliament in 1789 and the suppression of the Breton guerilla forces, all things Breton had been firmly crushed. Inter-Celtic relations, however, continued in spite of this, especially between Brittany and Wales. The first Inter-Celtic Congress was organised in 1867 at St Brieuc by the Association Bretonne (which legally had been banned by the French Government in 1858). Petitions to get Breton taught in schools (there were then about two and a half million Breton speakers) met with firm refusals. In 1870 Charles de Gaulle, a poet in the language and an uncle of General Charles de Gaulle, the late president of France, and Henri Gaidoz, editor of the *Revue Celtique*, petitioned that Breton be taught in schools. In 1895 Kevredigez Vreiz (Association Bretonne) published a manifesto asking for the teaching of the language in schools. The answer of the French government in 1903 was the prohibition of Breton in churches, despite the fact that all Breton deputies in the French Assembly supported the demand for the teaching of the language. In spite of this suppression, Breton literature flourished and philologists and scholars, such as Joseph Loth, Le Roux and F. Vallée, gave new possibilities to Celtic studies. In 1898 the Union Régionaliste de Bretagne was established which sought administrative and cultural freedom. In 1900 a Breton delegation attended the Eisteddfod in Wales and decided to establish a Gorzez Breiz, a Breton Gorsedd, on Welsh lines. The Gorzez Breiz was founded in 1901 under the direction of Le Fustec, Berthou-Kaledvouc'h and Taldir-Jaffrenou. From this time on Celtic Congresses between all the Celtic countries were held annually. In 1905 a language movement called Bleunn-Brug was formed to seek status for the language and further Breton literature.

The rumblings throughout the Celtic world were bound to have repercussions in Cornwall. But whereas, in the other Celtic countries, the great cultural revival movements became the spring-board of

11 Henry Jenner, 1848-1934, 'Father of the Cornish Language Revival', first Grand Bard of Cornwall (Gwas Myghal), 1928-34

12 Robert Morton Nance (Mordon), 1873-1959, second Grand Bard of Cornwall, 1935-59. He is pictured here at the Bodmin Gorsedd of September 1956

13 A. S. D. Smith (Caradar), 1883-1950, pictured here in the robes of a Welsh bard

15   R. St V. Allin-Collins (Halwyn), one of the most prolific story writers in the early days of the language revival

16 The first Celtic Congress to be held in Truro, Cornwall, in 1932, with Henry Jenner (centre) as president. The third person to Jenner's left is Dr Douglas Hyde, 1860-1949, Professor of Modern Irish at University College, Dublin, founder of *Conradh na Gaeilge* (The Gaelic League) who, in 1938, became the first President of Ireland

17 Cornish language lessons being given to pupils of Mount Pleasant House School, Camborne, by E. G. R. Hooper (Talek), the third Grand Bard of Cornwall, 1959-65

18 (opposite above)   The Cornish Gorsedd at Dawns Men, St Buryan, September 1971. Following the swordbearer, left to right, is the Grand Bard of Cornwall (Denis Trevanyon), Grand Druid of Brittany (Pierre Loisel), the Marshal of the Welsh Gorsedd, and Rev. Gwyndaf Evans (former Archdruid of Wales)

19 (opposite left)   A ceremony from the Cornish Gorsedd at St Buryan, September 1971, showing *Arlodhes a Gernow*, the Lady of Cornwall, Ursula Laws, with her pages and attendant dancers

20 (opposite right)   Swordbearer Edmund Hambly and Robert Morton Nance at the Lelant Gorsedd of September 1953

21 (below)   A scene from a Cornish Gorsedd showing, left to right, Richard Jenkin (Map Dyvroeth), editor of *New Cornwall*, E. G. R. Hooper (the Grand Bard, Talek), F. B. Cargeeg (Tan Dyvarow) and, bareheaded, Dr Laurent Erwan le Barzic of Brittany

22   A scene from the 1972 Cornish Gorsedd

movements for political and economic independence, which were quite strong at this time, in Cornwall such ideas of political independence were not to manifest themselves in any concrete form until the 1950s. The Cornish-language enthusiasts, having rediscovered their Celtic past, felt Cornwall should not be backward in becoming part of the greater pan-Celtic cultural revival. Throughout the Celtic world the Celts were beginning to realise more about their suppressed and forgotten histories, customs, languages and literatures. It was learnt that the kilt was not only the national dress of Scotland but had once been common to all Celtic countries. In Scotland the Hon. S. Ruadhri Erskine of Marr published a book on the Celtic renaissance which included observations on the kilt.[5] In Ireland, Gaelic Leaguers adopted the saffron or the green kilt, while Bretons adopted a kilt with less success. The secretary of Cowethas Kelto–Kernuak, Duncombe Jewell, was the first to introduce, or perhaps re-introduce, the wearing of the kilt into Cornwall. He wore a blue kilt and, in 1904, when he was admitted as a bard to the Welsh Gorsedd he chose the bardic name of Bardd Glas (Blue Bard). There are two styles of kilt currently worn by Cornishmen: a plain black kilt and a rather synthetic tartan called 'the Cornish National Tartan'.

The Celtic renaissance must also be seen in an even wider context. Throughout Europe there were many small nations incorporated into larger state territories, ruled by bigger nations. For example, from the thirteenth century until 1809 Sweden and Finland were considered one country until Finland was ceded to the Russian Empire. From 1380 Norway had been unified with Denmark and Danish had replaced the Norwegian language. Lithuania, on the other hand, was recognised merely as an annexed territory of Russia. Throughout their histories such small nationalities, including the Celts, had struggled against their imperialist conquerors in various ways. But the nineteenth century saw the rise of the great liberalism, the acceptance of the theory of national independence. The independence of small nations was, after all, supposed to be the main ideal behind the struggle of the First World War. In the nineteenth century, all over Europe, small nations were struggling to be free—the banners of Byron, Garibaldi, Mazzini, Bolívar and others inspired countless men and women. Throughout these small countries, as in the Celtic countries, the native cultures and languages had suffered greatly under the pressure of the imperial languages and cultures; in order to counteract this, language movements sprang up in the small nations. Generally, it was

F

the language movement which came first, giving the basis to the
national political and economic struggle. Strangely enough, it is only
in Ireland that we have a case of a small European nationality which
won, in part, national independence, and the successive governments
which pledged to restore the native language and culture, and failed
miserably in doing so. In every other country which gained independence at more or less the same time, and had to revive its language,
such revivals have been carried out with a marked success. The list
of nationalities is impressive: the Albanians, Armenians, Czechs,
Estonians, Faroese, Finns, Latvians, Lithuanians, Norwegians, Poles,
Rumanians, Slovakians, Slovenians and Ukrainians. We might also add
the Israelis, but their restoration of Hebrew (a dead language for
nearly 2,000 years) was carried out in exceptional circumstances.[6]

The Cornish-language enthusiasts, having started their language
revivalist movement, now found their sister Celtic nations somewhat
reluctant to recognise their claim to be a Celtic nation. J. Hobson
Matthews, the St Ives historian, was one of the first Cornish people
to be recognised as fellow Celtic bards by the Welsh. In 1899 he
became a bard of the Welsh Gorsedd as Mab Cernyw (Son of Cornwall)
with Reginald Reynolds (Gwas Piran) and Mrs Tangye Reynolds
(Merch Eia). Jenner was similarly honoured by the Bretons as Gwas
Mikael (Michael's Servant) at their third Gorsedd. During the same
visit to Brittany, in September 1903, Jenner was invited to address a
congress of the Union Regionaliste Bretonne at Lesneven, Finistere, on
why Cornwall should be recognised as a Celtic country. He afterwards
recalled: '. . . I tried the experiment of a Cornish speech on an
audience of educated Bretons. They understood almost all of it.'

In 1904 Jenner, addressing the Celtic Congress on why Cornwall
should be admitted to the congress as a Celtic nation, was met with
some scepticism. Delegates argued that Cornwall was no longer
Celtic. Jenner delivered an address on Cornish history entitled
'Cornwall: a Celtic nation'[7] which was well received and, when it
came to a vote, the majority of delegates supported Cornwall's ad-
mission. Jenner immediately received a telegram of congratulations
from Dr Hambly Rowe (Tolzethan) in Cornish. Jenner proudly
showed this to those delegates who had claimed everything Celtic in
Cornwall was dead.

With the gathering interest in the Cornish language, thanks to
the propaganda efforts of Cowethas Kelto–Kernuak, a demand was
growing for a suitable textbook by which to learn the language.

Lach-Szyrma's work with its first steps in Cornish was very elementary and so Duncombe Jewell suggested to Jenner that he should write a grammar. This grammar would become the basis of the revival. In 1904 David Nutt of London published Jenner's *Handbook of the Cornish Language*, which gave a brief history of the language as well as a grammar. The book proved to be the mainspring of the revivalist movement. In it Jenner tried to answer the question:

> Why should Cornishmen learn Cornish? There is no money in it, it serves no practical purpose, and the literature is scanty and of no great originality or value. The question is a fair one, the answer is simple. Because they are Cornish.

By 1907 Jenner had written a Cornish version of the Gorsedd ceremonies in preparation for the inauguration of a Cornish Gorsedd but there were not enough Cornish speakers or interested persons to establish a Gorsedd at this time. Why was the Gorsedd so important to the Cornish revivalists? The origins of the Gorsedd go back to the origins of the Celts themselves. The writers of Greece and Rome mention such gatherings. We can, with certainty, go back to the bardic competitions in Wales in the twelfth and thirteenth centuries. These gatherings became known as Eisteddfodau (*Eisteddfod,* a session— *eistedd,* to sit). It is popularly thought that the Lord Rhys ap Gruffydd held the first historical Eisteddfod in Cardigan in 1176. But the Eisteddfod was not just a meeting of poets. According to the Welsh *Chronicle of Princes* it was a contest 'between bards and poets, between harpists and crowders, and pipers and various classes of musical craft'. Eisteddfodau continued to be held in Wales under the patronage of the Welsh rulers, and after the English Conquest, to a lesser extent, under the Tudors. On 20 May 1594, an Eisteddfod was organised but was not successful and, by 1650, we find an anonymous Welsh poet lamenting the passing of the old bardic order. In September 1789, an Eisteddfod was held at Bala under the patronage of the London Welsh. The Eisteddfod movement grew and Eisteddfodau were held at St Asaph in 1790, Llanrwst in 1791 and Denbigh in 1792. The literary life of the country was reawakened and brought into a living tradition once again.

In 1792, however, Iolo Morganwg formed a Gorsedd of Welsh Bards as a rival to the Eisteddfod. The Gorsedd was not simply an arts gathering but involved what was then presumed to be Druidical

ceremony and costume. In 1819 at the regional Carmarthen Eisteddfod, arranged by the Cambrian Society of Dyfed, the Gorsedd became part of the Eisteddfod ceremony and today the Gorsedd is held on the day before the Eisteddfod when prize winners of the previous Eisteddfod are announced. It was with the great Eisteddfod of Llangollen, in 1858, that the gathering became a national festival and a recognised part of the Welsh way of life.[8] The Bretons had borrowed their Gorzez Breiz from the Eisteddfod in 1901 and Cowethas Kelto–Kernuak hoped they could inaugurate their own Gorseth Kernow. While the Cornish word is *Gorseth* I have used throughout the pan-Celtic word *Gorsedd*.

Shortly after the shelving of the Gorsedd scheme, Duncombe Jewell resigned as secretary of Cowethas Kelto–Kernuak and left Cornwall. Without his dynamism, his driving force, the movement lapsed. Nevertheless, it had created interest among a number of people and between 1901 and 1902 a number of poems in Cornish, written by Jenner, Duncombe Jewell and the Breton poet C. A. Picquenard (Ar Barz Melen) were published in the magazine *Celtia*, a pan-Celtic monthly published by the Celtic Association from Dublin between 1901 and 1903. Poems also appeared in the *Cornish Telegraph* during the same period. It was the beginning of a new Cornish literature.

Two Cornishmen learning the language at this time were to influence the revival movement. One was William Daniel Watson, of whom E. G. R. Hooper has stated: 'no one has spoken Cornish in so authentic a fashion as Watson';[9] the other was Robert Morton Nance who was to originate the Unified Cornish spelling system and thus become the principal figure of the revivalist movement. Watson was thirteen years old, attending Mylor National School, when he saw a footnote in a book in Cornish: '*kemer uith na rey gara an vor goth rag an vor noueth*' (take care not to forsake the old road for the new road). Watson wrote, 'neither Cornish language nor Cornish history were ever mentioned in school'.[10] In the winter of 1901 Watson met a man called J. W. Bull, a french polisher, who had a good knowledge of the language and even had traditional knowledge of Cornish words and phrases. Watson started studying Cornish from books in Falmouth Free Library. In 1904, after an accident on a boat in Mylor Creek, Watson found himself in Falmouth Hospital where he met an old lady with traditional knowledge of the numerals. Jenner's *Handbook* helped Watson's study and he corresponded with the Rev. H. L. Leverton of Mawnan Sanctuary for some years. Leverton also knew

the language. Watson spent some time going round the country picking up traditional pieces of the language from people such as George Hall of Mylor, George Bray of Lanner, Mr Dunn of Trevarth, John George of Mullion and others. It was not until 1918 that A. P. Jenkin of Trewirgie introduced Watson to Jenner and Morton Nance and later Richard Hall of St Just-in-Penwith, the leading figures of the revivalist movement.

Robert Morton Nance had been born in Cardiff in 1873 of Cornish parents. His father was from Padstow, one of the Nances of Trengove, Illogan. In 1878 the family moved to Penarth where he spent most of his youth. He studied art in Cardiff and in Bushey, Hertfordshire, marrying a fellow student, Beatrice Michell, who was to die in 1900. Nance began to write poetry and illustrate it for Arthur Quiller-Couch's famous *Cornish Magazine*. He won an art prize in the Welsh Eisteddfod at Cardiff in 1899:[11]

My own interest in Cornish came, I expect, from my father's comparison of Cornish names with Welsh, of which he knew a little, having had at least enough interest in it to get a dictionary and grammar. Living then in Wales, this was an obvious thing to do, but to learn Welsh was more difficult for a Victorian in Wales than it is now. Myself, I associated with Welsh speaking boys at school, but got practically nothing from them, their instinct seeming to be to guard their language as a private one amongst themselves: though later, of course, I met with others who realised that a Cornishman or a Breton was a sort of cousin.

Nance learnt his first Cornish from Borlase's *Antiquities* and Sandys's *Specimens of Cornish Provincial Dialect*. When Jenner's *Handbook* appeared he devoured it eagerly but

even the *Handbook* did not get me to the stage of attempting to write or speak the language, as the projected book of exercises might have done had it been printed. If I could puzzle out such things in Cornish as were printed in a Penzance newspaper that seemed enough.

In 1906 Nance had remarried to Annie Maud Cawker and settled in Cornwall at Nancledra, between St Ives and Penzance. While there he wrote a number of dialect plays for children now published collectively

as *The Cledry Plays*. In 1909 Jenner, having retired from the British Museum, settled at Hayle. The two men met while Nance was researching at Falmouth for a book, *A Glossary of Cornish Sea Words*, which was not to be published until after his death as a memorial volume in 1959. The two men became firm friends.

During the next decade Jenner and Nance devoted themselves to research on the language and, with other enthusiasts, gathered as much traditional Cornish as they could. The result of this research appeared in a series of papers which were read to the Royal Institution of Cornwall and to the Royal Cornwall Polytechnic Society and subsequently published in the annual volumes of those bodies. Jenner tried to get the Royal Institution to take an interest in a systematic study of the language for the purpose of translating place names. At the annual meeting of the Institution on 9 December 1909, Jenner proposed: 'That it is desirable that the Royal Institution of Cornwall should take some steps towards promoting a systematic general survey and collection of Cornish place and family names, with a view to their correct interpretation.' In making the proposition as an introduction to a paper on 'Cornish place names', Jenner remarked:[12]

> The spoken language may be dead, but its ghost still haunts its
> old dwelling, the speech of West Cornish country folk is full of
> it, and no one can talk about the country and its inhabitants in
> any sort of topographical detail without using a wealth of
> Cornish words.

Jenner translated many songs and poems from English into Cornish and also wrote several original sonnets in Cornish, particularly '*Gwaynten yn Kernow*' (Spring in Cornwall) and '*An Pempthack Pell*' (The Fifteen Balls), which is dated August 1921, and included in the Cornish manuscripts of the National Library of Wales.[13] He also wrote '*Dho'm Gwreg Gernauk*' (To My Cornish Wife), which he composed in 1904 and used to preface his *Handbook*:

Kerra ow Holon! Beniges re vo
Gans bennath Dew an dedh a'th ros dhemmo,
Dho whelas gerryow gwan pan dhetha vi,
Tavas dhe dassow, ha dho'th droyva di.
En cov an dedh splan-na es pel passyes;

En cov idn dedh lowenek, gwin 'gan bes,
War Garrak Loys en Cos, es en dan skes
Askelly Myhal El, o 'gan gwithes;
En cov lias dedh wheg en Kernow da,
Ha ny mar younk—na whekkah vel er-ma
Dhemmo a dhig genev an gwell tra,
Pan dhetha vi en kerh, en ol bro-na;
Dheso mi re levar dha davas teg,
Flogh ow empinyon vi, dho'm kerra Gweg.

Dearest of my heart! Blessed has been the day that God's blessing
gave you to me. Coming to seek words of the language of my
fathers I found you. In memory of that great day, long ago. How
happy we were. On St Michael's Mount the shadow of the
archangel's wings preserved us. In memory of many sweet days
in good Cornwall. And I so young—and not better now. The
best thing happened to me when you came. To you I have given
this beautiful language child of my mind—to my dearest wife.

The work of Jenner appeared in some unexpected places. In 1916,
during the First World War, the London *Daily Mirror* published the
soldiers' marching song 'It's a long, long way to Tipperary' in
the languages of the British Empire. Jenner supplied a Cornish
version. It was also thanks to Jenner that Cornish adorns the walls
of the entrance porch of the Pool of Bethesda in Jerusalem. The
miracle of Jesus Christ curing the sick man at the Pool of Bethesda is
recounted in the fifth chapter of St John's Gospel. Inside the city of
Jerusalem, near St Stephen's Gate, known to the Moslems as Bab
Sitti Maryam (Lady Mary's Gate), is situated the pool which, in
1878, became the property of the Society of Missionaries to Africa
(the White Fathers) who established a training college there for
Byzantine clergy. It was they who rediscovered and repaired the old
pool and on the walls of the entrance porch started to carve the
pertinent biblical passage from John 5: 1-14. The passage was carved
in the various languages of the world and after the British took
Jerusalem from the Turks, in 1917, Jenner supplied the Cornish
version which is headed:

*Awell san Jowan, an pempes cabydul, gwersy un dhe beswarthek
treylys yn Kernewek gans Henry Jenner.*

The inscription was last reportedly seen by J. L. Palmer when editor of the *Cornishman*, who visited Jerusalem in 1931.[14]

In 1914 Nance had settled in Carbis Bay, St Ives, but had volunteered for army service during the war years. After the war Nance and Jenner decided that a new movement must be formed to replace Cowethas Kelto–Kernuak so that a new direction would be given to those interested in the language. In 1920 they formed the first Old Cornwall Society at St Ives with the motto '*Cuntelleugh An Brewyon Us Gesy Na Vo Kellys Travyth*' (Gather Ye The Fragments That Are Left That Nothing Be Lost!). The aim of the society was the preservation of all that was Celtic in Cornwall, especially the language. Jenner became president and under a resurgence of interest in things Cornish, the society grew and new societies had to be formed to meet the demand in various parts of Cornwall. By 1924 there were enough societies in Cornwall to form a Federation of Old Cornwall Societies with Jenner as president and Nance as recorder. Another Cornish scholar and historian, A. K. Hamilton Jenkin, became secretary. He did a lot in helping the foundation of more societies and at the present time there are thirty-four societies in existence. In 1925 the Federation started the publication of *Old Cornwall*, a twice yearly journal averaging fifty pages which has been published regularly ever since. The journal is a must for all students of Cornish and in its early editions it carried short stories, mainly by Nance, and articles on grammar, place names, as well as articles on the history and remains of the language.

There were at this time five leading spirits in the revivalist movement. Jenner and Nance were the undisputed leaders of the movement. Of Nance, E. G. R. Hooper comments: 'As editor of the *Old Cornwall* magazine he wrote articles of lasting value, both interpreting Late Cornish spelling that had baffled many and being able to write Middle Cornish handwriting with exactitude, and today the authority on Cornish place names and folk-lore.' The other three prominent revivalists were W. D. Watson (Tyrvab), R. St V. Allin-Collins (Halwyn) and Richard Hall of St Just-in-Penwith. These five men were the first to really revive conversational Cornish.

In London Trelawney Roberts was conducting Cornish classes and so was Allin-Collins, who was a professional translator. It was Allin-Collins who insisted that his pupils should talk the language rather than merely write it, proving, by his example, that it could be done. E. G. R. Hooper recalls 'his keenness sometimes led him to make unsubstantiated statements as in his paper in the *Zeitschrift für Celtische*

Philologie XV. 3'. This was, in fact, mentioned in a London *Times* editorial: 'A Cornishman born as late as 1878 and writing quite recently in the *Zeitschrift für Celtische Philologie* has claimed to be a living repository of a few phrases which he learnt through family tradition in early childhood.'[15] Allin-Collins re-endorsed this claim in his *Cornish Grammar*, published in London in 1927, in which he writes: 'It is wrong to conclude that Cornish is a dead language; neglected, it has fallen into disuse, but there are still some who know it as a living language, not excepting the writer of this grammar.' Hooper comments: 'Unluckily his *Grammar* . . . fails to show his ability; he tried to compile a class-book but was unable to attend to the proof pages and his illness prevented travel to Cornwall.' Nevertheless, Allin-Collins, under the bardic name of Halwyn (he was to become a bard of the Cornish Gorsedd in 1933 by examination in the language) was a prolific writer of short stories in Cornish and did a great deal to interest the London Cornish Association in the language. A number of his short stories were published in the *St Ives Times* and some short stories of his also appeared in a small book *An Den ha'y Dheu Wreg* (The Man and his Two Wives) by Nance, published in St Ives in 1927, with the subtitle 'and some short stories in the Cornish language by Edith Grenville and Halwyn'. Other tales of Halwyn may be found in the National Library of Wales dated between May and December, 1928. Among them is '*Clappiansow an Treghas Treus*' (The Dour Tailor) and '*Davydd Trewortha*' ('An improbable tale of love and war').[16]

In 1923 a noted scholar, Professor Henry Lewis, published a handbook of Middle Cornish in Welsh, *Llawlyfr Cernyweg Canol*. It provided Welsh students with an excellent guide to the language and a second edition was published in 1946. However, during the twenty years which elapsed between editions Nance and A. S. D. Smith had done a vast amount of research and work on the language. Hooper comments: 'Unfortunately, Lewis ignored all this work in his 1946 edition—partly because it might have been said, that the work of Nance and Smith could not be effectively published there being no university not even a learned journal, which might help.'[17]

In 1924 Ernest George Retallack Hooper from St Agnes contacted Nance, who was then running classes in St Ives. He learnt the language from Jenner's *Handbook*. Later he went to work in London and seized the opportunity to attend Allin-Collins's classes in Fenchurch Street. Hooper became one of the first five bards of the Cornish Gorsedd to be admitted by proficiency in the language, under the bardic name Talek,

in 1932. In 1924, also, Trelawney Roberts had read a paper on the language to the London Cornish Association which was well reported in the press and a great deal of enthusiasm was aroused. During the same year Nance, the historian C. C. Henderson, and Canon G. H. Doble (historian of the lives of Cornish saints) formed the Cornish delegation to the Celtic Congress in Brittany. A Celtic Congress due to be held in Cornwall two years later had to be cancelled because of a rail strike.

Interest in the language was growing steadily but there were many difficulties for learners. Not the least of these were the many discrepancies in spelling and finding new words to express modern concepts. The subject occupied Nance and he set to work to find a unified system of spelling based on the surviving Middle Cornish literature. In 1929 Nance published *Cornish For All* embodying his unified spelling system; henceforward students adopted his instructions on phonology, spelling and punctuation and the history of the language passed into a new phase—Unified Cornish. Writing in the magazine *Gwalarn*, M. Roparz Hemon (author of *Précis Grammaire Bretonne, Geriadurig—dourne* and *Brezonek—Gallek*, etc.) described *Cornish For All* as 'a work that may serve as a basis for the revival of Cornish'.[18]

The number of students and interested persons had now grown to such a proportion that it was felt the time had come to make Jenner's long-cherished dream of a Cornish Gorsedd into a reality. In August 1928, Jenner and Nance attended a meeting of the Welsh Gorsedd at Treorchy for initiations as bards. Jenner took the bardic name of Gwas Myghal (the Cornish equivalent to his Breton bardic name of Gwaz Mikael) and Nance took that of Mordon. Jenner and other Cornish writers such as Allin-Collins, who was honoured as a Breton bard, Lokmaria Ker, on 10 September 1928, wrote articles explaining the importance of the establishment of a Cornish Gorsedd and the recognition of the hegemony of the Gorsedd y Beirdd Ynys Prydain. Allin-Collins made two pleas in the *Cornish Guardian*: 'Cornish is an ancient language: a plea for its study' and 'The Gorsedd: what it should mean for us'.[19] The day before the first Cornish Gorsedd the *Cornish Guardian* wrote of the revivalists:

> They believe, as most Cornishmen do, that the preservation of
> the Cornish spirit in this levelling age is a good thing in itself.
> They see no better way of doing it than by the revival of the ideal
> of Celtic culture. And this means by which they seek to preserve
> that ideal is the same that the Welshmen have used for many

centuries and the Bretons have recently adopted—the study of Celtic history and literature, certainly: but more broadly the general cultivation of the Cornish people as they are, without any attempt whatever to archaise them.

But there was little publicity in the newspapers when, on 21 September, at the ancient stone circle of Boscawen Un, the first Gorseth Kernow ceremony was held, despite the thousands of spectators and mayors and civic dignatories who attended to see Jenner installed as the Barth Mur (Grand Bard) of Cornwall. The Archdruid Pedrog of Wales (Rev. Howell Elvet Lewis) assisted by two Welsh bards Dr J. Maurice Jones (Elfed) and D. Rhys Phillips (Beili Glas) conducted the inauguration and initiation of twelve Cornish bards. These were Sir Arthur Quiller-Couch; A. K. Hamilton Jenkin, the historian; John Coulson Tregarthen, president of the Royal Institution of Cornwall and a naturalist; the Rev. Canon Thomas Taylor (author of *The Celtic Christianity of Cornwall*, Longmans Green, 1916); Charles Henderson, history lecturer at Corpus Christi, Oxford; William Tregoning Hooper, an exponent of Cornish wrestling; John Dryden Hosken, a poet; and George Sloggett of the Cardiff Cornish Association. The ceremony has been held every year since 1928. It is usually held on the first Saturday in September when the blue-robed Cornish bards (there are no Druids or Ovates in the Cornish Gorsedd such as there are in Wales and Brittany) meet to declare the loyalty of Cornishmen to Cornwall, their language and Celtic culture. There are usually delegates from Wales and Brittany as well as from the other Celtic countries who bring fraternal greetings. The Cornish bards are distinguished from their Celtic bardic cousins by the black and gold bars on their head-dresses. Bards are admitted to the Gorseth Kernow—as in Wales and Brittany—when they have been adjudged worthy for the work they have done in the arts, or other fields. Since 1932 bards have also been admitted for knowledge of the language. Initially bardship was given to those who submitted an essay or story or verses of their own composition in the language which reached a sufficient standard. There were five such bardships given in 1932. Today bardship for knowledge of the language is given when candidates have passed three exacting examinations in Cornish which they may not take in less than two successive yearly sittings. The Gorsedd's literary competitions, dating from 1940, have done much to foster a modern Cornish literature.

The 1930s was an exciting decade for the revivalists. One of the most significant events was the arrival of a Sussex schoolteacher named A. S. D. Smith among the revivalists' ranks. Smith, who was born in Hurstpierpoint in 1883, had already applied himself to Welsh and had written a Welsh textbook called *Welsh Made Easy*, which ran to three editions between 1925 and 1929. It was regarded as the best Welsh instructional book of its time. Smith learnt the basis of Cornish through Henry Lewis's book *Llawlyfr Cernyweg Canol* but, seeking more knowledge, he wrote to Lewis for further information. Lewis put Smith in touch with Nance and with the aid of *Cornish For All* Smith became quite fluent. In 1930 Smith was teaching modern languages at Blundell's School, Tiverton, and decided to teach Cornish to a group of interested boys as an extra curricular subject. The progress his class made inspired Smith to produce a small work entitled *Lessons in Spoken Cornish* which appeared in 1931. The booklet immediately sold 500 copies. A second edition was prepared with the collaboration of Nance but its publication could not be financed until 1962. Smith was convinced, because of the progress his pupils had made, as Halwyn had been before him, that Cornish could be revived as a generally spoken language. The same year as Smith's *Lessons in Spoken Cornish*, W. D. Watson produced a little phrase book called *First Steps in Cornish*. Mr Hooper remarks, 'he was better qualified than others to record words and phrases known to a few old people and which he passed on to Nance.'

In 1932—an especially busy year—the Celtic Congress met in Cornwall for the first time, with Jenner as president. Delegates heard speeches in Cornish from eight Cornish bards. They were also entertained by the performance of the first one-act play to be written in modern Unified Cornish. This was *An Balores* (The Chough) written by Nance. The chough is a bird which used to frequent Cornwall and is to Cornwall what the dragon is to Wales or the lion to England. The play takes the form of an inquiry into the apparent death of the bird in which lived the national spirit of Cornwall. Eventually the 'bird of King Arthur' revives and flies away to a general rejoicing and the singing of '*Can Palores*' (Song of the Chough). The play was published shortly afterwards. As president of the Celtic Congress Jenner seized the opportunity to state that Cornish ought to be an optional subject in the schools of Cornwall. Apart from a headline in the *Western Morning News* there was no reaction at all from the educational authorities. The year 1932 also saw Canon Doble presenting an

English version of *Beunans Meriasek* or, in the new spelling *Bewnans Meryasek*, at Redruth in order to interest people in the old Cornish dramas. At the Gorsedd that year five bards were admitted by examination for their knowledge in the language. Three of them were to become important leaders of the revivalist movement—A. S. D. Smith (Caradar), E. G. R. Hooper (Talek) and Edwin Chirgwin (Map Melyn).

It is Edwin Chirgwin (1892-1960) who has been acclaimed as, perhaps, the foremost of modern Cornish poets. As headmaster of St Cleer school, Chirgwin had taught his pupils the Lord's Prayer and Creed in Cornish and was supported by a school inspector, Mr Guest, who was in sympathy with the idea of teaching children some knowledge of their past. Professor J. J. Parry, writing in 1946,[20] commented that Chirgwin deserved first place among Cornish poets for such works as '*An Jynjy gesys dhe goll*' (The Deserted Engine Room), '*Den Hanternos*' (At Midnight), '*An Velin Goth*' (The Old Mill) and '*Gorthewer*' (Evening).[21] While '*An Velin Goth*' shows considerable metrical ability, *Gorthewer* is, perhaps, the best example of Chirgwin using a sonnet form in Cornish:

Ny-allaf-vy leveral, oll a-dheth
ajy ow holon omma yn ow saf
Pan es ow-merwel deth pur-snell yn Haf
Ha gallas war y forth an howl dh'y veth.
A-ugh an bron y-teth yn hell an lor
Ha powes whek wor all an bys a-goth,
Yma y'n ebron haneth steren-goth
Ha golow-lor a-gram a-hes an dor.
Hem yu an ur hag oll a whyla cres
A-ugh ow fen comolow munys a
Rag tewlel war ken tyrgow aga skes
Ha codha wor an gwelyow yn glaw da
Mis ot! guth cuf gorthewer plas a-re
Ha gans gonesek coth y-whylaf tre.

I cannot tell of all the things that came
into my heart as I was standing here
while the summer day
was quickly dying and the sun had gone
upon the road that leads him to his grave.

Above the hill slowly the moon goes up
and sweet response falls upon all the earth
in the sky tonight there is a shooting star
and all along the ground the moonlight creeps.
This is the hour when all things seek for peace
over my head the small clouds move along
to cast their shadow upon other lands
and fall in good rain on the open fields
But lo! evening giving way to kindly dew
with the old worker I seek a home.

'*An Jynjy gesys dhe goll*' (The Deserted Engine Room) is another example of Chirgwin's poetry worthy of note. Here he has captured the spirit of the deserted Cornish mines in three verses using alternate rhymes:

My a gews hep let, my a gan a goll
War ow fossow los ydhyow gwer a dyf
Lun a wakter of, ynnof lyes toll
Genefbryny du powes where a gyf

My a lever whath a'n bledhynnow pell
Pan o lun a whel pyth yu gwak yw gwyr;
Kynth of trygva taw, gwyns ha glaw a dell
Kepar del o tellys gans tus yn lür.

Agan spyrysyon y'm mysk-vy a vew
Avel kerens da y a dryk ajy
Tarosvan of-yn gwel oll yn few
Nyns us mes nos a guth ow notha-vy.

I talk without hindrance, I sing of a loss,
On my walls green ivy grows
I'm full of emptiness, in me many holes
Crows find their rest in me.

I tell still of the distance years
When what is empty now was full of work.
Though I'm a silent dwelling,
wind and rain bore like the old men used to bore.

Their spirits live among me
like good friends staying with me
Phantom I am in sight of life
only night covers my nakedness.

A shorter example of Chirgwin's poetry is the following piece
entitled 'Ro dhymmo-vy dha dhorn' (Give me your hand):[22]

Pan vo whans dhyso rak car,
Pan vo'n forth unyk hep par,
Ha'th gwaytyans yu gwan hep mar,
Ro dhymmo-vy dha dhorn.

Pan vo'n genef pur dhu,
Hag hep golow nos a sew,
Y'n ancombrynsy ha gew,
Ro dhymmo-vy dha dhorn.

When you want a friend,
When the way is lonely, indeed,
and your hope is weak,
Give me your hand.

When my outlook is dark,
and night is following on,
in trouble and woe,
give me your hand.

On 31 December 1932, the Western Morning News published a
speech of Jenner's concerning Cornish patriotism in which he used
the phrase 'Bedheugh Byntha Kernewek' (Be forever Cornish). A group
of politically active young Cornishmen and women banded together
and formed what can be described as Cornwall's first national political
movement—Tyr ha Tavas (Land and Language). They took Jenner's
phrase as their motto and became a pressure group which lobbied
Members of Parliament and other authoritative bodies. Led by Dr
E. H. Hamblin (Gwas Arthur), with C. H. Beer (Map Kenn'yn) as
secretary and B. Y. Couch (Scryfer Cudhys) the movement was made
up mainly of students and young people under the age of thirty. It
marked a tremendous change in Cornish thinking. Nance commented
at the time:[23]

The young people of this group are among those who 'see visions' and from the response to their clarion call, there is ground for hoping that they represent a new and growing force which will help to revive in Cornish people a consciousness of their race and destiny, and to create a bond of affinity and unity between the remnants of the Cornish Nation throughout the world.

Tyr ha Tavas instituted the first Cornish church service. *The Times*[24] published a news story with the heading '*Bedheugh Byntha Kernewek*' announcing that An Tredden, the executive committee of Tyr ha Tavas, had organised a church service at Towednack where the last Cornish sermons were preached in 1678. The service at Towednack, near St Ives, took place on Sunday, 9 September, at 3.30 p.m. and was attended by Mr Justice and Lady Hawke. The vicar, the Rev. L. V. Jolly read evensong and a sermon, written by Smith, was read by Edwin Chirgwin. The first lesson was read by Henry Trefusis (Map Mor) and the second by E. G. R. Hooper. Prayers were then said by W. D. Watson. The publicity given to the service, in which the Form of Evening Prayer from the Anglican Prayer Book (*Pesadow Doghajeth*) together with a number of hymns, had been translated and published by Nance, caused the London *Times* to devote a leading article to the revival, headed 'A revival of Cornish':[25]

> The older book Cornish, therefore, has not wanted for sound expository; but it is not the poetical Cornish of the middle period so much as the eighteenth century colloquial which the new movement seeks to revive and reduce to uniformity. With what success this object has been attained is plain from the religious service which has now become possible again. It is hardly likely that there will be a clamour for compulsory Cornish in the schools, but that a voluntary pride should be taken in the language is all to the good. It fosters patriotism, brings out the meaning of hundreds of mysterious place names, and reminds the Saxon that the Duchy has, when it likes to wear it, a culture which is beyond that of the more standardised counties to the east.

In 1933 Smith, then aged fifty, moved to Cornwall and started to conduct evening classes. A move to accommodate the growing

demand for Cornish classes had to be made by the Federation of Old Cornwall Societies which opened new classes in seven towns that year. But the revivalists were still handicapped by lack of a proper vocabulary. Jago's dictionary had long since been outdated and an improved second edition was never published. This had been presented to the Royal Institution of Cornwall in 1909, along with a Cornish grammar, and some annotations on the language. The Federation of Old Cornwall Societies had grown so much that it was now able to sponsor a new dictionary which would fix spelling and forms of verbs and so forth. Nance and Smith worked hard on the project and the publication of the small *English–Cornish Dictionary* in 1934 fulfilled the widely felt need for such a work. All the work of preparation for the press had been supervised by Smith. In Wales, T. Eurwedd Williams added a Welsh section to the new dictionary but, unfortunately, this English/Cornish/Welsh dictionary, in two manuscript volumes, was not published and is now in the National Library of Wales.[26]

Smith launched the first all-Cornish magazine called *Kernow* (Cornwall) in April 1934, and it became the official journal of Tyr ha Tavas. It first appeared as a monthly but no issues were published in August or September of that year. In March 1935, it became a quarterly and, after fourteen numbers, ceased publication when Smith returned to Sussex to live. The aims of *Kernow* were threefold: (1) to act as a bond between all of the Cornish who loved the language; (2) to furnish reading matter in Cornish, and (3) to raise up new Cornish writers who would form and develop a new literature for Cornwall. *Kernow* found one hundred subscribers. It was the most important vehicle for spreading work in Cornish. It contained such articles by Smith as '*Dasserghy a-wra an Kernewek?*' (Will the Cornish language revive?); a translation of an article by Elizer Ben Yehuda, 'Father of the Hebrew Language Revival', from *The Times* of 1 January 1924, and an account of the chief features of the Cornish revival. Nance also wrote twelve very important articles on the revival for *Kernow*. As well as articles and short stories, poets like Chirgwin found an outlet for the publication of their poetry.

Before the revival, surviving Cornish literature had been produced by male writers. The revival attracted many women writers. One of the most prominent of these to emerge in the columns of *Kernow* was Mrs Phoebe Proctor, *née* Nance (Morwennol). Her poem '*Pyu a Wor?*' (Who Knows?) gives an excellent example of her metrical skill:[27]

Pyu a wor an den a garaf / Who knows the man I love
Deryvys yu dhe'r molghas du / It is proclaimed to the blackbirds
Y hanow ker kyn na lavaraf / His dear name although
Colonnek gansa kenys yu / I do not say it
  A Dhew yu nos / O God at night
  yn ow hanros / in my dreams
Danvon ef arta dhym dydros / Send him again to me

My a wel yn y dheulagas / I shall see in his eyes
Golow glas an stergan oll / The blue light of the stars
Hag y lef yu tecca ages / And his voice is sweeter
Anal whek an whybanal / Than the wind of the pipes
  A Dus yn scon / O come quickly
  Ow cuf colon / Dear heart
Rag confort yu govjyon / for comfort in sorrow

An tecca blejyow a vyth terys / The most beautiful flowers then
Garlont whek a rosennow / will be picked
Lylyow rag ow gwella kerys / Fine garland of roses
Dyworth ros ha scorennow / Lilies for my best beloved
  War les an nor / Spread on the world
  Ha ton an mor / Or the waves of the sea
A garaf nefra—pyu a wor? / He who I love forever—who knows?

In 1934 at the age of eighty-six, Henry Jenner, 'Father of the Cornish Language Revival', died. He had seen the dream he had expressed in 1904 becoming a reality—Cornwall was becoming Cornish again. The natural successor to Jenner as *Barth Mur* (Grand Bard) of the Cornish Gorsedd was Robert Morton Nance. On 7 September 1934, he was installed in office at Padderbury Top, Liskeard. In 1935 the BBC broadcast a programme of choral music in Cornish and for the first time '*Bro Goth agan Tasow*' (Land of Our Fathers) was heard sung in a language that was supposed to be dead. The broadcast had been achieved due to the efforts of the Rev. Denys Hoey, chaplain of Bodmin Mental Hospital. The choir taking part was the St Austell Choir under the direction of Mr Bernard Smith. The programme was so popular that the BBC at Plymouth was induced to broadcast many other such programmes using six Cornish choirs.

In 1936, the year Smith left Cornwall to return to Sussex to be with his invalid mother, he published his first major literary work in the

language, *An Awayl herwyth Sen Mark,* a complete translation of St Mark's Gospel. A second edition of this was published by *An Lef Kernewek* in 1960. Smith was not to return to Cornwall for any length of time but, until his death in 1950, he continued his work for the language. The Royal Institution of Cornwall had a special Jenner Medal struck for work on Cornish subjects and Smith became the first recipient of it at the Institution's annual meeting in 1936. Smith said:[28]

I was both surprised and delighted when your secretary informed me that I was to be the first recipient of the Jenner Memorial Medal: surprised to find myself singled out for this honour among so many and delighted that your first award should be for work in connection with the language of Cornwall; that lost language which Mr. Jenner did so much to restore.

In 1933 Smith had started a correspondence course with students and now, as an extension of this, F. B. Cargeeg (Tan Dyvarow) started a correspondence circle to encourage writing in the language. Each member took it in turns to write in rotation. The circle continued until the outbreak of the Second World War. Chirgwin, who was winning many Gorsedd prizes with his verses and short stories, produced a small handbook in 1937 containing 240 conversational pieces on everyday topics entitled *Say It In Cornish.* It proved extremely popular.

Nance completed what he described as his 'life work'—a *Cornish–English Dictionary* in 1938. Some £2,000 was raised by voluntary donations to pay for the publication of this epic work which has been described as the most modern work on Cornish in existence and which was the fruit of many years hard work. The following year Nance published *Lyver an Pymp Marthus Seleven,* a collection of authentic folk tales from the parish of St Levan written in imitation of the style of the miracle-play writers. This became one of the most important reading books in Cornish. In spite of his removal to Sussex, Smith was as active as ever, and in 1939 he published what is possibly his most important work—*Cornish Simplified.* He had been approached by Dr Hambly of Tyr ha Tavas, in 1938, and asked to prepare a Cornish textbook for learners. Hambly pointed out that there were many people who would learn the language if they had the right book, a not-too-academic 'teach yourself' book. The assignment was a tough one as Smith wrote to J. J. Parry of the University of Illinois:[29]

The compilation of this little book gave me more trouble than did my *Welsh Made Easy*. Everything is known about Modern Welsh, whereas we are still uncertain about some features of Cornish, and you will find much in this little book that no one has attempted to explain previously. This meant many months of research, and in the end I had amassed so much material that it took another whole year to arrange it in the form of short lessons! I did not dare to call the book *Cornish Made Easy* but I do claim to have simplified matters.

Cornish Simplified has been reprinted twice and sold 2,500 copies. It has become one of the standard works on the language for students.

By the time the storm clouds of the Second World War were beginning to erupt the revival movement was firmly on its feet. New words for modern concepts were coined such as the following:

jyn-ebron	sky machine	aeroplane
margh-tan	fire horse	locomotive
margh-horn	iron horse	bicycle
gwaya-myr	moving show	cinema

The 1930s had seen a tremendous activity among the revivalists. Sympathetic help had been given them by J. L. Palmer, as editor of the *Western Morning News,* who printed short Cornish texts in that newspaper. Later, as editor of the *Cornishman,* he once printed the whole text of a sermon in Cornish. But with the war came an inevitable decline in activities. The Gorsedd continued to meet but in private session while Tyr ha Tavas became the first casualty, ceasing to function as its young members were caught up in various branches of the armed services. Nevertheless, in 1940 the Gorsedd began to award its annual literary prize which that year went to a witty adaptation of a miracle play called *Bewnans Alysaryan* by Peggy Pollard (Arlodhes Ywerdhon) which was later published. Another play, *Synt Avaldor*, based on Middle Cornish dramas, won the first prize in 1941. Peggy Pollard wrote a third play, *Synt Tanbellen*, a light-hearted skit on the Gorsedd characters but lack of funds prevented the publication of these last two plays and they have since become lost.[30]

The war years also cut off contact with other Celtic countries especially Brittany, ties with which were of particular importance for Cornwall. A number of Breton national groups had been in negotiation with Germany which had promised to set up an independent Breton

state if the Bretons remained non-partisan and did not aid the French in the war. After France's armistice with Germany and the establishment of the Vichy French régime under Marshal Pétain, such promises were not fulfilled and Vichy became an ardent persecutor of the Breton national movements. Although negotiations with Germany were confined to a small band of right-wing extremists, the French Maquis started a wholesale persecution of Bretons in 1943. This drove some Bretons into forming a special military unit, Unit Jean-Marie Perrot, which fought with the Germans against Maquis operations in Brittany. The unit was formed when Father Jean-Marie Perrot, the ageing parish priest of Scrignac, was shot to death on the steps of his church on 12 December 1943, by the Maquis. His only claim to Breton nationalism was that he had been a member of a Breton language society. The activities of this military unit, which was never more than 50-100 strong, caused a massive persecution of all Bretons with any 'nationalist' tendencies during the period 1944-8. Well over a hundred were executed and thousands imprisoned in special camps while sentences of banishment, confiscation of property, civic degradation (loss of civil rights and consequently the loss of the right to earn a living) were imposed on many more. Ill treatment under interrogation caused many deaths and one famous Breton novelist was driven insane. The Breton language was prohibited by law, despite the fact there were one and a half million native speakers at this time. The persecution in Brittany was overlooked by the rest of the world because of French propaganda which announced that they were merely dealing with collaborators and Fascists. In fact, France was using the pretext of an attempted collaboration by a few extremists, prior to 1939, to smash the Breton nation. It was even found that Bretons who had fought in the French Underground against the Germans had been interned or executed if they had connections with Breton language or national movements. Due to the efforts of Dewi Powell, special correspondent of the Welsh newspaper *Baner ac Amserau Cymru*, the facts were revealed and petitions and protests were sent to the French authorities which eventually yielded to pressure.

One interesting sidelight on Cornish during the war years was that Edwin Chirgwin, who was in Gibraltar, kept up a correspondence with Smith and others in Cornish. The fact that Cornish was accepted by the military censors was noted by the *West Briton* newspaper. Chirgwin became secretary of the Cornish Gorsedd in 1944 and retained the office until his death in 1960.

With the close of the war the Cornish Gorsedd resumed its public meetings at Perran Round in 1946. Smith attended this Gorsedd— it was to be his last visit to Cornwall. He had not been inactive during the war years and in 1947 he published *Nebes Whethlow Ber,* a number of short stories in Cornish; a small pamphlet history of the language *The Story of the Cornish Language* and *How to Learn Cornish.* In 1948 he published *Whethlow An Seyth Den Fur A Rom* (The Seven Sages of Rome). This was a remarkable work that originated in India in 500 B.C. and found its way to the West. The tale became popular in the Middle Ages and a version was written in Welsh by a priest called Llywelyn in the 'Red Book of Hergest' (A.D. 1400-25). This was edited by Professor Henry Lewis under the title *Chwedleu Seith Doethon Rufein* in 1925. It was from Lewis's book that Smith made his translation into Cornish.

In 1949 a major find occurred for Cornish enthusiasts. In April of that year the noted Celtic scholar John Mackechnie (author of *Gaelic Without Groans,* 1934, and editor of *The Dewar Manuscripts,* 1964) discovered a new Middle Cornish manuscript in the British Museum.[31] It was in a collection of papers of the Puleston family of Emral and Worthenbury in Flint, Wales, which had just been purchased by the Museum. This was the 130-page Tregear manuscript containing a translation of Bishop Bonner's *Homilies, circa* 1560. Mackechnie got in touch with Nance who delivered a paper on the find to the Royal Institution of Cornwall on 20 December 1949.[32]

In 1950 a Cornish version of part of the miracle play *Bewnans Meriasek* was performed before the Celtic Congress by a Camborne– Redruth drama group formed by Helena Charles. The extract from the drama had been published in Unified Cornish by E. G. R. Hooper. Performances were given in Truro, St Day, Redruth and Camborne and Mrs Collingwood Selby, the county drama organiser, helped in the production when the play was submitted as an associated production of the Cornwall Amateur Drama Festival. It was the only play to be produced in Cornish during the Festival at Perran Round. The play was also entered as Cornwall's contribution to the Festival of Britain in July 1951.[33]

On 22 November 1950, A. S. D. Smith died, aged sixty-seven, a great loss to the revivalist movement. Mrs F. M. Willis of Par (Sulwen) wrote: 'This great man has gone from us and what can we do, who have had so much from him, but carry on in our small way, the fine work he has so nobly begun, the spreading of the Cornish language.' Smith had left some very clear instructions behind him on how to

spread the language. Writing in the *Cornish Review* just before his death he proposed that students should bind themselves into a Unyans an Cows Kernewek (Cornish-Speaking Union) to meet at regular intervals for discussions and that the Gorsedd extend its scope to include an oral test, reading of a passage and extempore conversation.[34] Smith left a number of Cornish texts unpublished. Among these was his 8,000-line work *Trystan hag Ysolt*, the story of Tristan and Iseult retold in Cornish verse. He had written it during the long war nights when he was an Air Raid Precautions Warden, but it was incomplete at his death. E. G. R. Hooper, in co-operation with Smith's widow, Dorothy, edited the work and published it as a memorial volume in 1951. The unfinished part of the story was taken by D. H. Watkins (Carer Brynyow) and finished in 1,000 lines which won him the Gorsedd award in 1962. Watkins had learnt Cornish in the days of Jenner but was lost to the revivalist movement until his retirement in the 1950s. He then applied himself with vigour to the language writing two or three one-act plays and some poetry—notably '*Spyrys an Meneth*' (The Spirit of the Mountain) and '*Tarth an Jeth*' (Daybreak).[35] The completion of *Trystan hag Ysolt* was his main work but due to lack of funds it lay unpublished for many years. Thanks to the generosity of his widow *An Lef Kernewek* published the work, with a short introduction, in 1973.

Lack of funds has also prevented another major work by Smith from being published; this is the '*Mabinogion*' which Smith left in manuscript form. As well as his work on the technical side of the language Smith remains one of the important figures of the new Cornish literary movement. Although he was passionately involved in the revival he was not above joking as in his poem '*An Gwlascarer*' (The Patriot):[36]

Ny allaf-vy kewsel Kernewek	I cannot speak Cornish
Ny allaf y scryfa ha whath	I cannot write it either
Re gales yu tavas mar uthek	Such a terrible language is too hard
Predery anodho a-m-lath!	It kills me to think about it!

This extract from his short story '*Tremenyans Arthur*' (Passing of Arthur)[37] gives a good indication of Smith's prose style:

Golya dhe ves a wruk an gorhel, ow casa Bedwyr down yn prederow war an treth. Omlesa a wruk an gol kepar hag askel

ledrek, hag y teth dhe glew Bedwyr war awel an gorthewer
ylow a'n whecca hag a lowenhas y enef. Awotta an gan gologhas
marthys a dhuk an awel y dhywscovan-ef:

'Yn hans dhe'n bys yma pow hep cleves nag ola na henys.
Plema henna? Yndella yu Enys Avallon. Y'n vro hudhyk-ma yma
hunrosow re wruk hebaskhe ownow an osow: ena yma gwaytyans
ow pewa bynytha; ena yma frutys agan towlow ughel. Nanyl
fowt fyth, na forth meth, na colon trogh ny dhe nefra dhe'n
pow-ma rak y dhyswul. Ena yma tan pup awen a ganno den;
nerth kyfyans, tan colon an gwlascarer—ena ymons-y oll, ow ry
crefter dhe nep a vynno gwaytya. Coth by vydhyn nefra y'n
pow-ma. Ynno yma anal bewnans agan kenethel-ny.'

Nebes ha nebes an ylow eth gwanna y'n pellder, erna
ve avel whystrans whek, kens es tewel yn tyen.

Dyworth an lyn y sevynewl, ha'n gorhel eth yn mes a wel
kepar ha tarosvan.

Bedwyr, tryst hag unyk, eth wardhelergh dhe'n bys.

The ship sailed away leaving Bedwyr [Bedivere] deep in thought on
the beach. The sail spread itself like a sloping wing and on the
evening breeze there came to Bedwyr's ear the sweetest music,
gladdening his soul. This was the song of praise that the breeze
brought to him:

'Beyond the world there is a world without sickness, weeping
nor old age. Where is that place? It is Avallon. In that happy land
there are dreams which have soothed the fears of all the ages:
There is Hope there, existing forever: The reward of high
endeavour is there. No crime, no way of disgrace, no broken
heart ever comes to that land so as to harm it. Every invocation
sung by man is there—strength, the great heart of the patriot—
they are all there, giving power to all who wait. We shall never
be old in that land. The breath of life of our own nation.'

Little by little the music became weaker in the distance until
it was a charming whisper before falling silent.

From the lake a mist arose, and the ship went out of sight
like a phantom.

Bedwyr, sad and alone, went back to the world.

Smith had brought a new vitality to Cornish and made the language
a living thing, not just an academic curiosity.

In 1951 the Old Cornwall Societies began to publish a series of booklets containing extracts from the Middle Cornish texts which Nance and Smith had edited in Unified Cornish and translated in collaboration. They included *Bewnans Meryasek* (a second enlarged edition was published in 1966); *An Tyr Marya* (The Three Maries); *Sylvester Ha'n Dhragon* (Silvester and the Dragon); *Abram hag Ysak* (Abraham and Isaac); *Adam ha Seth* (Adam and Seth); *Davydd hag Urry* (David and Uriah) and *An Venen ha'y Map* (The Woman and the Son).

In January 1952, Richard R. M. Gendall (Gelvynak), a bard by examination in 1949, launched a new all-Cornish magazine called *An Lef* (The Voice). This was designed as a monthly to fill the gap left by the loss of Smith's *Kernow*. Gendall was the writer of some original Cornish poetry such as '*Hunros Dyvres*' (An Exile's Dream) and '*An Dewys*' (The Choice)[38] and a short play *Ascra Lan Dyogel hy Ferghen* (Secure is he who has a clear conscience). With the twentieth issue the magazine passed under the editorship of E. G. R. Hooper with the new title of *An Lef Kernewek* (The Cornish Voice). It has appeared ever since as a quarterly entirely in Cornish, Mr Hooper agreeing with Smith's argument that a bilingual journal soon becomes slave to the stronger language. E. G. R. Hooper has built a publishing house around *An Lef Kernewek* and his contribution to the furtherance and development of the language has been outstanding. Gendall, in the meantime, launched another all-Cornish magazine *Hedhyu* (Today), 'an occasional magazine to encourage the use of everyday Cornish'. The magazine was launched in May 1956 but ceased publication in 1961.

Nance still worked tirelessly on improving modern Cornish and in 1952 and 1955 new editions of the two dictionaries were published. He had been elected president of the Royal Institution of Cornwall during 1951-5; was for ten years chairman of Penzance Library and for six years president of the Cornish branch of the Celtic Congress. This was in addition to his twenty-five years as president of the Federation of Old Cornwall Societies and a similar period as Barth Mur of the Gorseth Kernow. In 1954 records of Nance reading the story of *Jowan Chy an Hor*, Boorde's 'Colloquies' and the Lord's Prayer were produced. But in the autumn of 1957 Nance was taken ill. He managed to preside at the Gorsedd at Perran Round in 1958 but on 27 May 1959, aged eighty-six, he died at St Michael's Hospital, Hayle. He was taken to Zennor for burial and on his memorial stone is

the sentence: *Oberow y vewnans yu y wyr govath* (His life's works are his true memorial). He left all his books and manuscripts to the Royal Institution of Cornwall. Before he died Nance remarked: 'One generation has set Cornish on its feet. It is now for another to make it walk.'

Chapter Eight

The Growth and Future of the Revival

The growth of the Cornish political national movement is inseparable from that of the language revival; you cannot revive a language without reviving the idea of nationhood and the aspiration of nationhood is independent statehood. Tyr ha Tavas had been the first Cornish national political pressure group but they had faded away in the early days of the Second World War. For a short time a Young Cornwall Movement replaced Tyr ha Tavas. On 6 January 1951 in a Redruth hotel a number of Cornish men and women, some of whom had been members of Tyr ha Tavas and Young Cornwall, formed Mebyon Kernow (Sons of Cornwall). Their aim was to act as a political pressure group, along the lines of Tyr ha Tavas, 'to maintain the character of Cornwall as a Celtic nation, to promote the interests of Cornwall and the Cornish people and to promote the constitutional advance of Cornwall and its right to self government in domestic affairs'. It also aimed to 'foster Cornish studies and culture, including language, literature, history and sport'. Miss Helena Charles, who had convened the first meeting, was elected chairman, Lambert Truran became secretary and G. P. White became treasurer. From a ridiculed pressure group Mebyon Kernow grew within two short decades into a respectable political party.

Mebyon Kernow wanted a 'domestic self government' in Cornwall. They demanded that the central government at Westminster recognise Cornwall not as an English county but as a Celtic country with a special position within the United Kingdom. They believed the only way Cornwall could develop economically and culturally was for the county to be given the same limited domestic self-government as the Channel Islands or the Isle of Man. They were quick to point out that the Isle of Man, one-sixth the size of Cornwall, managed its own affairs extremely well, had the lowest rate of taxation in the British Isles and yet still could afford to give interest-free loans to the United

Kingdom government. Mebyon Kernow envisaged this domestic self-government as a *Cuntelles Kernow*, (an Assembly of Cornwall), rather like the county council but with more extensive powers. Mebyon Kernow's life president, Robert A. Dunstone, stated that his movement 'requires only the reorganisation of the United Kingdom, not the dissolution or lessening of it, on the lines which are already admitted in the cases of the Isle of Man and the Channel Islands'.

Initially, members of all political parties could belong to the Mebyon Kernow pressure group. By 1966 three of Cornwall's five Members of Parliament were openly advocating many of Mebyon Kernow's major policies. John Pardoe, Liberal M.P. for North Cornwall, and Peter Bessell, then Liberal M.P. for Bodmin, advocated in the London *Times* in 1968 'that Cornwall must be regarded not only as a separate region, but as a separate country. Transference of government is a just claim in Wales and Scotland and we must demand it equally for Cornwall.' John Pardoe emphasised: 'I want to see devolution of power away from Whitehall and London to the people of the regions and nations of the United Kingdom. I look forward to a parliament for Wales, Scotland and Cornwall.' A third M.P. John Nott, a Conservative member for St Ives, claimed to be fully in agreement with Mebyon Kernow's aims. When Peter Bessell retired from Parliament in 1970 another Mebyon Kernow member was elected, David Mudd, who became a Conservative Member. At the same time that Plaid Cymru (Party of Wales) and the Scottish National Party were achieving election successes in Wales and Scotland, Mebyon Kernow were reflecting these successes in Cornish local council elections. In 1967 Colin Murley became the first 'official' Mebyon Kernow candidate to sit on the Cornwall County Council. Numerous Mebyon Kernow members had been previously elected to councils as 'independents'. In the 1970 General Election Mebyon Kernow decided to field its own Parliamentary candidate and Richard G. Jenkin stood for Falmouth–Camborne, polling 2 per cent of the total votes.

As a political pressure group Mebyon Kernow organised a successful resistance to a government proposal to close the world-famous Camborne School of Mines and re-establish it in London. Mebyon Kernow aided the formation of the Cornish Transport Committee to fight government rail closures, inadequacy of roads, slightness of air connections and disuse of ports. The movement has also pressed for a University of Cornwall and, although the government rejected the

idea, and even removed the degree courses from the Technical College, Mebyon Kernow 'created a sentiment which may yet be strong enough to succeed during the next decade'.[1] Mebyon Kernow printed a special report on the subject of Cornish education in 1966. They claimed, 'it is necessary that Cornish boys and girls see what is Cornish tradition and what is English influence. Otherwise an English education is being applied to Cornish children making them less Cornish. Some do this innocently, some ought to know better.'[2] In regard to the Cornish language revival Mebyon Kernow say that they wish for a realistic solution. While recognising that Cornwall must go on using English as a medium 'learning Cornish must be an option available to each child, with other languages, all equally provided with means, equipment, books and teachers. Cornish must be given examination status.' At the same time, Mebyon Kernow asks that Cornish history be taught in schools together with English history because, at the present time, Cornish children have no way of learning about their Celtic background at school.

Economically, Mebyon Kernow believes that the once thriving Cornish fishing industry could be revived again if better protection were given to Cornish fishing fleets. Similarly, the Cornish mines are far from worked out. 'The Cornish mines went out of production not because they were worked out but because it was found cheaper years ago to produce tin in Malaya and South America than in Cornwall.'[3] Mebyon Kernow claim that if government gave tax concessions to mining firms for an initial five-year period, as many other countries do, the mining industry would come alive and be viable again. It is a plan that Harold Wilson, leader of the Labour Party, once advocated in the early 1960s when in Opposition. Failing central government giving concessions, Mebyon Kernow feel that Cornwall, as a separate political unit, could grant such concessions herself. John Pardoe M.P. stated :'I have little doubt in my mind that Cornwall's economy could be a viable and an independent unit, and that we would then be able to give tax incentives.' An economic programme *What Cornishmen Can Do—The Economic Possibilities before Cornwall* was published by Mebyon Kernow in September 1968, and their policy document for the General Election of 1970 is contained in *Cornwall Tomorrow*. In their economic planning, Mebyon Kernow received support from economics expert Professor Northcott Parkinson who has advocated that Cornwall ought to be a separate economic and administrative unit.[4] Leopold Kohr, Professor of Economics and Public Administration at the

University of Puerto Rico, who has lectured at the University of Wales, also supports Mebyon Kernow economics.[5]

Unlike the Welsh and Scottish national movements, Mebyon Kernow are hampered by the fact that Cornwall is not recognised except as an English county and it was to gain such recognition that Mebyon Kernow started their 'postage stamp campaign'. In 1958 permanent regional postage stamps were issued for Wales, Scotland, Northern Ireland, the Isle of Man, Jersey and Guernsey 'in recognition of the ancient status and of the current constitutional position of the regions and islands concerned'. In 1963 a plea for a similar stamp for Cornwall was rejected by the postmaster-general's office with the comment 'if we were to issue a Cornish stamp we would not very well be able to refuse requests for similar recognition for all other counties'. On 6 March 1967, John Nott M.P. rose in the House of Commons and asked the postmaster-general whether in commemoration of St Piran's Day (5 March) he would give consideration to the production of a Cornish stamp, 'Cornwall being the only Celtic country in the United Kingdom which is without its own postage stamp'. Edward Short, then postmaster-general, refused. On St Piran's Day, 1968, Mebyon Kernow produced a St Piran's Day card with a demand for a stamp and Peter Bessell M.P. tabled no less than eight questions. In face of refusals, Mebyon Kernow started to produce their own 'unofficial' stamp as the Welsh and Scots before them. St Piran has now become the patron saint of Cornwall, whose day is honoured on 5 March, although St Petroc seems to have a better claim on the title. A story in the Gotha Manuscript, says that the men of many nations were in a ship during a fierce storm and each cried to the patron saint of their nation for help. A Cornishman cried to St Petroc and the storm ceased. The relics of St Petroc were stolen in the twelfth century and Petroc is then described as 'chief of the Cornish saints'. The same wording is used in a sixteenth century manuscript which describes the saint.

Mebyon Kernow also has its own Fabian Society or Bow Group in Cowethas Flamank (The Flamank Group), named after one of the leaders of the 1497 Cornish uprising. Formal approval for its foundation was given at the annual meeting of Mebyon Kernow on 31 May 1970. The group is bound by the rules of Mebyon Kernow and within its framework it pursues an independent course in searching out information and presenting new ideas. 'As a long term project, the group is anxious to inaugurate a series of comprehensive economic,

social and environmental studies for the whole of Cornwall. . .'[6] The group has its own publication *Keveren* (Link).

In 1952 a chemistry teacher of Leedstown, Hayle, Richard G. Jenkin (Map Dyvroeth) and his wife, Ann, started a publication called *New Cornwall,* a magazine which, although independent, made Mebyon Kernow policies known to the Cornish people. The symbol of the magazine, appropriately enough, shows a phoenix rising from the flames of rebirth and underneath is the legend '*Dasserghyn*' (Resurgence), denoting the Cornish renaissance. It includes regular articles in Cornish. In 1968 Mebyon Kernow began its own publication called the *Cornish Nation* and in 1971 it launched another publication *Kernow* which is described as 'an open forum for students at Cornish schools and colleges'. Mebyon Kernow is associated with the League of Celtic Nations, a political and cultural movement representing all six Celtic countries.[7] The aim of the Celtic League is to foster co-operation between the Celtic peoples, developing the consciousness of the special relationship and solidarity between them, making their national struggle and achievements better known abroad, and encouraging the acceptance of the need for a formal association of the Celtic nations once two more of them have attained independence, advocating the use of the natural resources of each Celtic country for the benefit of all its people. The League, which has branches in all six Celtic countries and a general secretariat in Dublin, Ireland, published a quarterly *Celtic News* and an annual volume, but from Spring 1973, now publishes a quarterly periodical called *Carn*. Mebyon Kernow also sends delegates to the Federal Union of European Nationalities, a body based in Denmark representing national minorities throughout Europe. Younger members of Mebyon Kernow also subscribe to the Celtic Youth Congress, a radical political and cultural Celtic movement not to be confused with the purely academic Celtic Congress (formed in 1858). A Cornish branch of the Youth Congress was formed in 1970 at a meeting in the Bishop Philpott Library, Truro, when secretary general Keith Bush urged Cornish youth to 'become part of the international brotherhood with a mission to change the world— for the better'. At the Celtic Youth Congress held in Dublin on Monday, 4 April 1966, the then president R. O. F. Wynne (Wales) said the aim of the Congress was the independence of the Celtic countries and their unification in a Celtic union. 'Co-operation— even integration—is our aim and it is the duty of this Congress to explore every means of achieving it.'[8]

In May 1964, Mebyon Kernow published its revised aims. These were now to 'maintain the Celtic character of Cornwall and its right to self government in domestic affairs; to foster the Cornish language, literature, culture and sport, and to demand that Cornish children have the opportunity in school to learn about their own land and culture'. Because of Mebyon Kernow's aim of 'domestic self government' within the United Kingdom structure, those Cornishmen who were of a more radical persuasion decided to break away and form their own political party. In June 1969, Leonard C. Trelease, a former national secretary of Mebyon Kernow, established the Cornish National Party. Mr Trelease's party, whose leader was Robert Holmes who had won a seat on Liskeard council as a Mebyon Kernow candidate in 1968, issued a leaflet on their political aims entitled *Cornwall—Forward with Confidence*. They explained:

What is certain is that the future government of Cornwall must have control over all Cornish matters unfettered by the dead hands of Westminster and Whitehall. This does not mean total separation for Cornwall. There will certainly be a need for a great deal of co-operation between the peoples and countries of the British Isles. What we envisage has been described as Commonwealth Status.

The advent of Mebyon Kernow and the Cornish National Party was, perhaps, one of the most important events for the revival movement for the political agitation began to develop a Cornish national consciousness which started an awakening of interest in the Cornish language and its literature.

With the death of Nance, E. G. R. Hooper (Talek) was elected as Barth Mur of the Cornish Gorsedd and installed in office at Callington in 1959. Rules governing the election of the Grand Bard were changed so that a Grand Bard was elected for a three-year term of office. He could serve for two successive three-year periods but could not stand for a further term. Hooper has been a great benefactor to the revival by his publication of much work that would otherwise have gone unnoticed. Perhaps his most notable achievement has been the editing and production of the all-Cornish periodical *An Lef Kernewek* in which has appeared much of the most notable writing in Unified Cornish. He has edited many of Smith's works for publication, making them available through *An Lef Kernewek* publications. A prolific translator

and writer, he edited *Kemysk Kernewek,* a miscellany of letters, verse, stories, etc. in Cornish, published in 1964. *An Lef Kernewek* publications have also published, in 1962, *Lyver Hymnys ha Salmow,* containing 100 hymns and psalms in Cornish, as well as an updated version of Smith's *The Story of the Cornish Language,* in 1969. Many of Nance's and Smith's notes were published under the title *Cornish Studies* in multigraphed form. Mr Hooper has been the acknowledged authority on the language since the death of Nance. Unfortunately lack of finance precludes the publication of a large number of works in Cornish, such as Smith's '*Mabinogion*', but Mr Hooper has made a valiant struggle in supplying the revivalists with an increasing published literature. He has also reprinted Smith's *Cornish Simplified, Lessons in Spoken Cornish, An Awayl herwyth Sen Mark, Nebes Whethlow Ber* and *Whethlow an seyth den fur a Rom.* Mr Hooper is fully aware of the difficulties of his task and he states the problem in an article '*Dasserghys a Wra an Tavas*' (Will Cornish be resurrected?).[9] Although Mr Hooper is passionately dedicated to the language, like Smith he too can joke about his dedication as illustrated by the following verse:[10]

Yth esa den coynt yn Cambron	There was a queer fellow in Camborne
a scryfas Kernewek, del won	who wrote Cornish, as I know
ha gul tra yu mar fol	and doing such a silly thing
y teth anedhy dhe goll	he came to disaster
na dhyndylys bythqueth y gon.	and never earned his supper.

It was Mr Hooper who first tried to put into practice Jenner's call, made in 1933, for Cornish to be introduced as an optional subject in Cornish schools. In 1933 Tyr ha Tavas had organised a Cornish-speaking camp and the exercise was repeated by Mebyon Kernow in 1953. But the Cornish language as a school subject having a place in the normal curriculum has long been an aim of the revivalists. It was first tried by Mr Hooper in the private school of Mount Pleasant House, Camborne, and later in another private school, Strangways House School, Truro. It was not until some time had been spent on Cornish history and place names that any study of the language was introduced to the interested pupils. Under Miss J. E. Petchey (Elowen) girls at Strangways House were instructed in the language and two of them managed to pass the elementary grades of the new Cornish Language Committee's examination. Miss Petchey now runs an annual summer school, *Scol Haf Kernewek.* Mr Hooper writes:

G

An unexpected result of teaching Cornish to Cornish children has been improvement in their English writing—they understand that their 'Cornicism' is a trace of their own language with its own dignity of expression, neither a quaint relic nor merely a 'West Country' dialect of the imaginary district of the British Broadcasting Corporation.

Television was quick to cash in on the new phenomenon and Alan Whicker made the Cornish-language classes into something of a public entertainment. He was followed by Westward Television and finally Welsh Television, who treated the subject with more sympathy. The idea of Cornish in schools was ridiculed by an academic at Liverpool University who put forward the proposition that the Cornish people did not exist anymore.[11] At the time of the television interest in Cornish, 1962, a long correspondence appeared in the *Daily Telegraph* concerning the lack of interest shown in the subject by Cornwall education authorities. The school was closed by the Cornish education authorities in 1969 and David Mudd, the prospective Conservative Parliamentary candidate and Mebyon Kernow member, immediately started an investigation into the reasons behind the closure. He was assured by the authorities that the department of education 'accepts without question the right of Cornish teachers to hold personal views on the culture of their own county'.

There is a lot of interest among school children in the language and more and more young people are taking the Gorsedd examinations. However, at the present time they are only able to learn the language outside normal school hours. In 1971 a fourteen-year-old girl from Truro High School for Girls, Mary Truran, wrote an essay '*An Le Rak Kernewek Yn Kernow Avorow*' (The place of Cornish in Cornwall tomorrow), which is indicative of the feelings of many young Cornish people:[12]

Nyns-yu nep pell, an düs yowynk Kernewek ny-wruk gothvos mur a daclow adro dh'aga thavas. Herwyth an gys o leverys 'Tavas degensete yu, nyns-yu a hedhyu.' Lemmyn, bytegens, ny a-yl gweles y vos tavas a hedhyu, mes a avorow ynweth. Ny a-vyn gweles moy Kernewek scryfys y'n trevow y'n forthow, hag oll a'n leow a'n bobel. Moy es henna, yma mur a düs yowynk nep a-wra dysky an tavas-ma y'n geryow Henry Jenner, 'Awos agan bos Kernewek'.

Mur a jyow yu henwys yn Kernewek yn ur-ma mes drok yu dhyn nag-yu a daclow Kernewek dyskys yn scolyow Kernewek.

Mur a düs yowynk ny-yl dysky Kernewek, awos aga bos purvysy:
alemma-rak res yu dhedha gweles agan tavas scryfys y'n eglosyow,
chyow, cowethasow, kewsys y'n forthow, yn lavarow, hag yn
gorhemmynadow Menestrouthy a'n bobel yu kerys gans an düs
yowynk—res yu dhe ganoryon cana y'n tavas—ma ha res yu
dhe'n scryforyon a vusyk scryfa mur a ganow yn Kernewek kepar
han canow a-wra scryfa Richard Gendall.

Res yu dh'agan denythyans gwaynya le rak Kernewek y'n
termyn a-dhe.

Not long ago, Cornish youth knew little of their language. It
was fashionable to say 'It's a language of yesterday, not of today.'
Now, however, we can see that it is a language of today and
tomorrow. We want to see more Cornish written in the towns,
in the roads, and in all public places. Moreover, there are many
young people who learn this language, in the words of Henry
Jenner, 'Because we are Cornish'.

Many houses are already named in Cornish, but we are sorry
that little of Cornish things are taught in our schools. Many
young people cannot learn Cornish because they are too busy;
from now on they must see our language written in churches,
houses, societies and spoken in the streets, in slogans and in
greetings. Folk-music is popular with young people—the singers
must sing the language and composers must write more songs
in Cornish like those Richard Gendall writes.

Our generation must secure a place for Cornish in the future.

Mr Hooper retired after his two terms of office as Barth Mur in
1965 and was succeeded by G. Pawley White (Gunwyn), who had
been admitted to the Gorsedd by examination in the language, with
his wife, in 1947. He had been a marshal of the Gorsedd, a council
member, secretary of the examinations board, and a vice president of
the Federation of Old Cornwall Societies. On the expiration of his
two terms of office, he retired according to the Constitution and
Mr Denis Trevanion (Trevanyon) was elected to succeed him in 1970
and duly installed in office at the Gorsedd of 1971.

In spite of the lack of money an increasing number of Cornish
books, such as *Lyver Henwhethlow* (1965), eighteen fables in Cornish by
D. R. Evans (Gwas Cadok), were being published. D. R. Evans, a
Welshman who was a close friend of Nance and deputy Grand Bard

for some years, did much translation into Cornish including parts of the Bible and some hymns. A new Cornish publishing company, Lodenek Press of Padstow, is also contributing much to the growth of the new Cornish literature. Its list includes: *Bewnans Meryasek*, a new translation for the theatre; *Gwyrans an bys, Names for the Cornish* (300 Cornish Christian names) and *Lyver Lavarow Kernewek* (A Cornish Phrase Book). The last three works are by Christopher Bice (Gwythenek), a bard by examination in the language. New textbooks have also been produced including *Cornish For Beginners* by P. A. S. Pool (Gwas Galva) in 1961. This was based on a series of lessons prepared for an evening class under the auspices of the London Cornish Association. In this volume Pool gives a simple 'teach yourself' book which takes one to the Intermediate Standard of the Language Board's examination. The most up to date work on the language, in way of a textbook, however, was published in 1972 by Kesva an Tavas Kernewek entitled *Kernewek Bew* (Living Cornish) by Richard Gendall (Gelvynak). This is a modern approach to learning the language by the direct method, complete with illustrations. Gendall had written a series of Cornish Lessons published by the monthly *Cornish Magazine*, starting in 1960. The Cornish Language Board, whom we shall deal with later in this chapter, also published a Unified Cornish version of *Passyon agan Arluth* (The Passion Poem) by Nance and Smith, edited by Mr Hooper. A Cornish song book went a long way to interesting young people in the language via folk songs. This was *Canow Kernow* by Inglis Gundry (Ylewyth), published in 1966. Dr Ralph Dunstan had produced *A Cornish Song Book* in 1929 which included several pages of songs in Cornish. Pamphlet histories of the language were also produced to create a better understanding. Between the publication of Jenner's *Handbook,* in 1904, and Smith's *The Story of the Cornish Language,* 1947, nothing was published except academic papers. In Breton the late J. R. F. Piette (Arzel Even), who lectured on Cornish at Aberystwyth, published *Istor ar yezhou keltiek*, vol. i, 1959, which included two chapters on Old Celtic, including Cornish. In 1969 Mr Hooper published an excellent updated version of Smith's *Story* and, at the same time, Geoffrey H. Sutton, a member of the staff of the Universal Esperanto Association, Rotterdam, published a history of the language in Esperanto: *Konciza historio pri la Kornala lingvo kaj gia literaturo*.[13] Another pamphlet history of the language was produced by the Tor Mark Press of Truro.[14]

As far as literature is concerned, there are a number of writers who

deserve mention. F. J. B. McDowell (Map Estren Du), a bard by examination in 1943, was a zealous correspondent in Cornish, producing translations and a large number of original poems amongst which are 'Den Hep Fyth' (A Faithless Man), 'Farwel dhe'n Haf' (Farewell to Summer), 'An Fyllor a Sparnon' (The Fiddler of Sparnon) and 'An Barth Perfyth' (The Perfect Bard).[15] L. R. Moir (Car Albanek), a bard by examination in 1957, is a Scot who retired to Cornwall with his Cornish wife and was for many years secretary of the Federation of Old Cornwall Societies working closely with Nance and becoming, on Nance's death, editor of Old Cornwall. His command of the language led to his being awarded the Gorsedd prize for his story in verse An Map Dyworth an Yst (The Boy from the East) in 1965, which was published in 1967; he wrote 'Gwythoryon an Eglos' (Builders of the Church) in 1967 and 'An Gwary Myr' (The Miracle Play) in 1969. Women are still well represented among revivalist writers, among them Miss Ivall (Morvran) and Mrs Royle (Pendenhow) have made some interesting contributions.[16] But Margaret Norris (Brosyores), a bard by examination in 1944, is perhaps the most prominent of the modern women writers. She is the writer of some delicate poems, notably 'Clew Galow an Orseth' (Hear the Call of the Gorsedd), a triolet which won the Gorsedd prize in 1947. The following poem, 'Poldice', gives an indication of her style. Poldice was famous for a mine which used to employ 1,000 men. Now it is merely a deserted ruin:[17]

Cudhys yn tyen os yn nans
Ha breow adro dhys a bup tu
Ynnos pupteth y synsyn sans
Covyon mar wyr ha gwyw
A'n dhedhyow-na abell yu passys
Covyon hyrethak a'th sowynyans
A whel-sten bryntyn pan vue gwres
Ow ry dhe lyes den y vegyans
Lemmyn ellas oll yu chanjys
Nyns ys travyth oll a sef
Cofhe dhyn a'th vraster mes
Cuth an whel, los, whath cref—
An keth re-na yu dha wythysy
Bys vynary dha woskes-ejy.

You are completely hidden below
and hills all around
in you we hold as sacred
the true and worthy memories
and the days long ago of the
noble tin-mine that gave its
livelihood to so many men
Alas all is now changed
Little enough stands to remind
us of the greatness but the
husk of the works, grey yet strong,
these are your guardians
forever in your shelter.

M. C. V. Stephens (Keybalhens) and J. A. N. Snell (Gwas Kevardhu),

both bards by examination in 1954, are also well known as is W. M. Bennetts (Abransek).[18] W. A. Morris (Haldreyyn), a bard by examination in 1966, experimented with Welsh poetical patterns in Cornish and also produced a number of translations. He has written some short stories but is noted for his glossaries of technical words and phrases. Probably the most able young writer in the language today is N. J. A. Williams (Golvan), a worthy successor to Edwin Chirgwin (Map Melyn). Williams is a Celtic scholar, whose play *Trelyans Sen Powl* (Conversion of St Paul) written in traditional style, won the Gorsedd award in 1961. *Trelyans Sen Powl* closely follows the *Ordinalia* style and spelling and in its use of 'fill-up words'—e.g. 'indeed', 'verily', etc. (*yredy, yn tefry, yn gwyr, hep wow, defry, oll*, etc.)—it copies *Bewnans Meryasek*. Mr Hooper says if it had been written on old paper and in medieval script it 'could have been a beautiful literary forgery'. The work begins:[19]

Hic pompabit Saul et postea dicit

Ym gylwyr Saul yredy	Saul, I am called,
aswonys dres oll Judy	known through Judea
avel compyer an lagha	as champion of the law,
ow punsya an Grystoryon	punishing the Christians
Cryst bos myghtern Yedhewon	if they will not deny
mara ny vynnons nagha . . .	that Christ is King of the Jews . . .

The following four separate verses which appeared in *An Lef Kernewek,* in autumn, 1962 (no. 79), are difficult to translate because of the abstracts and the ideas contrasted. In the first verse note particularly the alliteration:

Lowsys yu logh lagas glas	The lake's blue eye is dulled
ganow gwyn gensy gallas	It's white mouth gone away
ny bew bennath beth bytteth	The blessing of the grave doesn't exist
mes moreth ha mallath meth	but misery and the curse of shame
a calses clewes dhys canen	if you could hear me I would
ha devra dagrow dughan.	sing you and shed tears of woe.
Yma an gwyns ow rustla	The wind is rustling through
dres del gwyth dro dhymmo	the trees around me
marthys cref yn y nerth ef	amazing strong its power
yn town us synsys genef	that I feel intensely

mes creffa dhym yun cof coth
ahanas hag y'm bus both
dha anakevy y'n tor-ma.

but yet stronger is the
old memory of you
and yet my desire is to forget you.

Gwaynten ma yn Breten Vyhan
Trelys yu an vledhen ros
Eythyn tek banal melon
a gweth pup yu an ros
Gans tonyow spilan kmmya y can
an gucu der an cos.

It is Spring in Brittany
the year's wheel is turned
Pretty furze, yellow broom,
Clothe each of the downs
with splendid tones, now sings
the cuckoo in the wood.

Gwavyv an hens, gweles den-vyth
Ny yller yn nep le
Mes an byasen lowenek
A nyj adro dhe'n ke
Hy fluf fyn ha glas ha gwyn
A lever bos haf de.

The park is empty—one can't
see anyone anywhere
But the happy magpie
flies about the hedge
her fine blue and white
feathers say that summer is come.

Another example of Williams's prosody is given in 'Can Myghtern Arthur' (A Song of King Arthur)[20] which begins:

Nyns yu marow myghtern Arthur
nyns yu marow whath yn sur
rag un jeth y whra dewheles
dh'agan rewlya-ny gans gwyr
mes ny'n hembronk-ny gans cledha

King Arthur is not dead
indeed, he is not dead
for one day he will return
to rule us with justice
but he will not lead us with a
    sword

rak may fedhyn-ny y'n gas
mes yn cres ha dre gerensa
a Vap Marya lun a ras.

so that we win in battle
but in peace through love
and grace of Mary's Son.

As a final example of Williams's poetry, the following is the last verse of a five-verse poem called 'Scusow'.[21] The word *scusow* can mean shade, shadow, uneasy feeling or dread. In this case Williams, whose work shows a strong religious quality, is expressing his unease about his beliefs:

Scus! deryf dhym kerensa
Dew agan Tas awortha
garmeleugh-ef hep anken
may hyllyf-vy daseafos

Doubt! Tell me about
the love of God
Our Father above.
Praise him without 'hind-thought'

ow eyjyans dhodho y'n cos   so that I can find again my faith
kellys del welyn mapden.   lost in the wood, as I see mankind.

Most revivalist literature has dealt mainly with religious themes,
nature poetry or legends and fables. Many writers attempt merely to
imitate the topics and style of the Middle Cornish 'miracle play'
period. Tales of saints, folk-tales and like subjects abound in revivalist
literature although Chirgwin and Williams have done much to
'broaden' the Cornish literary field. This fact, however, has caused
some bitter attacks on the 'revivalist establishment' by some young
radicals. One such attack was made by a young student of Celtic
studies named Tim Saunders in an article which he entitled 'Scubyon
Lyenegyl' (Literary garbage). The Cornish word for garbage is, in
fact, lyenak. Tim Saunders rejects many of Nance's Unified Cornish
and coins words from Breton or Welsh sources which does make for
confusion among revivalists who follow the Unified system. Saunders,
who is currently attempting to translate into Cornish some writings of
the Irish Marxist revolutionary James Connolly (executed following
the 1916 Irish uprising), accused the revivalists of being afraid of real
life 'so they are continually fleeing to a world of romantic illusions':[22]

> Poetry must have a substance—that is, the substance of the life
> around us. We have no past, so we must build a future—through
> our literature. A native literature can show us our own character-
> istics: also what is to be done? Fighting to realise our potential
> is the only justification for literary activity in our ancient tongue.

Mr Hooper has dismissed most of Saunder's criticisms as nonsense:

> It is easy to write in a language by adopting and respelling scores
> of Welsh or Breton words—but what about the readers who have
> Cornish dictionaries? It is true that words lacking in Cornish
> have to be adopted from Welsh and Breton sources but these new
> words must be agreed upon and made available in a new
> dictionary.

As for Saunders criticism of lack of 'down to earth' literature, Mr
Hooper feels that the language must walk before it can run. 'Who
is going to read this 'down to earth' stuff he wants to see? Writers
here wish to learn the language before they write!' Nevertheless,

radical criticism, especially by a younger generation of Cornish writers, can only give new impetus and dimension to revivalist literature. Perhaps a new, more earthy, modern literature may be produced which will have more relevance and appeal to the young people who are now being attracted by the revival.

Academic studies on the language since the Second World War to the present time have come mostly from America. In December 1944, J. J. Parry of the University of Illinois read a paper to the Celtic Group of the Modern Language Association of America entitled 'An Dasserghyans Kernewek: the Cornish language revival'. Interest spread in several American universities and the University of Washington in Seattle contained a special School of Cornish Studies, something no United Kingdom university possessed until 1972. Dr Eugene van Tassel Graves of Columbia University published the first important work to appear on the language in America on Old Cornish.[23] This was an edition of the *Vocabularium Cornicum* of the twelfth century. Explaining the work in an article 'outline of a doctoral thesis' Dr Graves commented: 'It is indeed basic to the history of the Cornish language, being almost the whole body of Old Cornish.'[24] Quoodle of the *Spectator*[25] lost no time in poking fun at this serious study. He claimed that Dr Graves was the only person to receive a degree in Cornish from Columbia University. 'Bully for Graves. But if I am right that the Cornish language is virtually extinct, who then, examined him?' Dr Graves's degree was in general linguistics. As *Old Cornwall* commented: 'This comment is as unenlightened as it is unfair. The Latin language is dead and yet Quoodle must have studied it and suffered examination in it. The hieroglyphs of the Rosetta Stone illustrate a dead language; are they and it of no human value?'[26] Quoodle's concern was probably to denigrate the language revivalists but, unfortunately, he had chosen to do this by denigrating a serious scholastic study.

Other work on Cornish appeared in America such as *The Cornish Ordinalia*, a new translation by Markham Harris.[27] This is quite an extraordinary work. The version seems prepared solely for the American market in a prose style which is a mixture of North American English dialect and a Victorian civil service English. Characters in the play use such phrases as 'hard work out'; 'some real hell'; 'all-fired'; 'gonna'; 'oughta'; 'kinda rough'; interspersed with 'redirect your attention' and 'permanent basis', etc. Mr Hooper, reviewing the work, says: 'the present book is entertaining but the remark of Bentley

G*

to Pope concerning his Iliad comes to mind, "You have made a pretty poem, Mr. Pope, but you must not call it Homer." ' Professor Markham Harris, of the Department of English at the University of Washington, writes: 'My goal was to produce, insofar as possible, a rendering that would prove responsible to the original and, what I think of as equally important from a literary point of view, responsive to the considerable range of tone to be found in the Cornish.' He is currently working on a translation of *Beunans Meriasek*. The University of Bristol's English-language production of the *Ordinalia*, which was staged in Perran Round, during July 1969, was prepared by Neville Denny of the University (Drama Department) and Professor Harris. A sound recording was made of the performances and the University of California made a documentary film based on them which was released in September 1971.

Dr Phyllis Harris, Professor Harris's wife, prepared an edition of the *Origo Mundi* drama from the *Ordinalia* for her doctoral dissertation. This was supervised by Professor David Fowler and published as *Origo Mundi, A New Edition* by Phyllis Pier Harris (University Microfilms, Ann Arbor, Michigan, 1964). Dr Harris prepared her text from the MMS. Bodley 791 with a literal translation and an exhaustive glossary, the whole reflecting what has been done in Middle Cornish scholarship since the Edwin Norris edition of the *Ordinalia*.

Mr Hooper writes:[28]

There is a revival of interest in old Cornish religious plays especially in America where it is possible to get published studies such as Longsworth's *The Cornish Ordinalia* [Harvard University]; and others make use of Norris or Nance and Smith to experiment with metres and English embellishments for stage production but which have little to do with Cornwall and nothing at all to do with the subject of this essay which concerns the language itself. Nance's work was done only for the better understanding of the original.

Mr Hooper has also commented:[29]

The revival has dangers, e.g. 'scholars' like the Americans who paraphrase Norris-Nance-and-Smith and call it a 'translation'. They wouldn't do that in Breton or Welsh—too many native speakers would have shot them down. But Cornish is safe for exploitation.

What has been missing for a long time has been an institute devoted solely to Cornish studies. Mebyon Kernow, in pressing for a *Penscol Kernow* (Cornish university), had this idea in mind. Until 1972 there was little scholastic work done in Cornwall on the linguistic field outside of the revivalist movement. In 1969 the University of Exeter put forward the idea of a board of Cornish studies on the model of the board of Celtic studies maintained by the University of Wales. Co-operation was sought and made with the Cornwall county council and by 1972 the two bodies jointly sponsored an Institute of Cornish Studies which became fully operative on 1 October 1972, operating from Trevenson House, Pool, Redruth, Cornwall. The Institute is not a direct teaching institution; its initial aim is to provide 'a focus for, and the co-ordination and encouragement of, all forms of research in Cornwall'.

The first director of the Institute is Professor Charles Thomas, a forty-four-year-old professor of archaeology, a native of Camborne, president of the Council for British Archaeology and president of the Royal Institution of Cornwall. Dr Frank A. Turk was appointed Senior Research Fellow, Natural Sciences, responsible for the Institute's Biological Research Centre. Miss Myrna M. Combellack, from Carharrack, near Redruth, was appointed personal assistant to Professor Thomas. Oliver J. Padel was appointed Place Names Research Fellow and Miss Ann Carreck and John P. Stengelhofen were appointed China Clay Research Fellows. There is a strong interest in the Institute on the Cornish language. Professor Thomas, the director, is particularly interested in the phonetics of spoken Middle Cornish and the enlargement of the Old and Middle Cornish lexical material from place names and certain aspects of the 'miracle plays', their origin and details of physical performances. Miss Combellack, who finished a year of Middle Cornish at Leeds University before taking up her appointment, is concerned with the propagation of the Institute's linguistic work in Cornish while Oliver Padel, who spent two years with Professor Kenneth Jackson (one of the foremost Celtic authorities) in Edinburgh, is concerned with a place-name study as well as working with Professor Thomas and Miss Combellack on a corpus of the fifth to eighth century A.D. south western inscribed stones as a source for British (Celtic) names. The Institute, which issues an annual journal called *Cornish Studies*, should add a new scholastic impetus to the revivalist movement. Both Professor Thomas and Miss Combellack represent the Institute on the Cornish Language Board. But, of course,

the scholars have 'academic reservations' on the revivalist movement. Professor Thomas writes:[30]

> Our Institute takes the view that the so called 'Unified Spelling' invented by Nance has never been explained, i.e. we have never had any real discussion of the principles on which it was based. We regard the dictionaries with their high proportion of words invented by the comparative method as suspect, because they don't give dated forms, and we feel that some of the lost words can probably be recovered from dated Middle Cornish place-names and may prove to be other than the forms invented for them by Nance. Lastly, following the work of the Leeds Survey of English Dialects, we suspect that the pronunciation currently used for modern Cornish (based on an ultimate form of Wessex Middle English) may be wrong and that the true phonetic range is still just recoverable from an area west of an isogloss that cuts off the Land's End and part of the south side of the Lizard.

Professor Thomas made a similar criticism in 1963 when, as president of the Cornish Branch of the Celtic Congress, he delivered a paper on the language revival to the congress at their meeting at Carbis Bay, St Ives, in April:[31]

> More serious criticism comes from the rarified world of Celtic scholarship. It has been pointed out, justly, that no really reputable linguist has worked over the remnants of Cornish, that definitive editions of the major texts, the medieval miracle plays are lacking; and that the reconstructed language is full of assumptions, accretions and inaccuracies.

Although this statement is strongly disputed by the revivalists, Professor Thomas points out that modern Celticists, like Professor Jackson, unite in ignoring any of Nance's or Smith's work and almost all of Jenner. When they are obliged to quote Cornish words they do so from Williams's *Lexicon*. Giving the O'Donnell lecture at Oxford in 1958 Professor C. L. Wrenn observed:

> Yet the most recent Cornish dictionary, that of Mr. Morton Nance, having access to a fairly up to date linguistic apparatus though much condensed through lack of space, displays that

scarcely scientific revivalist local patriotism which is still so
commonly associated with Cornish studies.

Professor Thomas asked, 'are these criticisms, is this widespread
ignoring of Nance's work, justified? In the field of the Cornish
revival, no. In the field of European scholarship, I have to say yes.'
In 1963 he urged the compilation of a comparative dictionary of the
Cornish language in its Old, Middle and Late phases, giving all
variant forms, however wild, all cognates, all derivations and—
most important—sources and dates for each form. He also urged that
full editions of the 'miracle plays' and associated fragments be published and, third, that a series of analytical studies on grammar be
made, to place the study of Cornish on the same footing as that of all
other Celtic languages. The revivalists have answered that it is easy
to make such proposals but quite another thing to find the money to
finance such projects. It seems that with the foundation of the
Institute of Cornish Studies under the directorship of Professor
Thomas some funds might be forthcoming and we may look forward
to new directions and discoveries in the linguistic field.

How do the revivalists answer academic criticisms? The general
secretary of the Cornish Languages Board, Mr G. Pawley White,
answers: 'no rejoinder is needed by the Board, the attitude of which
to Unified Cornish and its recognition that it is not intended for
advanced linguistic students, is set out fully in its policy statement,
sections 3-5.' This appears later in this chapter. In answer to criticisms
of Nance's work, Mr Hooper has replied:

Nance's aim was simple: to choose the best form on both phonetic
and historical grounds. He changed his own spelling somewhat as
can be seen by reading each story in *Old Cornwall* from 1925 to his
last in 1959—always leaning towards the 'old texts' spelling,
discarding the letter 'i' altogether, which was perhaps a pity.
Whims and arbitrary spellings are not absent, I admit, but who
could he consult? He had to harmonise Old, Middle and Late
Cornish and there are words in all three which are not found
in the others. On the other hand an ancient word is found in the
Anglo-Cornish dialect which is not written in Cornish.

Nance's problem was a tremendous one. According to Hooper,
'Nance introduced hyphens which are useful to learners, I think.

But away from exercises they tend to make Cornish look silly, especially joining particle *a* to the verb. Nance followed Breton grammar. They are not used now except to join some enclitics like -ny; -vy; -ma; -na; etc.' In fact, F. J. B. MacDowell (Map Estern Du) wrote a poetical dig at Nance's hyphens called '*Hyphennow*'. Most revivalists think that Nance fully explained his Unified system in the introductions to his dictionaries.

For all the criticism made of the revivalist movement, it must be pointed out that, had it not been for the revivalists, 'the rarified world' of scholarship might have by-passed Cornish studies altogether and a great many remains of the language would probably have been lost. As Professor Thomas has stated: 'Unquestionably the most important result [of the revivalist movement] has been the preservation of a very large amount of the Cornish language, mostly from the period labelled Middle Cornish before the declining of the language got right out of hand.'

But the world of scholarship apart, the Cornish language revival has left distinct visible signs on everyday life in Cornwall. For example, new houses, roads and housing estates are being named in Cornish. In this respect Dr Bannister's and Dr Charnock's pioneering work on Cornish names was continued by T. F. G. Dexter who published a very useful survey in 1929 which contained 1,600 Cornish names, their meanings and how to name one's house in Cornish.[32] Nance's work on place names and personal names remains invaluable.[33] His pamphlet *A Guide to Cornish Place Names*, published by the Federation of Old Cornwall Societies, has run to numerous editions while *An Introduction to Cornish Place Names* by P. A. S. Pool is another important survey. The recent publication of *Names for the Cornish*, containing 300 Cornish Christian names, by Christopher Bice (Lodenek Press) has enabled many Cornish people to name their children with traditional names. With such guides the visitor to Cornwall, and more importantly the Cornish people themselves, are no longer confused by what appears to be a meaningless jumble of syllables in place names. Cornish now becomes a visible sign of expressing Cornish nationhood. A public house in Mabe Burnthouse bears the sign 'New Inn/*Tavern Noweth*' while the Cubert post office has the sign '*Lytherva*/Post Office'. Another example of the visible signs of the revival are the numerous schools, societies, even rugby clubs, which adopt mottoes in the Cornish language. Also the number of memorials, tombstones or commemoration stones appearing which are inscribed in Cornish. They

keep the language not only before the visitors but the people themselves. Examples of these are John Davey's memorial in Zennor, erected by St Ives Old Cornwall Society in 1930; the plaque to commemorate the 'last Cornish sermon' unveiled by Mr Hooper in Landewednack on 11 June 1960; the plaque in St Keverne churchyard commemorating the 'An Gof' uprising in 1497, unveiled by Alderman Foster, chairman of the county council in 1966; and many others.

The language has distinct commercial possibilities in attracting Cornwall's annual two and a half million tourists. In 1966 Cornish Co-operative stores were selling bread in wrappers decorated with choughs, fishing boats, miners and fishermen, bearing the inscription *Bara an gwella dyworth Kernow!* (The best bread from Cornwall!) Binoculars are advertised with the name *Kernow* as a sign of quality. Serviettes and tea towels, bearing Cornish words on them, have proved popular as well as Christmas cards in Cornish and a Cornish calendar (published every year since 1955 by Mebyon Kernow); car plaques bearing the name *Kernow* in silver on a black background have also proved their commercial value. A Truro cinema, in 1968, advertising the spectacular musical *Camelot* about King Arthur had *Arthur Myghtern A Ve Hag a Vyth* (Arthur, Once and Future King) in high letters across its frontage.

The resurrection of a church service in Cornish by Tyr ha Tavas in 1934 has put the language back into religious life. Mr Hooper translated the Church of England order of matrimony into Cornish and this was first used in practice at a wedding at Perranwell on 3 October 1964, at a ceremony conducted by the Rev. D. R. Evans (Gwas Cadoc). On Saturday, 20 November 1965, P. A. S. Pool (Gwas Galva) and Miss Audrey Humphris (Keltya) were married in Cornish and English in Truro Cathedral. The Bridal March was 'Kernow agan Mamvro' and the three hymns were all in Cornish. The bride and groom gave their responses first in Cornish and then in English while the lessons were read in Cornish and the dean of Truro blessed the ring in the language. Cornish was also used at the reception afterwards in the many congratulatory telegrams and messages.

Another outward display of the revival is the performance of old Celtic folk customs, such as the Midsummer Bonfires, now well established and popular. The Midsummer Bonfires are an ancient Celtic custom connected with the old Celtic religion. According to Cyril Noall, 'these bonfires were supposed to have been kindled by the Druids on the first of May on all their sacred places, and on the tops

of their cairns, in honour of Bel. . .'.[34] Bel represented the sun,
the life force of the world. There are no records of the Cornish tradition
of Celtic gods but the survival of the Midsummer in Cornwall indicates
similar worship in Cornwall as in the other Celtic countries. For
example, in Scotland the first day of the May month was called *La
Buidhe Bealltuinn,* the golden yellow day of the fires of Bel. It was an
apt description for the whins would be in bloom across the hillside
making a golden yellow carpet and the tiny whinchat, the small bird
which frequented the yellow gorse, would add its colouring to the
vivid shade of yellow. *La Buidhe Bealltuinn* was the old Druidic new
year, the day on which the ceremony of *Bealltuinn* was held. Praise
would be offered up to Bel for having brought victory to the powers of
light over darkness and for bringing his people within sight of yet
another harvest. Prayers were offered so that Bel, the sun, might
shine the light of his countenance upon the harvest and the people
might not starve. On that day all the fires of each household were
extinguished. Then, at a given time, torches were kindled by the
priests from the sacred fires of Bel and taken to each house where the
household fires were rekindled to give each household a fresh start
in the eyes of Bel for the new year. A number of cattle from each herd
was driven sun-wise in the ancient circles of Bel, through close-set
fires as a symbol of purification by fire—the earthly embodiment of
Bel. With the spread of Christianity native superstition and customs
were incorporated into the service of the new religion, although the
Christian clergy preferred to replace the name of the month *Bealltuinn* with the Latin *maius,* the month the ancient Romans held sacred
to Maia, mother of Mercury. Illogically they reasoned that as Rome
was the Holy City, Roman pagan deities were more acceptable than
their own. The May month is still called in Irish *Bealtaine* and although
the month is now called *An Ceitean* in Scottish Gaelic, Scots Law
continued to name its May Term as the *Beltane* term up to the nineteenth century. The Cornish name *Mys–Me* for the May month is
obviously derived from Latin/English influence. Incredibly the old Celtic
religious custom survived in Cornwall as late as 1914. Bottrell, writing
in 1873, indicates the tradition was fast dying out.[35] But according
to Cyril Noall although the fires appeared to have been discontinued
elsewhere, Camborne still had its traditional May Day bonfires until
1914. In 1929 the Old Cornwall Societies revived the Celtic custom
with a chain of bonfires from Chapel Carn Brea, overlooking Land's
End, through the eighty-mile length of the Cornish peninsula to Kit

Hill on the Devon border. It is now an annual festivity growing in popularity each year.

Another Celtic revival is that of wrestling. As we have observed Cornwall was particularly renowned for its wrestling, especially during the medieval period. The style is similar to that used by wrestlers in Brittany, Wales and Cumberland, all of which share the Celtic tradition in common. In 1811 it is recorded that 4,000 spectators saw a contest at Bodmin. After 1826 interest in Cornish wrestling faded until 1923 when the Cornish Wrestling Association was formed. In 1927 William Tregoning Hooper (Bras y Golon) joined forces with the Breton Dr Cottonac of Quimper and decided to revive the connections between the two Celtic countries by means of annual wrestling tournaments. The Breton province of Cornouaille has a similar style to that of Cornwall. Since 1927 Cornish wrestlers have visited Brittany and Breton wrestlers have paid reciprocal visits to Cornwall. Although the Celtic style of wrestling is popular in Cornwall only Truro Cathedral School currently teaches it as part of its physical education syllabus.

Jenner and Nance formed the Federation of Old Cornwall Societies basically to create an interest in the language. The Cornish Gorsedd became for many years the focal point of the revivalist movement. But there has never been a Cornish Language Society, such as advocated by Smith. Under E. G. R. Hooper's guidance a Cornish Language Committee was formed which updated the Cornish-language examinations, but it had long been felt that there should be a central unifying body, which would look after all aspects of the revivalist movement. In November 1967, Kesva an Tavas Kernewek was established under the co-chairmanship of the Grand Bard of the Gorseth Kernow and the president of the Federation of Old Cornwall Societies. A policy statement was issued on 11 November 1967:

1   The Board exists to promote the study and revival of the Cornish language, initially by continuing the Publications, Examinations and Competitions formerly sponsored by the Cornish Gorsedd and the Federation of Old Cornwall Societies, but also by any other means which may prove possible.

2   The Board has no connection with any political organisation.

3   The Board considers that Unified Cornish provides an acceptable common basis for spelling modern writings in the Language, such a basis being essential if the revival is to secure any degree

of public acceptance. For this reason all works intended for students or for general reading should continue to use Unified Spelling and no deviation therefrom should be encouraged. It is however recognised that Unified Cornish has little significance for more advanced linguistic studies.

4   The Board accepts the prime need for publication of texts and translations of the medieval Cornish literature, and considers that where possible the original texts should be printed as well as the Unified. If however this is prevented by expense, the Unified texts could be published alone (with translation).

5   The Board recognises that the resources available in Cornwall may be insufficient to bring about proper research into and publication of all necessary texts in the foreseeable future, and for that reason welcomes and where possible will encourage competent projects for such research and publication originating outside Cornwall.

6   The Board believes that the object of the revival of Cornish should be to make it readily available as an optional second language for those Cornish people who want it. It does not aim at seeing Cornish replace English as first language of the Cornish people.

7   While attaching the greatest importance to Cornish being taught as an optional language in as many schools in Cornwall as possible, the Board has no wish to force the Language on school pupils or anyone.

8   The Board considers that Cornish should be available as a subject at all GCE and CSE examination levels, and until this is achieved it will hold its own examinations. It would wish to encourage the study of the language at Universities.

9   The Board recognises that, if Cornish is to be effectively revived for modern use, considerable extensions of the existing vocabulary will be necessary to cover things not in existence when Cornish was traditionally spoken. In evolving new words every due care should be taken to ensure that each has a sound linguistic basis, and due attention given to the way in which such problems are dealt with in other Celtic countries, especially Wales and Brittany.

Under the guidance of the Cornish Language Board the revivalist movement has consolidated its position. Its first *Scryvynyas Kemyn*

(secretary general) was P. A. S. Pool who was succeeded by the former Grand Bard, G. Pawley White, in 1970. The Board has reprinted the dictionaries, and Pool's *Cornish for Beginners*. It has also published Gendall's *Kernewek Bew* (Living Cornish), a Unified version of *Passyon agan Arluth* by Nance and Smith, edited by Mr Hooper, and works such as *Lyver Pysadow, Ordenal Mythynesow, An Venen ha'y Vap* and *John of Chyannor*. The Board has also issued an LP record made by a variety of Cornish speakers.

The number of people learning the language is growing all the time. During the year 1971-2 there were nearly 150 learners taking Cornish classes in Cornwall. An idea has already been mooted to issue a 'bezant' or round button hole badge to all who can speak Cornish which would encourage recognition of such speakers by each other and so help to promote conversational Cornish. This would be similar to the Irish *Fainne,* the Manx *Yn Fainey* and the Scottish *Cruinne*. Already *New Cornwall* magazine provides a regular column in Cornish under the title *Urth an Besont*. Miss Petchey maintains the corresponding tradition with *An Kelgh Keltek* (Celtic Writing Circle), encouraging correspondence in the language. It is difficult, however, to get an idea of exactly how many people have a knowledge of the language because, of course, one must define the degree of knowledge. By 1969 there were eighty Bards of the Cornish Gorsedd who had been admitted after passing the Gorsedd examination in the language. Mr Hooper writes: 'As for speakers of Cornish, that's like asking how many speakers of Latin, French and Spanish there are in Cornwall.' However, he continues, 'there are more people than we can guess who know enough to read *An Lef Kernewek* but often, alas, as if it were a crossword puzzle, translating it as they go; this would infuriate Caradar (Smith).' According to G. Pawley White, 'of the hundreds who have already passed examinations a considerable number should be able to conduct a simple conversation'.

What is the future of the language revival and what are the aims of the revivalists? Speaking in 1963 Professor Thomas said that the aims

include, not so much the revival of Cornish as a spoken vernacular, an impossible task, but preparation of conditions under which any moderately intelligent person can learn a form of the Cornish language; as a concomitant of this, the reduction of the highly confused spelling of the existing texts and manuscripts

to an artificial system of orthography which R. Morton Nance invented, and called 'Unified Spelling'; the creation, by means of various societies, journals and other means, of a climate of opinion towards this linguistic revival which, if not a nationalist movement, closely resembles the conditions from which nationalist movements are liable to emerge; and, lastly, the preservation within the framework of a rapidly changing social and economic environment of all those aspects of Cornish life that recall on the one hand the period of spoken Cornish, on the other the isolated life of Cornwall prior to the industrial revolution.

The aims of the majority of language revivalists were expressed by Richard Gendall, the author of *Kernewek Bew,* in an article entitled 'Cornish as an optional subject in schools' which appeared in *New Cornwall* and is reproduced here in its entirety:[36]

The basis of the arguments against the study or use of Cornish at all, in or out of school, is generally that the language is supposed to have been dead by 1800 A.D. and that its resuscitation as a living language is unrealistic and irrelevant to the modern world; that any study of it is bound to be of academic interest only.

To see Cornish in perspective, however, a valid simile can be made with a camp fire that has been allowed to die down so that the flames and smoke are no longer visible, yet whose ashes cover a quantity of charcoal, itself already mostly black and apparently lifeless, but capable of rekindling if raked together and blown upon, with the addition of a little fresh combustible material. Before long, a bright fire is again burning. The size and life of the fire thereafter depends on the will of the stokers.

Enough living embers were, in fact, gathered together by Henry Jenner in the last century, and a small fire rekindled. That fire is not only still alight but has grown considerably in intensity. Cornish is alive and it is undeniable that an ever increasing number of people from all walks of life are taking an interest in it.

Why take this trouble to save Cornish? Few sensitive people question the good sense of attempting to save rare animal and plant life from extinction, having almost too late become aware of the appalling destruction which human progress leaves in its

wake. A great deal of trouble is also taken to preserve the works of man himself . . . even industrial buildings such as mine-engine houses, scarcely a century old, to say nothing of Georgian, Restoration and Tudor buildings and so on into the past; the more ancient (or often the more 'useless') the object the greater the interest in preservation.

Why not preserve a language? What could be a greater work of art—on a national scale too. What is a greater or more revealing treasure-house of a given community than the language which it has itself developed, and which should hold the key to its character or way of thought?

My own interest in Cornish—not necessarily an argument for teaching it in school—is due simply to my love for it, and its representing for me the epitome of Cornwall and the Cornish. I find Cornwall in the Cornish language. At the same time I am convinced that over the past few generations the Cornish have been steadily losing their self respect in the same measure as they have been losing their traditions. This is not a rare phenomenon in the history of the world. Too remote from the South East to ever be truly in the 'national' swim, further, indeed, from the 'capital' of the South West Region, Bristol, than Bristol is from London, and having, moreover, her own history (sadly neglected in schools, if not completely overlooked), Cornwall must, I am convinced, be Cornwall, take a pride in her self, recognise herself for the entity she is. In practical terms, the outcome would be less complaining and more application to the job in hand: ultimately a more flourishing, contented and useful community. I am not saying that the answer is that we should all learn Cornish, but even a little knowledge of Cornish would help engender, or revive and strengthen this necessary sense of self-respect.

Recently, persons publicly recognised as responsible citizens—Members of Parliament—have become convinced of Cornwall's need to manage to a greater or lesser extent her own affairs, and have said so openly. This may, of course, be no more than political expediency on their part, but that they could say this in public is almost entirely due to those who first began to revive the Cornish language with all its implications, not vice versa. *Mebyon Kernow,* for instance, the focal point of these trends today, was itself a product of the language revival movement. 'Without

language, without land' say our nearest relations, the Bretons.
The French have realised the truth of this saying and have long
been trying to belittle and ultimately stifle Breton. They do not
wish Brittany to have peacefully what Ireland had by force, and
was the better for. The Cornish language has already begun,
through peaceful means, to raise heads of Cornish people; to wish
otherwise is to ill-wish.

I am glad that at school I was taught, largely against my will,
French, Spanish, and Latin. Cornish I had to teach myself as well
as a schoolboy could. After the War, when I was training as a
teacher, my tutor leaned over backwards to convince us that the
learning of language has cultural and 'entente' value, but had
been 'proved by research' to have no value as a mental exercise.
My own experience has been to the contrary—I am convinced
that the study of any language is an excellent means of mental
development.

In spite of this, I do not advocate compulsory Cornish: far from
it! Yet those who do study it will find that, as in the case of other
languages, it demands self-discipline, gives in return some
insight into the character of the people who have developed it,
and rewards one with new horizons. Perhaps only linguists can
get the maximum out of a language but one can both learn and
enjoy an idiom without being a linguist. My most enthusiastic
Cornish class was composed of children from a Secondary
Modern school, none of them linguists, and some, I am tempted
to say, finding more difficulty with their English than with their
Cornish! But they were delighted to discover the Cornish
language and to know it belonged to them; it seemed to give a
decided boost to their morale, and they were remarkably quick
at picking up the spoken idiom.

Cornish, alas!, has very little literature, and in this respect
is at a great disadvantage. Though it seems that great, inter-
nationally famous works such as Tristan and Iseult and also the
Arthurian tales were originally in Cornish, these works, if they
were written down at all, have disappeared. When Cornwall lost
her independence, and her native rulers, Cornish became the
language of the people—such literary remains as there are were
written for the common people, not for an élite of high society.
It might be argued here that since this literature is almost
entirely Christian in content, being a dramatised version of the

underlying facts of the Old and New Testaments, this makes it more worth while of study than much of the censurable works of doubtful moral content which often 'get through' as literature.

But it was, after all, the common man who kept Cornish alive, and it comes down to us today as he developed it from the parent British tongue. This language is, therefore, an inalienable part of Cornwall's heritage—even of Britain's heritage—and it should be put within reach of Cornwall's children.

Is it at all reasonable to expect the language to be put within reach of Cornish children, to hope for the introduction of the Cornish language and literature into the school's curricula even as an optional subject? J. G. Harries, secretary of education for the Cornwall county council, states: 'the Education Committee have not given any directive to schools on the teaching of the Cornish language. Heads are free to prepare their own syllabus and the Committee are satisfied that much teaching of Cornish history is at present done by environmental studies.'[37] None of the Committee's schools teaches the Cornish language although 'the committee would certainly raise no objection to the Cornish language being taught in the Secondary Schools as an optional subject, but they give no direction to Heads on this matter, as the curriculum of each school is the responsibility of the Head'. Nevertheless, the Education Committee have appointed a representative, F. L. Harris O.B.E., M.A., C.A. of Redruth, to serve on the Cornish Language Board. The Education Committee endorses the evening classes in the language which, in the 1972/3 period, were held in nine centres in Cornwall. Should any school wish to include the language in its curriculum 'any school which needs text books on the language can purchase them out of their annual capitation allowance for books etc.' But, 'teachers of the language are normally required to have passed the Final Examination which is set by the Cornish Language Board.'[38] This means that the revivalists have to try to persuade each individual head master as to the value of including the language and its literature as an optional subject in his school.

The Cornish language revival is, as we have seen, part of the wider Celtic renaissance which started at the end of the nineteenth century, waned a little, and since the early 1960s has flared up again with increasing determination. Trevor Fishlock recently phrased the situation in this way:[39]

On the edge of north-west Europe the Celts are making their last stand. As distinct peoples they have been for 2,000 years a bright thread in the evolution of European civilisation and now they have reached the ultimate crisis in their long march and decline. They are a tough remnant, not a relic, and by the end of the century it will be possible to judge whether they have gouged out for themselves a worthwhile or valid future existence, or have been effectively erased by the progress to which they have contributed much.

The nationalism which manifests itself in all six Celtic countries is basically a linguistic and cultural struggle and therefore part of a world movement. It is a reaction to the growing world sickness. All over the globe there is a groping new individualism rising in revolt against the mass society of our day. The revolt is against the tremendous drive of 'big power' politicians towards a world state, a world government and a world language and culture. Unity through uniformity would be the end result, a world where there are no 'national barriers'. This is a simplistic way of achieving world peace and co-operation by an attempt to destroy natural differences between national groupings (language and culture). It would be the achievement of that fallacious dream of a *Brave New World*.[40]

It is often said that language is merely a means of communication. If this is true then the development of the vast range of different languages spoken throughout the world has been one of the great catastrophies of human history. If this is true then we must hope that the countless languages of the world may soon be reduced so that we can have a confrontation between the thirteen major languages to see which one will emerge dominant. But language is more than a material means of communication. Culture is that very distinct quality of living that is to the community what personality is to the individual. The main medium of mental cultivation, or culture, is language and diversity of language is absolutely necessary for a rich diversity of culture. Brennan has written:[41]

If this ever growing uniformity of the material side of our life is not offset by rich cultural diversification, then man will face an awful crisis of a deadly sameness and monotony of life, a frightening prospect of utter boredom of spirit which would deprive him not merely of the will to achieve but the very desire to survive.

Indeed, T. S. Eliot, in his *Notes Towards the Definition of Culture*, maintained:

It is an essential part of my case that if the other cultures of the British Isles were wholly superseded by English culture, English culture would disappear too. It is probable, I think, that complete uniformity of culture throughout these islands would bring about a lower grade of culture altogether.

The more the individual, the community and the national community feel that they have something particular of their own to contribute to mankind, the more they will respect themselves and thereby respect others; the more they will be heartened to develop that unique set of values which they possess. It would seem that diversification of language and culture is the product of a very fundamental law of human nature. Critics claim that languages are barriers but barriers need not be purely negative things: they can be creative. Barriers to reproduction between originally interbreeding sections of plant and animal life have been the means of enabling these to speciate and produce the present rich variety of living forms. At the cultural level, the partial barrier of languages enables different groups to develop, diversify and enrich their own inherited cultures instead of having their individuality finally washed out in a flat uniformity. Language is a product of many centuries of cultural development, a vehicle of all the wisdom, poetry, legend and history which is bequeathed to a people by its forbears. Rough hewn, chiselled and polished with loving care it is handed down as a beautiful work of art— the greatest art form in the world—the noblest monument of man's genius. The repression of minority languages and cultures is due not only to a cynical expansionist policy but also to a materialistic lack of understanding of the values enshrined in language and culture. It is generally believed that a language that does not possess a rich literature is a poor vehicle of expression. Eduard Sapir writes:[42]

The most primitive South African Bushman expresses himself with the help of a rich symbolic system which in essence is quite comparable to the language of a cultured Frenchman. . . Many primitive languages have a richness of form, a wealth of possibilities of expression which surpasses anything known in the languages of modern culture.

Language, thought and culture are inseparable. According to Simeon Potter:[43]

> Purely verbal thinking—thinking in words without images—is the highest form of conceptual cognition of which a human being is capable. If this is so, may it not follow that a man's outlook on life is in some measure determined for him by the structure of the language he learns as a child? After all, in those formative years between seven and twelve a normal child devotes a very great part of his mental energy to the acquisition and control of a working vocabulary and his whole vision is coloured accordingly. His view of the world becomes his private thought world and, as Eduard Sapir observed, 'the thought world is the microcosm that each man carries about within himself, by which he measures and understands what he can of the macrocosm.' This theory was further emphasised and elaborated by that profound American thinker Benjamin Lee Whorf (1897-1941) who made a deep study of Hopi, Shawnee, Nootka and other aboriginal languages. This so-called Whorfian hypothesis 'that a man's world outlook is determined by his linguistic upbringing' has probably been exaggerated by its more exuberant exponents, and yet few experienced philologists would gainsay its intrinsic truth.

Whorf says:

> We are inclined to think of language simply as a technique of expression and not to realise that language first of all is a classification and arrangement of the stream of sensory experience which results in a certain word order, a certain segment of the world that is easily expressible by the type of symbolic means that languages imply. In other words, language does in a cruder form but also in a broader and more volatile way the same thing that science does.

The destruction of languages and cultures is merely another all-important facet of the world's growing environmental sickness of which ecological pressure groups are becoming increasingly aware. Throughout the last hundred years we have witnessed many language struggles in Europe (see Chapter Seven). These have been the struggles of small nations, dominated and incorporated into large

states, which have sought, first, to regain their cultural and linguistic identity and then, as a natural process, their political, economic and social independence. Such struggles have always been built up from a language struggle; the effort to reconstruct a healthy community environment which has a prime concern for the health, welfare and integrity of the individual. In the countries where such struggles have taken place the native languages have been repressed by imperialism to the point of extinction or near extinction. Language movements have sprung up to revive the language and in the cases cited in Chapter Seven, have done so successfully.[44] There has, however, been only one example where a language, which completely ceased to be spoken as a vernacular, was restored as a modern language. This is the example of Hebrew in Israel, which died as a spoken language in the second or third century B.C. but its knowledge (like Latin) was kept for use in religious worship. Now it is the everyday speech of two and a half million Israelis. So in spite of destruction and desolation which follows man's search for material gain and empire, language revivals can work and have worked.

Those countries which have fallen under the influence of the major western languages, English, French, Spanish and German, have always found a remarkable degree of intolerance shown by the majority linguistic groups. It is interesting to compare this state of affairs with that prevailing among the nations under the influence of the Russian linguistic group. Out of the total 232 million people in the USSR today there are 125 million native Russian speakers while a further 35 million consider themselves Russian speaking in the latest census. Naturally enough the language is widely propagated through the educational programme of the Soviet Republics and used for technical advancement, political philosophy and so on. Most new words in other Soviet languages take their derivation from Russian. The language now shows signs of ousting some of the minor languages such as Samoyedic, Tungusic and the Palaeo-Siberian varieties simply because Russian has become the language with which to 'get on'—not because the other languages are ignored or suppressed but merely because Russian is the 'international language' in the Soviet world. Soviet policy is actively to encourage linguistic and cultural minorities to the extent that unwritten country vernaculars have acquired literary status; for example, a great many Soviet languages such as Abkaz, Chukchee, Dorgwa, Gilyak and others have only been written languages since the 1920s and 1930s. This encouragement contrasts

very strongly with the attitude of western countries such as England, France and Spain towards their linguistic minorities.[45] This is not to suggest that the USSR has no 'nationalities problem' but the linguistic situation of Soviet nationalities is far better than that of the Basques, Catalans, Celts, Frisians, Wends, etc.

Events in Cornwall, therefore, are neither unique nor parochial. Bearing in mind the need for the maintenance of human individuality in our growing world of uniformity and deadly sameness we can, if we are wise, wish the Cornish language revivalists well in their search for self and in their efforts not to lose all contact with the world of their forefathers. For when all argument is exhausted on the question why should Cornishmen learn Cornish, it is Henry Jenner's answer which remains clearly in the mind—'Because they are Cornish'.

Postscript

Since completing my manuscript, the Cornish language movement has continued to gain in strength. The Cornish Language Board still issues a very impressive amount of literature, not only dictionaries and grammars, but textbooks, religious works and general works. In the past year the Board has produced the missing 1,000 lines of *Trystan hag Ysolt*, left unfinished by A. S. D. Smith at his death. These were completed by David H. Watkins (Carer Brynow) who, with this work, won the Mordon-Caradar Bowl in the 1962 Gorsedd. Watkins was born in Trelewis, Wales, in 1892, and was made a Welsh bard (Bryn Ceri) at the Gorsedd Beirdd Ynys Prydain, Aberfan, in 1966. He first learnt Cornish when studying ancient Cornish history and, after a teaching career, he retired to Cornwall and aided the newly-formed Cornish Language Board. He died in 1969.

The Language Board have, this year, introduced the study of the history and literature of the language as a separate additional paper in the Advance Grade examination in the language.

The Federation of Old Cornwall Societies have not been idle and in the summer of 1973 they produced *Place Names of West Penwith* by P. A. S. Pool which is one of the most authoritative works on Cornish place names. The work consists of a glossary of the settlement-names of West Penwith, the Land's End peninsula, with a long introduction and explanation of Cornish words most commonly found in place names. On the subject of personal names *A Handbook of Cornish Surnames* by G. Pawley White also became available.

The Language Board are soon to publish *Whethlow an Mabinogion*, the Cornish version of the Mabinogion by A. S. D. Smith. Hitherto unpublished, this has been corrected and revised by E. G. R. Hooper.

Records and tapes for learners are not lacking now. Tapes of the lessons connected with Richard Gendall's *Kernewek Bew* are now available. There is an LP record of *Jowan Chy an Hor*, *Abram hag Ysak* and other tales in Cornish. Also, as a guide to the growing popularity of interest, came the release of the first commercial

stereo LP record of songs and poems in Cornish from Sentinel Records in 1973. This was *Crowdy Crawn*, which means a framework covered in skin, a drum-like receptacle for keeping useful odds and ends in. The songs and poems are sung and recited by the well known folk singer Brenda Wootton aided by Richard Gendall. *Crowdy Crawn* has proved so popular that it undoubtedly will be only the first of many such records.

It is true that many people still associate the revivalists with grey-haired academics. The *Sunday Times* of 7 April 1974, dispelled the idea when they published an article on 17-year-old Mary Truran. In 1972 Mary became the youngest bard of the Cornish Gorsedd, taking the name of Tamon (sea-pink, a rock plant found along the coast of Cornwall), having proved her proficiency in the language. Mary is now studying Celtic at Newnham College, Cambridge. She told the *Sunday Times*: 'What I hope to see is the Cornish language used again by ordinary people, not just an esoteric minority. A first step must be the introduction of the language as an optional subject in schools. There was great enthusiasm among schoolchildren when I conducted an experimental session and we played games in Cornish.' Mary Truran is one of the rising new generation of Cornish who may well achieve Morton Nance's dream of making Cornish 'walk' now that it has been so firmly set upon its feet.

Notes

Abbreviations

ALK	*An Lef Kernewek*
BM	British Museum
JBAS	*Journal of the British Archaeological Society*
JRIC	*Journal of the Royal Institution of Cornwall*
NLW	National Library of Wales
OC	*Old Cornwall*
PBA	*Proceedings of the British Academy*
PMLA	*Publications of the Modern Language Association of America*
PRO	Public Record Office
Report RCPS	*Report of the Royal Cornwall Polytechnic Society*
TPS	*Transactions of the Philological Society*

Introduction

1 *Speculum Magnae Britanniae pars Cornwall*, circa 1610.
2 *New Cornwall*, vol. xiii, no. 3.
3 P. A. S. Pool, *An Introduction to Cornish Place Names*, 2nd ed., privately published, Penzance, 1971.
4 *Macmillan's Magazine*, April, 1867.
5 A. S. D. Smith, *The Story of the Cornish Language*, revised by E. G. R. Hooper, *ALK*, Camborne, 1969.

Chapter One   Old Cornish

1 Max Müller, *Biographies of Words and the Home of the Aryas*, Longmans, London, 1888.
2 Eoin Mac Neill, *Phases of Irish History* (first published 1919), new ed. Gill, Dublin, 1968.
3 Liam Mac Mathúna, 'The Celtic languages', *Annual Book of the Celtic League*, 9 Bothar, Cnoc Síon, Baile Átha Cliath 9, Éire, 1971 and 1972.
4 Trevor Fishlock, 'The Celts: Europe's vanishing tribes', *The Times*, 11, 12 and 13 September 1972.
5 Joseph Raferty (ed.), *The Celts*, Mercier Press, Cork, 1964.

6 H. M. and Nora K. Chadwick, *The Growth of Literature*, 3 vols, Cambridge University Press, 1932.

7 Proinsias Mac Cana, *Celtic Mythology*, Hamlyn, London, 1970.

8 Henri Hubert, *The Greatness and Decline of the Celts*, Routledge & Kegan Paul, London, 1934.

9 Ibid.

10 Melville Richards, *The Laws of Hywel Dda*, Liverpool University Press, 1954; Laurence Ginnell, *The Brehon Laws*, Unwin, London, 1894; M. J. Macauliffe, *Gaelic Law*, Hodges & Figgis, London, 1924; John Cameron, *Celtic Law*, Hodge, London, 1937; Sophie Bryant, *Liberty, Order and Law under Native Irish Rule*, Harding & Moore, London, 1923, and *Ancient Laws of Ireland*, 6 vols, Dublin, 1865-1901.

11 *Ancient Laws of Cambria*, trans. from the Welsh by W. Probent, 2 vols, E. Williams, London, 1823.

12 Summarised by Edmund Spenser in *The Faerie Queen*, intro. by J. W. Hales, 2 vols, Everyman's Library, London, 1910, Book ii, stanza 39.

13 Nora K. Chadwick, *The Druids*, University of Wales Press, Cardiff, 1956.

14 Nora K. Chadwick, *The Celts*, Penguin Books, Harmondsworth, 1970; Jan Filip, *Celtic Civilisation and its Heritage*, Publishing House of Czech Academy, Prague, 1962; Anne Ross, *Everyday Life of the Pagan Celts*, Batsford, London, 1970 and Carousel Books, London, 1972.

15 Patrick Crampton, *Stonehenge of the Kings*, John Baker, London, 1967.

16 Sir John Morris-Jones, *Pre-Aryan Syntax in Insular Celtic*, Oxford University Press, 1900.

17 Kenneth Jackson, 'The Irish language and the languages of the world', in Brian Ó Cuív, (ed.), *A View of the Irish Language*, Stationery Office, Dublin, 1969.

18 Charles Woolf, *Introduction to the Archaeology of Cornwall*, D. Bradford Barton, Truro, 1970.

19 Nora K. Chadwick, 'The colonisation of Brittany from Celtic Britain', *PBA*, 1965.

20 Kenneth H. Jackson, *Language and History in Early Britain*, Edinburgh University Press, 1953.

21 David Greene, *The Irish Language*, Cultural Relations Committee of Ireland, Dublin, 1969.

22 Nora K. Chadwick, 'The British or Celtic part in the population of England', in *Angles and Britons*, University of Wales Press, Cardiff, 1963.

23 Mario Pei, *The Story of the English Language*, Allen & Unwin, London, 1968.

24 Kenneth Jackson, 'Angles and Britons in Northumbria and Cumbria', in *Angles and Britons*, University of Wales Press, Cardiff, 1963.

25 Anthony Conran (trans. and ed.), *The Penguin Book of Welsh Verse*, Penguin Books, Harmondsworth, 1967.

26 Henry Jenner, 'History of Cornish place names', in *Report RCPS*, vol. ii (n.s.), 1911-13.

27 Geoffrey Ashe (ed.), *The Quest for King Arthur's Britain*, Pall Mall Press, London, 1968. See also Henry Jenner, 'The Arthurian legend', *JRIC*, vol. lviii, 'Some possible Arthurian Place Names in West Penwith', *JRIC*, vol. xxi; and P. A. Lanyon Orgill, 'Cornwall and the Arthurian legends', *Cornish Review*, no. 6, winter, 1950.

28 Joseph Bédier, *Le Roman de Tristan par Thomas*, Paris, 1902-5.

29 Henry Jenner, 'The Tristan romance and its Cornish provenance', *JRIC*, vol. xviii. See also Loth in *Revue Celtique*, vol. xxxiii, 1912.

30 Joseph Loth, *Des Nouvelles Théories sur l'origine des Roman Arthurian*, privately published, Paris, 1892.

31 C. A. Ralegh, 'Report on the excavations at Castle Dore', *JRIC*, vol. i (n.s.), 1957.

32 R. Bromwich, *Trioedd Ynys Prydain*, University of Wales Press, Cardiff, 1961.

33 Gertrude Schopperle, *Tristan and Isolt, a study of the sources of the romance*, Frankfurt and London, 1913. See also the Ottendorfer Memorial Series of Germanic Monography of New York University, nos 3 and 4.

34 H. P. R. Finberg in *Antiquarian Journal*, vol. xlviii, 1968.

35 Henry Jenner, 'Cornwall—a Celtic nation', *Celtic Review*, vol. i, 1905.

36 Henry Jenner, 'The Bodmin Gospels' and 'The Manumissions in the Bodmin Gospels', *JRIC*, vol. xxi, 1922-5. See also F. E. Halliday, *A History of Cornwall*, Duckworth, London, 1959.

37 'Merlini prophetica cum expositione Joannis Cornubensis cod. membr. 8 Octob. 1474. Seac. XIV', Vatican Library, Rome. See also *Spicilegium Vaticanum Frauenfeld*, 1838, p. 92; and Whitley Stokes, 'Cornica', in *Revue Celtique*, vol. iii.

38 Jenner, 'The Tristan romance and its Cornish provenance'.

39 R. A. S. MacAlister, *Corpus Inscriptionum Insularum Celticarum*, vol. i, Stationery Office, Dublin, 1940.

40 F. Madam and H. H. E. Craster, *A Summary Catalogue of Western Manuscripts in the Bodleian Library*, Clarendon Press, Oxford, 1922-53.

41 MS. Bodley 572 for 14 S.C. 2026 (3).

42 Johann Casper Zeuss, *Grammatica Celtica*, Berlin, 1871, pp. 1060-3.

43 BM Additional MS. 9381. See also Jenner, 'The Bodmin Gospels'.

44 Halliday, op. cit.

45 P. Berresford Ellis, *A History of the Irish Working Class*, Gollancz, London, 1972.

46 BM, MSS. Cotton Vespasian, A XIV.

H

47 Eugene van T. Graves, *The Old Cornish Vocabulary*, University Microfilms, Ann Arbor, Michigan, 1964.
48 Henry Jenner, *A Handbook of the Cornish Language*, Nutt, London, 1904.
49 Sir R. C. Hoare (ed.), *Itinerarium Cambriae Giraldus Cambrensis*, London, 1804.
50 See Jenner, 'The Royal House of Damnonia', in *Report RCPS*, vol. ii, 1911/13 and vol. iv, (n.s.), 1916-22.
51 Ibid.

Chapter Two   Middle Cornish

1 Henry Jenner, 'Some possible Arthurian place names in West Penwith', *JRIC*, vol. xxi.
2 L. Elliott-Binns, *Medieval Cornwall*, Methuen, London, 1955.
3 See *JRIC*, vol. v, 1874-8.
4 *OC*, vol. i, p. 18; vol. iii, p. 29; vol. vii, p. 27.
5 L. C. J. Orchard, 'Some notes on the Cornish language in the fourteenth century', *OC*, vol. iii, no. 2.
6 Elliott-Binns, op. cit.
7 R. Morton Nance, 'The Cornish language in the seventeenth century', *OC*, vol. vi, no. 1.
8 Henry Jenner, *A Handbook of the Cornish Language*, Nutt, London, 1904.
9 Smith quoting Nance in *The Story of the Cornish Language*, A. S. D. Smith, Camborne, 1947; ed. by E. G. R. Hooper, *ALK*, Camborne, 1969.
10 Thurstan Peter, *The Old Cornish Drama*, Elliot Stock, London, 1906.
11 'The Cartulary of the collegiate church of St Thomas of Canterbury at Glasney', English trans. by J. A. C. Vincent, *JRIC*, vol. vi, 1879.
12 Henry Jenner, 'Some miscellaneous scraps of Cornish', in *Report RCPS*, vol. vi, 1928.
13 A. S. D. Smith, op. cit.
14 William Sandys, 'On the Cornish drama', *JRIC*, vol. iii, 1865.
15 David C. Fowler, 'The date of the Cornish Ordinalia', Records of the Pontifical Institute of Medieval Studies, *Toronto Medieval Studies*, vol. xxiii, 1961.
16 Bodleian Library, MS. Bodley 791 (SC 2639).
17 R. Morton Nance, 'A Cornish poem restored', *OC*, vol. iv, no. 10.
18 Thurstan Peter, op. cit.
19 Peniarth MS. 105. See also Nance's report on the MS. in the Nance papers in the Royal Institute of Cornwall, Truro.
20 A. L. Rowse, *Tudor Cornwall*, Cape, London, 1941. 2nd ed., Macmillan, London, 1969.
21 BM MS. Add. Chart. 1949. See also *Athenaeum*, 1 December 1877; *Revue Celtique*, vol. iv; Henry Jenner, 'The fourteenth century charter

endorsement', *JRIC*, vol. xx, 1915/16; and Nance's 'Unified Spelling' version, *OC*, vol. ii, no. 4.

22 BM, Harl. MSS. Harl. N. 1782. There are also two copies in the Bodleian Library and an incomplete copy in the Gwavas Collection (BM) and a fragment version with a Welsh and English translation BM Add. MS. 14,934. See also 'Unified Cornish' version in *Kernow*, 1933-5, and in *ALK*, nos 81-103. Also complete version *Passyon agan Arluth* in Unified Cornish by R. M. Nance and A. S. D. Smith, ed. Hooper, *Kesva an Tavas Kernewek*, 1972.

23 R. Morton Nance, 'The Plen an Gwary or Cornish playing places', *JRIC*, vol. xxiv, 1933-6.

24 Thurstan Peter, op. cit.

25 Henry Jenner, 'Cornish drama', *Celtic Review*, April/July, 1907.

26 Elliott-Binns, op. cit.

27 Mario Pei, *The Story of the English Language*, Allen & Unwin, London, 1968.

28 *Polychronicon*, 1364.

29 David C. Fowler, 'John Trevisa and the English Bible', *Modern Philology*, University of Chicago, vol. lviii, no. 2.

30 David C. Fowler, 'Piers Plowman and the Cornish Ordinalia', *PMLA*, 1961. See also *OC*, vol. v, no. 12.

31 Basil Cottle, *The Triumph of English 1350-1400*, Blandford, London, 1969.

32 Philip Ziegler, *The Black Death*, Collins, London, 1969.

33 A. R. Myers, *England in the Late Middle Ages*, Penguin Books, Harmondsworth, 1972.

Chapter Three   Tudor Cornwall

1 R. Morton Nance, 'The Cornish language in the seventeenth century', *OC*, vol. iv, no. 1.

2 Fred. W. P. Jago, *The English-Cornish Dictionary*, Simpkin Marshall, London, 1887.

3 *Historical Basis of Welsh Nationalism* (lectures), Plaid Cymru, Cardiff, 1950.

4 Gerald Morgan, *The Dragon's Tongue*, Triskel Press, Cardiff, 1966.

5 Henry Jenner, 'Cornwall: a Celtic nation', *Celtic Review*, vol. i, 1905.

6 R. Polwhele, *The History of Cornwall*, 7 vols, London, 1816.

7 H. A. L. Fisher, *The History of England*, London, 1928.

8 Ibid.

9 Francis Bacon, *The Life and Reign of Henry VII*, Brewman, London, 1790. See also Polydore Vergil, *Anglica Historia,* ed. Denis Hay, Historical Society of Great Britain, 1950; Edward Hall, *Chronicle*, ed. Sir Henry Ellis (collated with ed. of 1548-50), London, 1809; *The Great Chronicle of London*, eds A. H. Thomas and I. D. Thornley, Longmans, London, 1938.

10 Bacon, op. cit.
11 Ibid.
12 *The Great Chronicles of London*.
13 L. J. Smith (ed.), *Leland's Itinerary*, Centaur Press, London, 1964.
14 Fortescue Hitchins, *History of Cornwall*, 2 vols, Helston, 1824.
15 Letters & Papers of Henry VIII v. 1093 (PRO).
16 Ibid. Addenda 1324.
17 Nance, op. cit.
18 Polwhele, op. cit.
19 A. L. Rowse, *Tudor Cornwall*, Cape, London, 1941. 2nd ed., Macmillan, London, 1969.
20 Richard Carew (ed. T. Tonkin), *Survey of Cornwall*, Truro, 1811.
21 Rowse, op. cit.
22 Polwhele, op. cit.
23 Jago, op. cit.
24 S. D. 10/86 printed in Rose Troupe App. G.
25 Joseph Polsue, *The Complete History of Cornwall*, 4 vols, William Lake, Truro, and Hopten, London, 1867-73.
26 Printed in Poccoche 141 foll.
27 William Borlase, *Natural History of Cornwall*, 1758.
28 John B. D. Whitaker, *Ancient Cathedral of Cornwall*, 2 vols, London, 1804.
29 Corpus Christi College, Cambridge, MSS. Synddalia no. cxxi and BM MS. Egerton 2350 f. 54.
30 BM, Spanish State Papers, Add. MSS. 28, 420.
31 R. Morton Nance, 'More about the Tregear Manuscript', *OC*, vol. v, no. 1.
32 BM Add. MS. 46397.
33 R. Morton Nance, 'Something new in Cornish', *JRIC*, vol. i, part 2 (n.s.), 1952. See also R. Morton Nance, 'The Tregear Manuscript', *OC*, vol. iv, no. 11 and 'More about the Tregear Manuscript'.
34 Henry Jenner, 'The Arthurian legend', *JRIC*, vol. lviii.
35 Henderson MSS. Truro Museum, vol. x, p. 124.
36 Henderson MSS. Truro Museum, vol. x, p. 176.
37 See *Report RCPS*, 1929, and *OC*, vol. vii, p. 43.
38 BM MSS. Cott. Jul. C IV.
39 Richard Carew, op. cit.

Chapter Four Late Cornish

1 Henry Jenner, 'A Cornish oration in Spain in the year 1600', 90th Annual *Report RCPS*, 1923.
2 King James version: verse 5: 'His glory is great in thy salvation. Honour and majesty hast thou laid upon him.'
3 Jenner, op. cit.

4 R. Morton Nance, 'The Cornish language in the seventeenth century', *OC*, vol. vi, no. 1.

5 'Gwreans an bys: The Creation of the World', trans. and ed. Whitley Stokes, Appendix, *TPS*, 1864.

6 'Gwreans an bys', Bodleian Library MSS. Bodley 219 (S.C. 3020) and BM. Harley MSS. 1867.

7 Henry Jenner, 'Some miscellaneous scraps of Cornish', *JRIC*, vol. vi, 1927-30 (n.s.).

8 Davies Gilbert, *The Parochial History of Cornwall*, 4 vols, London, 1838.

9 R. Polwhele, *The History of Cornwall*, 7 vols, London, 1816.

10 Mary Coates, *Cornwall in the Great Civil War*, Oxford University Press, 1933.

11 Nance, op. cit.

12 William Scawen, *Observations of an Ancient Manuscript entitled Passio Christi, written in the Cornish Language, and now preserved in the Bodleian Library; with an account of the Language, Manners and Customs of the People of Cornwall*, London, 1777.

13 Charles E. Long (ed.), *Diary of the Marches of the Royal Army during the Great Civil War. Kept by Richard Symonds*, Camden Society, London, 1856.

14 Ashley Rowe, 'The Cornish language during the Civil War', *OC*, vol. iv, no. 2.

15 Nance, op. cit.

16 Jenner, 'Some miscellaneous scraps of Cornish', see also *Western Morning News*, 15 December 1925.

17 William Borlase, *Observations on the Antiquities Historical and Monumental of the County of Cornwall*, 1754.

18 Scawen, op. cit.

19 Henry Jenner, 'The Arthurian legend', *JRIC*, vol. lviii.

20 P. Berresford Ellis and Seumas Mac a' Ghobhainn, *The Problem of Language Revival*, Club Leabhar, Inverness, 1971.

21 R. Morton Nance, 'Nicholas Boson's Nebbaz Gerriau dro tho Carnoack', *JRIC*, vol. xxiii, 1929-32.

22 W. C. Borlase, 'Nebbaz Gerriau dro tho Carnoack', *JRIC*, vol. iv, 1878-81.

23 Charles Henderson, 'Nicholas Boson and Richard Angwyn', *OC*, vol. ii, no. 2.

24 Nance, 'Nicholas Boson's Nebbaz Gerriau dro tho Carnoack'.

25 Bodleian Library, MS. 10714.

26 A. K. Hamilton Jenkin, 'The Dutchess of Cornwall's Progress', *JRIC*, 1924.

27 R. Morton Nance, 'Folk lore recorded in the Cornish language', Camborne, undated pamphlet.

28 Ibid.

29 *Gwalarn*, no. 20.

30 See Nance in *OC*, vol. iii, nos 4 and 5.

31 A. S. D. Smith, *The Story of the Cornish Language*, revised by E. G. R. Hooper, *ALK*, Camborne, 1969.

32 See collections in BM, Bodleian Library and NLW.

33 NLW, Llanstephan MSS. 97.

34 NLW, Penarth MSS. 428.

35 See also, R. Morton Nance, 'The Cornish of William Rowe', *OC*, vol. ii, nos 11 and 12 and vol. iii, no. 1.

36 *OC*, vol. i, no. 12 and vol. ii, no. 1.

37 Nance, 'Folk lore recorded in the Cornish language'.

38 BM Add. MSS. 28,554. fol. 135.

39 K. H. Jackson, *A Celtic Miscellany*, Routledge & Kegan Paul, London, 1951; Penguin Books, Harmondsworth, 1971. See also N. W. Lloyd in *Y Cymmrodor*, VI, and *Scottish Studies*, VII.

40 R. Morton Nance, 'Edward Chirgwin's Cornish Song', *OC*, vol. iv, no. 6.

Chapter Five The Death of the Language

1 BM, 'Gwavas MSS.', Add. MSS. 28,554.

2 PRO, E. 134 36 Chas. 2 Mich. 18.

3 William Kelynack, Richard Richards, Philip Kelynack and 116 others, fishermen, appellants, and William Gwavas Gent., respondent, 2 parts: *The Appellants Case, The Respondents Case*, London, 1730.

4 See Nance, *OC*, vol. i, no. 1.

5 R. Morton Nance, 'Parson Drake's Cornish certificate', *OC*, vol. ii, no. 2.

6 R. Morton Nance, 'William Allen's Cornish rhyme', *OC*, vol. iv, no. 9.

7 See *OC*, vol. i, no. 1.

8 R. Morton Nance, 'Celtic words in Cornish dialect', *Report RCPS*, vol. iv, 1918-22.

9 Anthony Conran (trans. and ed.), *The Penguin Book of Welsh Verse*, Penguin Books, Harmondsworth, 1967.

10 NLW, NLW MSS. 1662 (formerly Water Davies MSS.).

11 Glyn E. Daniel, 'Who are the Welsh?', *PBA*, vol. xl, 1954.

12 NLW, Llanstephan MSS. 84.

13 BM MSS. Cotton Vespasian, A XIV.

14 William Pryce, *Archaeologia Cornu-Britannica*, Sherborne, 1790.

15 Nance, 'Celtic words in Cornish dialect'.

16 Henry Jenner, 'The Cornish language', *TPS*, 1873-4.

17 R. Morton Nance, 'James Jenkins of Alverton', *OC*, vol. iv, no. 6.

18 Henry Jenner, *A Handbook of the Cornish Language*, Nutt, London, 1904.

19 W. C. Borlase, 'A collection of hitherto unpublished proverbs and

rhymes in the ancient Cornish language from the MSS. of Dr. Borlase',
JRIC, vol. iii, 1861-7.

20 Jenner, op. cit.

21 *Brice's Weekly Journal*, no. 52, 2 June 1727; see also T. N. Brushfield,
The Life and Bibliography of Andrew Brice, privately published, London,
1888; and Ashley Rowe, 'An Exeter printer & Cornish', *OC*, vol. v,
no. 1.

22 C. F. Vulliany, *Life of Wesley*.

23 P. A. S. Pool, 'William Borlase', *OC*, vol. v, no. 5.

24 William Borlase, *Observations on the Antiquities Historical and Monumental of
the County of Cornwall,* 1754.

25 W. C. Borlase, op. cit., see also *JRIC*, 1878-81.

26 Henry Jenner, 'Descriptions of Cornish manuscripts. 1. The Borlase
MSS', *JRIC*, vol. xix, 1912.

27 *Archaeologia*, vol. iii, London, 1776.

28 *Archaeologia*, vol. v, London, 1778.

29 A. S. D. Smith, *The Story of the Cornish Language*, revised by E. G. R.
Hooper, *ALK*, Camborne, 1969.

30 Joseph Polsue, *The Complete History of Cornwall*, 4 vols, William Lake,
Truro, and Hopten, London, 1867-73.

31 W. Treffry Hoblyn, 'The probable parentage of Dorothy Pentreath',
OC, vol. ii, no. 11.

32 Nance, 'Celtic words in Cornish dialect'.

33 John B. D. Whitaker, *Ancient Cathedral of Cornwall,* 2 vols, London, 1804.

34 Jenner, 'The Cornish language'.

35 Jenner, *A Handbook of the Cornish Language*.

36 Whitaker, op. cit.

37 John Bannister, *A Glossary of Cornish Names,* Williams & Norgate, London,
1871.

Chapter Six   The Embers

1 Henry Jenner, 'Cornwall: a Celtic nation', *Celtic Review*, 16 January 1905.

2 W. D. Watson, 'More traditional Cornish numerals', *JRIC*, vol. xxii,
1926.

3 Henry Jenner, 'Traditional relics of the Cornish language in Mount's Bay
in 1875', *TPS*, 1875-6.

4 R. Morton Nance, 'The 20th century tradition of Cornish numerals',
JRIC, vol. xxi, 1922-5.

5 W. S. Lach-Szyrma, 'The numerals in Old Cornish', *Academy*, London,
20 March 1875.

6 *Academy*, 17 April 1875.

7 Jenner, 'Traditional relics of the Cornish language in Mount's Bay in 1875'.

8 W. S. Lach-Szyrma, 'Le dernier echo de la langue Cornique', *Revue Celtique*, vol. iii, p. 239.

9 Nance, op. cit.

10 Watson, op. cit.

11 R. Morton Nance, 'A new found traditional sentence of Cornish', *JRIC*, vol. xxii, 1926.

12 R. Morton Nance, 'John Davey of Boswednack and his Cornish rhyme', *JRIC*, vol. xxii, 1922-5.

13 Nance, 'Folk-lore recorded in the Cornish language', Camborne, undated pamphlet.

14 Jenner, 'Traditional relics of the Cornish language in Mount's Bay in 1875'.

15 R. Morton Nance, 'Celtic words in Cornish dialect', *Report RCPS*, vol. iv, 1918-22.

16 *Cornish Magazine*, 1 August 1828.

17 Sir Aurel Stein, *Ruins of Desert Cathay*.

18 'The Irish Language', Thomas Davies Lectures, Radio Eireann, 27 September 1953.

19 Fred. W. P. Jago, *The Ancient Language and Dialect of Cornwall*, Netherton & Worth, Truro, 1882.

20 *Cambrian Journal*, 30 November 1861.

21 L. L. Bonaparte, *Some Observations on the Rev. R. Williams' Preface to his Lexicon Cornu-Britannicum*, 1866.

22 Henry Jenner, 'The Cornish MSS in the provincial library at Bilbao, Spain', *JRIC*, vol. xxi, 1922-5.

23 Edwin Norris, *The Ancient Cornish Drama*, Oxford University Press, 1859.

24 *Kernow*, no. 3, 1934.

25 BM MSS. Harl. N. 1782.

26 John Bellow, 'On the Cornish language', *Report RCPS*, 1861.

27 Bodleian Library MS. Cornish d 1 (SC 32544).

28 Thomas Quiller-Couch, 'The Cornish language', *JRIC*, 1864.

29 '*Gwreans an bys*: The Creation of the World', trans. and ed. Whitley Stokes, Appendix, *TPS*, 1864.

30 Whitley Stokes, 'A Cornish glossary', *TPS*, 1868-9.

31 Bonaparte, op. cit. See also J. Loth, 'Etudes corniques: Remarques et corrections au Lexicon Cornu-Britannicum de Williams', *Revue Celtique*, vol. xxiii, p. 236.

32 *Archaeologia Cambrensis*, 1869, p. 409.

33 Stokes, *A Cornish Glossary*.

34 Max Müller, 'Are there Jews in Cornwall?', *Macmillan's Magazine*, April 1867.

35 T. F. G. Dexter, *Cornish Names*, Longmans Green, London, 1926; new ed., D. Bradford Barton, Truro, 1968.

36 P. A. S. Pool, *An Introduction to Cornish Place Names*, 2nd ed., privately published, Penzance, 1971.

37 See *JRIC*, vol. xviii, 1910-11.

38 R. S. Charnock, *Patronymica Cornu-Britannicum*, Longmans, London, 1870.

39 Henry Jenner, 'The Cornish language', *TPS*, 1873-4.

40 Gerald Morgan, *The Dragon's Tongue*, Triskel Press, Cardiff, 1966.

41 Henry Jenner, 'The history and literature of the ancient Cornish language', *JBAS*, vol. xxxiii, 1877.

42 See *JBAS*, vol. xxxii.

43 Whitley Stokes (trans. and ed.), *Beunans Meriasek*, *TPS*, 1872.

44 *Archives für celtische Lexicographie*, 1, pp. 101, 161, 224.

45 *Revue Celtique*, vol. iii, pp. 85, 224.

46 Kitty Lee: author of *A Western Wildflower*, 1882; *In London Town*, 1884; *Katherine Blythe*, 1886; *An Imperfect Gentleman*, 1888; *Love and Mary Bentley*, 1891; *When Fortune Frowns*, 1895, etc. Also books on art, religion and poetry.

47 Henry Jenner, 'The fourteenth century endorsement', *JRIC*, vol. xx, 1915-16.

48 *Cornishman*, 1 May 1879.

49 *Cornishman*, 29 May 1879.

50 *Cornishman*, 19, 26 June and 3 July 1879.

51 *Cornishman*, 7 August 1879.

52 *Cornishman*, 14 August 1879.

53 Jago, op. cit.

Chapter Seven   The Revivalists

1 Matthew Arnold, *On the Study of Celtic Literature*, Smith & Elder, London, 1867.

2 Glyn E. Daniel, 'Who are the Welsh?', *PBA*, vol. xl, 1954.

3 *Y Celt*, 31 May 1899 suggests this date for the foundation of Cymru Fydd.

4 Henry Jenner, 'The Manx language: its grammar, literature and present state', *TPS*, 1875-6, p. 172.

5 S. R. Erskine, *The Kilt and How to Wear It*, Carruthers, Inverness, 1901.

6 P. Berresford Ellis and Seumas Mac a' Ghobhainn, *The Problem of Language Revival*, Club Leabhar, Inverness, 1971.

7 Henry Jenner, 'Cornwall: a Celtic nation', *Celtic Review*, 16 January 1905.

8 T. Parry, *Eisteddfod y Cymry* (The Eisteddfod of Wales), Cardiff, 1943.

9 Letter to author, 2 August 1972.

10 W. D. Watson, 'How Cornish came to me', *OC*, vol. v, no. 7.

11 R. Morton Nance, 'Cornish beginnings', *OC*, vol. v, no. 8.

12 Henry Jenner, 'Cornish place names', *JRIC*, vol. xviii, 1910-11.

13 NLW MSS. B 257.

14 Donald Attwater, 'Cornish in Jerusalem', *OC*, vol. vi, no. 1.

15 *The Times*, 6 September 1934.

16 NLW MSS. 6075 and 6076.
17 *Cornish Studies* No. 2 (pamphlet), *ALK*, Camborne.
18 *Gwalarn*, no. 20.
19 *Cornish Guardian*, 26 July 1928; 27 September 1928; see also R. Morton Nance, 'Cornish culture and the Cornish Gorsedd', *Cornish Review*, no. 1, Spring, 1949 and no. 7, Spring, 1951.
20 J. J. Parry, 'The revival of Cornish: An Dasserghyans Kernewek', *PMLA*, vol. lxi, no. 1, part 1, March, 1946.
21 Works of Edwin Chirgwin in *Kernow*: no. 1, 'Den Hanternos', 'Gorthewer'; 2, 'A Golonnow Cref'; 3, 'Dhe'n Kensa bryluen'; 4, 'Dhe'n awhesyth'; 5, 'Hyreth'; 6, 'An jynjy gesys dhe goll' and 'An Velyn Goth'; 10, 'Encledhyas Bran'; 11, 'Tran y honen a bys nefra'; 12, 'Dhe ber a Wlas' and 'Pan vo whas dhyso rak car'. *ALK*: no. 70, 'Nanjalyan'; 71, 'Gibraltar'; 73, 'Mebyon Arthur'; 75, 'Agan Avon'; 92, 'Whethel Coth'. See also *Kemysk Kernewek*, *ALK*, Camborne 1964, for 'An Velyn Goth' and 'Pan vo whans dhyso rak car'. See also contributions to *Lyver Hymnys ha Salmow*, *ALK*, 1962.
22 *Kemysk Kernewek*, *ALK*, 1964, p. 23.
23 *OC*, vol. ii, no. 5.
24 *The Times*, 25 August 1934.
25 *The Times*, 6 September 1934.
26 NLW MSS. 12514 and 12515.
27 *Kernow*, no. 12.
28 *JRIC*, vol. xxv, 1937-42.
29 Parry, op. cit.
30 See Mrs Pollard's contributions to *ALK*, nos 41, 59 and 86.
31 BM Add. MSS. 46397.
32 *JRIC* (n.s.), vol. i, part 2, 1952. See also *OC*, vol. iv, no. 12 and vol. v, no. 1.
33 'The drama in Cornwall', *Cornish Review*, no. 9, winter, 1951.
34 A. S. D. Smith, 'Resurrecting a language', *Cornish Review*, no. 4, spring, 1950.
35 See *ALK*, no. 117.
36 *Kernow*, no. 2.
37 'Tremenyans Arthur' gans Caradar, *Kemysk Kernewek*, *ALK*, Camborne, 1964.
38 See *ALK*, nos 104 and 105.

Chapter Eight   The Growth and Future of the Revival

1 William Greenberg, *The Flags of the Forgotten*, Clifton Books, Brighton, 1969.
2 *The Education of Cornish Children* (pamphlet), *Mebyon Kernow*, Falmouth, 1966.
3 Hansard (House of Commons Official Report), vol. 742, no. 161.

4 *Illustrated London News,* 4 August 1967.

5 Leopold Kohr, *The Breakdown of Nations,* Routledge & Kegan Paul, London, 1957.

6 John Fleet, 'Cowethas Flamank—The First Year', *Annual Book of the Celtic League,* 9 Bóthar, Cnoc Síon, Baile Átha Cliath 9, Éire, 1971.

7 Secretary General, League of Celtic Nations: Alan Heussaff, 9 Bóthar, Cnoc Síon, Baile Átha Cliath 9, Éire.

8 *Irish Times,* 6 April 1966.

9 *Annual Book of the Celtic League,* 1969.

10 *ALK,* no. 112.

11 D. Simon Evans, 'Story of Cornish', *University of Liverpool Studies,* autumn, 1969.

12 *Annual Book of the Celtic League,* 1971.

13 British Esperanto Association, London, 1969.

14 P. Berresford Ellis, *The Story of the Cornish Language,* Tor Mark Press, Truro, 1971.

15 F. J. B. McDowell's works have appeared in *ALK,* nos 21, 25, 33, 35, 40, 43, 45, 47, 50, 52, 55, 69, 70 and 71.

16 Miss Ivall, *ALK,* no. 116 and Mrs Royle, *ALK,* no. 118.

17 *ALK,* no. 112.

18 *ALK,* nos 107 and 114.

19 *ALK,* no. 76.

20 *ALK,* no. 85.

21 *ALK,* no. 90.

22 *Annual Book of the Celtic League,* 1972.

23 Eugene van T. Graves, *The Old Cornish Vocabulary,* University Microfilms, Ann Arbor, Michigan, 1964.

24 E. van T. Graves, 'Outline of a doctoral thesis', *OC,* vol. vi, no. 7.

25 *Spectator,* 10 January 1965.

26 *OC,* vol. vi, no. 8.

27 Markham Harris, *The Cornish Ordinalia,* Catholic University of America Press, Washington, D.C., 1969.

28 A. S. D. Smith, *The Story of the Cornish Language,* revised by E. G. R. Hooper, *ALK,* Camborne, 1969.

29 Letter to author, 10 August 1972.

30 Letter to author, 19 July 1972.

31 Charles Thomas, 'An Dasserghyans Kernewek—The revival of the Cornish language', *OC,* vol. vi, no. 5.

32 T. F. G. Dexter, *Cornish Names,* Longmans Green, 1926; new ed., D. Bradford Barton, Truro, 1966.

33 See *OC,* vols iii, v and personal names in vol. iv.

34 Cyril Noall, *The Cornish Midsummer Eve Bonfires,* Federation of Old Cornwall Societies, St Austell, 1963.

35 William Bottrell, *Traditional and Hearthside Stories of West Cornwall*, London, 1873.

36 Richard R. M. Gendall, 'Cornish as an optional subject in schools', *New Cornwall*, June, 1968.

37 Letter to author, 24 July 1972.

38 Letter to author, 15 August 1972.

39 *The Times*, 11 September 1972.

40 See P. Berresford Ellis, 'The Celtic cultural problem', *Freethinker*, 20 June 1970 and 'Celtic nationalism', *Ecologist*, October, 1971.

41 Martin Brennan, S.J., 'The restoration of Irish', *Irish Studies*, autumn, 1964.

42 Eduard Sapir, *Languages: An Introduction to the Study of Speech*, Harcourt Brace, New York, 1921. See also David Mandelbaum (ed.), *Selected Writings of Eduard Sapir in Language, Culture and Personality*, University of California Press, 1949.

43 Simeon Potter, *Language in the Modern World*, Penguin Books, Harmondsworth, 1960.

44 P. Berresford Ellis and Seumas Mac a' Ghobhainn, *The Problem of Language Revival*, Club Leabhar, Inverness, 1971.

45 D. S. Parlett, *A Short Dictionary of Languages*, English University Press, London, 1967.

Index

Allin-Collins, R. St V., 158-9, 160, pl. 15
Aneirin, 20
Angwyn, Richard, 80, 84, 86, 88, 107
Arthur, King, legends of, 21-3, 25n, 26n,
    32n, 66n, 84n, 189
Arundell, Humphry, 61

Bédier, Joseph, 23n, 28
Bennetts, W. M., 188
Béroul, 23-4, 25
Bodener, William, 119-20, 123-4, 135
Bonaparte, Prince Louis Lucien, 135-7,
    139
Bonner, Edmund, 44-5, 64-6, 172, pl. 4
Borlase, Dr W., 62, 69, 80, 107, 113-15,
    121, 140, 143, 144, 155
Borrow, George, 138-9
Boson, John, 96-7, 101, 110, 111, 115
Boson, Nicholas, 79, 85-91, 95, 102
Brerewood, William, 74
Brittany: Celts in, 16-17; and Cornwall,
    52, 66, 82; end of independence, 52,
    66-7; language of, 6-7 20, 75, 150;
    literature of, 37-8, 40, 90; persecution
    in, 171

Carew, Richard, 39, 59, 69, 73, 105
Catholicism, see religion
Celtic: Nations, League of, 181, 183n;
    revival, 147-52, 205-6; studies, 147
Celts: and Christianity, 18; definition of,
    5-6; history of, 10-31, 102; languages
    of, 6-20, 28, 63, 75, 87, 104, 113-14,
    133-5, 141-3, 148-50, 206n, see also
    Cornish; literature, of, 9-10, 20n, 23,
    26, 37-8, 40, 84, 90, 147n, see also
    Cornish; nationalism of, 148-52, 171
Chadwick, Nora, 9, 13, 16, 19
'Charter Fragment', 41-3, 144
Chirgwin, Edwin, 163-5, 171
Christianity: and Celts, 18; in Cornwall,
    18, 26-7, 72; see also religion

Cornish language: and Civil War, 77-9;
    death of, 95-124; decline of, 52, 57-62,
    66-7, 74-86; insurrections caused by,
    52, 54-7, 61-2; Late, 73n, 74-89;
    Middle, 32-4, 35n, 45-51; modern,
    170; monoglot speakers of, 60-3, 77,
    80, 95; noted speakers of, 115-24,
    127, 129, 135, 144, pl. 10; Old, 6-7,
    20, 27-30; and Reformation, 57, 60,
    66; and religion, 33-5, 59-64, 70-3,
    166, 197; revival, 82, 84-5, 152-77,
    194n, 209n; in schools, 162, 183-5,
    202-5, pl. 17; Unified, 154-6, 160,
    194-6
Cornish literature: Late, 74, 89-94, 144;
    Middle, 35-45; Old, 21-5, 27; and
    religion, 40-1, 64-6, 69, 74, 81-3, 91-2,
    137, 175, pl. 5; surveys of, 90, 94, 95n,
    96-8, 132, 137, 144; Tudor, 64-8;
    see also drama, poetry, proverbs, songs,
    stories
Cornu-British words, 131
Cornwall: and Brittany, 52, 66, 82;
    medieval, 32-51; origin of name, 20-1;
    separateness of, 26; Tudor, 52-69;
    see also historical surveys of Cornwall,
    nationalism, politics
Cottonian Vocabulary, 29, 106-7, pl. 2

Daniel, Glyn E., 106, 147
Davies, John, 75-6
dictionaries, Cornish: by Nance, 167,
    169, 194-5; by Jago, 52n, 135, 146;
    by Williams, 136, 139, 194; see also
    vocabularies
Doddridge, Sir John, 75
drama, Cornish: dialect, 113, 155-6;
    Late, 76; modern, 162, 170, 172, 173,
    175, 187, 188; surveys of, 132, 137,
    144; see also miracle plays
Druids, 12-13, 18, 198